Mexican Americans

& the Environment

THE MEXICAN AMERICAN EXPERIENCE

Adela de la Torre, EDITOR

Other books in the series:

Mexican Americans and the Environment

Tierra y vida

Devon G. Peña

The University of Arizona Press   Tucson

The University of Arizona Press
© 2005 Arizona Board of Regents
All rights reserved
♾ This book is printed on acid-free, archival-quality paper.
Manufactured in the United States of America

10   09   08   07   06   05   6   5   4   3   2   1

Library of Congress Cataloging-in-Publication Data

Peña, Devon Gerardo
Mexican Americans and the environment : tierra y vida / Devon G. Peña.
    p. cm.—(The Mexican American experience)
Includes bibliographical references and index.
ISBN 0-8165-2211-1 (pbk. : alk. paper)
1. Mexican Americans—Politics and government. 2. Environmental policy—
United States. 3. Political ecology—United States. I. Title. II. Series.
E184.M5P395 2005
304.2′089′6872073—dc22
2004023856

Publication of this book is made possible in part by the proceeds of a permanent
endowment created with the assistance of a Challenge Grant from the National
Endowment for the Humanities, a federal agency.

I dedicate this book to two fallen heroes of the environmental justice movement, the late Jeanne Gauna and Edwin Sánchez.

■ CONTENTS

■ ILLUSTRATIONS

FIGURES

MAPS

■ TABLES

◼ ACRONYMS

BLM	Bureau of Land Management
BRU	Bus Riders Union
CPRs	common pool resources
EIS	environmental impact study
EJM	Environmental Justice Movement
EPA	Environmental Protection Agency
FLOC	Farm Labor Organizing Committee
G10	Group of Ten environmental organizations
GAO	General Accounting Office
GEOs	genetically engineered organisms
GR	Green Revolution
MELA	Mothers of East Los Angeles
NABC	North American Bioregional Congress
NAFTA	North American Free Trade Agreement
NEJAC	National Environmental Justice Advisory Committee
NEPA	National Environmental Policy Act
NSM	new social movement
NTC	National Toxics Campaign
OACC	Ozark Area Community Congress
SD	sustainable development
SNEEJ	Southwest Network for Environmental and Economic Justice
SWOP	Southwest Organizing Project
TEK	traditional environmental knowledge
UFW	United Farm Workers of America
UFWOC	United Farm Workers Organizing Committee
UNCED	United Nations World Commission on Environment and Development
USFS	United States Forest Service
WTO	World Trade Organization

■ ACKNOWLEDGMENTS

Many colleagues contributed to the development of this book. First and foremost, I thank Adela de la Torre for inviting me to develop it. I would also like to thank my colleagues at the University of Washington, especially Greg Hicks, Eugene Hunn, and Eric Smith. Thanks also go to my students in the Graduate Program in Environmental Anthropology; I am especially indebted to Lisa Meierotto, Rebeca Rivera, and Megan Styles. Teresa Mares, a student in the Graduate Program in Sociocultural Anthropology, was helpful in seeking permissions for reprinted materials and handling other correspondence. I would like to thank Miriam Kahn, chair of the Department of Anthropology, for her support. Other colleagues who merit acknowledgment include James K. Boyce, Robert D. Bullard, Teresa Cordova, Rubén O. Martínez, Ivette Perfecto, and Laura Pulido.

I am equally grateful to all the grassroots organizers and activists who shared their time and wisdom over the past fifteen years of research leading to this book: Joe C. Gallegos, Teresa Jaramillo, Adelmo Kaber, Charlie Maestas, Richard Moore, and Veronica Sánchez.

I am especially grateful to my family for their support and tolerance of my mixed temperament as I confronted the long hours of work it took to produce this book. They made many willing sacrifices. I thank my wife, Elaine H. Peña, and my stepchildren, Elisa, Eduardo (Wayo), and Eliana Yzaguirre. I also wish to thank my father-in-law, William Hastings, my mother-in-law, Grace Hastings, and my brother, Daniel J. Peña; all three were sources of constant feedback, and they never wavered in their insistence that this be a book the average person could read.

Finally, I would like to thank the acquisitions editor at the University of Arizona Press, Patti Hartmann, for her undying patience and support through the three years of hard work it took to go from planning to publication of this book.

■ INTRODUCTION

"La Tierra Es Vida"

"La tierra es vida" (The land is life) is a popular *dicho* (folk saying) used by the **Mexican-origin people** of northern New Mexico and southern Colorado to describe the belief that humans must respect the land because it is the source of life. This **land ethic** instructs people to act as caretakers of the earth.[1] It also requires of them a sense of political responsibility because the community must actively confront greed before it leads to abuse of the land. This aspect of the Mexican American land ethic is retold in folktales like that of the Forest Spirit. The "Forest Spirit drove the man out of the forests for cutting down too many trees, for he was greedy and without shame."[2] Folktales like this relate the folly of greedy people who act out of balance with nature and community because they suffer from *sinvergüenzas* —a shameless indifference to the harm that others suffer as a consequence of their actions, which are designed solely for individual gain.

Vergüenza is a complex norm that hints at an indigenous critique of the spiritual and moral maladies of modern life under capitalism, the philosophy of systemic greed. The vergüenza worldview alleges that shamelessness occurs because the individual is separated from nature and community, invariably leading to unethical behavior and social conflict. As global corporations take hold and use free market ideology shamelessly to overexploit the earth, many local communities are struggling to protect the environment and control their own ecological futures. Community activists are responding to these threats by creating grassroots **social movements** to challenge the forces of harmful ecological and social change and create a democratic, just, and **sustainable** future. This broad-based social movement for grassroots democracy and a sustainable society, known as the **environmental justice movement (EJM),** is the underlying theme of this book.

This introductory textbook in the Mexican American Experience series is written in the spirit of the opening dicho. It explores the relationship between **ecology** and **culture** in the Mexican American experience. Written for use by first- or second-year undergraduate students in ethnic studies or environmental studies, *Mexican Americans and the Environment* joins the scientific study of ecology with the social scientific study of culture, history, and politics.

In this book I address an apparent paradox: To study the Mexican American experience from environmental perspectives, we must understand the basic methods and theories of ecological science. Yet we cannot truly study ecology in this context without also understanding the unique culture and history of a diverse, multiethnic national-origin group. Ecology has often been deemed irrelevant to the study of the historical and contemporary problems of oppression, poverty, and discrimination that have defined much of **Chicana/o** studies. I contend that we have drawn too hard a line between people and the environment. Ecology is relevant to the Mexican American experience because **environmental risks** surround and affect all of us. Scientific ecology simply provides some of the conceptual tools we can use to further understand ecological issues in the context of this experience.

There are well-established scientific connections among race, poverty, and the experience of environmental risks. Mexican and Mexican-origin farmworkers are poisoned by pesticides every year while harvesting crops destined for our nation's collective table. Mexican women workers, many still teenagers, are poisoned, sexually assaulted, mutilated, or fatally injured inside the **maquiladoras** on the U.S.–Mexico border, while Juárez has become a killing field for serial murderers stalking young women. Many Mexican-origin farmers have lost their ancestral lands to government **enclosure** and private expropriation. Healthy forests and watersheds were damaged under the heavy hand of industrial exploitation in the aftermath of the U.S. appropriation of the Southwest in 1848. The children of America's longest-established farmers work at or below minimum wage cooking and cleaning up after the burgeoning masses of middle-class, urban tourists who come to gawk at nature, buy purportedly authentic Indian arts and crafts, and eat nouveau Mexican cuisine while they do their best to ignore the quaint local help. In polluted inner cities, Mexican American parents cannot take for granted the safety of schools and playgrounds in a landscape underlain with toxic wastes that sicken children. Environmental risks endanger Mexican Americans where they live, work, and play. Attention to the ecological dimensions of Mexican American history, culture, and politics helps us avoid drawing too hard a line between people and the environment. Such an approach requires basic awareness and understanding of ecological research methods and theories.

I also seek to introduce the conceptual vocabulary used in the studies of ecology, culture, history, and politics. These terms, highlighted in the text with **boldface** type, are defined in a glossary at the end of the book. Each chapter ends with a brief list of suggested readings for further study of topics addressed in it, as well as questions to guide discussion and further study.

■ Overview of Environmental Issues and the Mexican-Origin People

The ideas and experiences of Mexican Americans from all walks of life are at the heart of this book. I personally interviewed, or consulted the writings and speeches of, numerous Chicana/o activists, farmworkers, farmers, industrial and service workers, union organizers, small business owners, land managers, lawyers, educators, intellectuals, scientists, and community organizers. Their voices are featured throughout the book because they define environmental issues from a variety of perspectives that speaks to the diversity of the Mexican American experience. They also provide a clear overview of the most critical environmental issues facing the Mexican American people. I want to begin by introducing some of these voices.

AURORA CASTILLO was a fourth-generation Mexican American activist. As an elder, Castillo helped found the grassroots organization Madres del Este de Los Angeles (Mothers of East Los Angeles, or MELA). She participated in MELA campaigns against proposals to locate in East Los Angeles an incinerator, a prison, and a pipeline that would have harmed the community and environment. A recipient of the Goldman Environmental Prize, Castillo died in 1998 at the age of eighty-eight.

CÉSAR CHÁVEZ founded the United Farmworkers Organizing Committee (which later became the United Farmworkers Union, or UFW). One of the best-known leaders of the Chicano Movement of the 1960s and 1970s, Chávez played a major role in bringing attention to the health effects of pesticide exposure among farmworkers during early negotiations with California growers. He passed away on April 22, 1993.

JOSEPH C. GALLEGOS is a fifth-generation farmer in San Luis, Colorado. He lives and farms on land that has been in his family since 1851. He is an activist and writer in the fields of sustainable agriculture, watershed protection, and land-use planning.

LORRAINE GRANADO works for the American Friends Service Committee in Denver and is the project director for Community Justice Organizing. She is a founder of the Cross Community Coalition and

Neighbors for a Toxic-Free Community, which fought for the cleanup of the ASARCO Superfund site in Denver.

JUANA GUTIÉRREZ was born in Mexico and lives in Boyle Heights in the Los Angeles area. She is a cofounder of MELA, the previously mentioned grassroots **environmental justice** organization.

LOIS HEAD is a community organizer and staff member of the Southwest Organizing Project (SWOP) in Albuquerque, New Mexico. His work takes him to urban ghettos, Native American reservations, pueblos in New Mexico, **barrios** in Texas and California, and the **colonias** and maquiladoras along the U.S.–Mexico border.

TERESA JARAMILLO, a fourth-generation native-born daughter of San Luis, Colorado, is a medical missionary based in San Diego, California. She has a long history of activism in the human rights, peace, and environmental justice movements.

AUBIN MAESTAS is a sixth-generation native-born son of a farming family in San Pablo, Colorado. In 1995, at age twelve, he was among the youngest of the two dozen anti-logging protestors arrested in Colorado during the start of a long struggle to prevent destruction of the local watershed by industrial timber companies.

RICHARD MOORE has lived and worked in the Southwest most of his life. He is executive director of the Southwest Network for Environmental and Economic Justice (SNEEJ) in Albuquerque, New Mexico, and was a founding organizer of the first National People of Color Environmental Leadership Summit held in October 1991.

ROSEANNE "ROCKY" RODRÍGUEZ is a native of Denver, Colorado, where she works with the National Chicano Human Rights Commission. She teaches English as a second language to immigrant workers and was an organizer of the Peace and Dignity Journey, which celebrated five hundred years of resistance by indigenous peoples.

EDWIN SÁNCHEZ, a sixth-generation native-born son of **acequia** farmers from Chama and San Luis, Colorado, was an apprentice in the carpentry and art of homemade *compuertas,* the traditional wooden gates used on farmers' acequia irrigation ditches. He studied computer graphics and loved hip-hop music. In 1995, at age fourteen, Edwin was arrested during the first protests by acequia farmers and environmentalists against logging on the Sangre de Cristo land grant. Edwin passed away in July 1999.

VERONICA SÁNCHEZ was a fifth-generation native of San Luis, Colorado. She worked on the family farm with her husband, Adelmo

Kaber, and was active in local campaigns to stop logging destruction of the village common lands. A seed saver, Veronica preserved squash and maize seeds that have been in her family for a hundred years. She passed away in May 2004.

These are some of the individuals who contributed to this book. Each has important stories about the struggles to protect the environment and communities. The idea that local communities speak for themselves is an important ethic of the environmental justice movement.[3] These voices define the range of environmental issues addressed in this book.

Los Campesinos: Farmworkers Resist Pesticides, Poverty, and Powerlessness

Farmworkers have struggled for union representation and collective bargaining rights to strengthen their efforts to create safe working and living places. Here is one of their voices. César Chávez asks us to consider the people dying in the farm labor camps and surrounding communities:

> What is the worth of a man or a woman? What is the worth of a farm worker? How do you measure the value of a life? . . . The chemical companies that manufacture pesticides and the growers who use them want us to believe that they are the health-givers. . . . They have convinced the politicians and the government regulators that pesticides are . . . the key to the abundance of food. . . . We accept decades of environmental damage these poisons have brought the land. . . . [Is it] acceptable to . . . farm workers and their children who have known tragedy from pesticides? . . . There is no acceptable level of exposure to any chemical that causes cancer. We cannot tolerate any toxic substance that causes miscarriages, stillbirths, and deformed infants. . . . Isn't that the standard of protection you would ask for your family and your children? Isn't that the standard of protection you would demand for yourself? Then why not for farm workers?[4]

El Racismo Tóxico: Urban Communities Resist Environmental Racism

Mexican American residents of inner-city barrios face decades of abuse caused by toxic racism. Aurora Castillo and Juana Gutiérrez of MELA write of their experiences:

Because we are a poor and Hispanic community they think we will accept destructive projects if they promise us jobs. But we don't want our children working as prison guards or in incinerators. We need constructive jobs—nurses, doctors, computer specialists, skilled workers, who can make a contribution to our community. . . . The state wants to place all of society's problems in our community—a prison, a pipeline, and an incinerator . . . they will have to solve those problems, not just dump them from one place to another.[5]

Drawing a distinction between Chicana/o and mainstream environmentalism, Richard Moore of SNEEJ and Lois Head of SWOP note that

Few people of color have been attracted to the mainstream environmental groups. . . . This does not mean that there is a lack of concern among Chicanos, Mexicanos, or other people of color. Environmental justice issues are bringing disenfranchised communities into the environmental arena. Many of these issues have historically been perceived as a poverty issue, an issue of social and racial justice inseparable from others, such as housing, unemployment, lack of health services, or poor educational opportunities. . . . Our communities are threatened by the environmental problems caused by racism inherent in land use decisions that result in the location of dirty industries, toxic dumps, incinerators, and military bases close to low-income communities of color.[6]

This struggle also confronts the role of the state in institutionalized **environmental racism,** as Moore and Head describe:

The EPA Campaign . . . [was] initiated in July 1991, when the [Southwest] Network submitted an open letter to the EPA that documented more than a decade's lack of enforcement of environmental regulations in communities of color. . . . The Network chose to confront the EPA because it had rarely if ever opened its doors to people of color or their organizations in the past.[7]

Tierra y Agua: Hispano Farmers Fight for Land and Water Rights

Over the past century, Mexican Americans across the Southwest have been fighting to protect their ancestral land grants and water rights. Joe Gallegos writes of these struggles:

A family has lived off their small acreage for generations. . . . No big paychecks but a consistent food source and a beautiful place to live. Then comes the great offer that Richie Richard [sic] makes and the family is spinning in turmoil. The modern day advocates will use the argument that the new millennium is a time to make way for different thinking. The school of thought that uses money instead of land to make a living is being echoed throughout the adobe house and the elders are near tears when they hear the words, "Sell it." . . . This battle is becoming more and more prevalent with the expansion of the rich man's domain within our watershed. . . . The old way holds that money and land are like two opposites. . . . It is difficult to make the modern advocates see that land is not here to make money but to make life.[8]

El Saber: Recovery of Traditional Cultural and Ecological Knowledge

Mexican Americans have deep knowledge of ecology—of the plants, animals, soils, rivers, grasslands, and forests. This knowledge is important to the survival of the culture and community. As Veronica Sánchez writes:

I built a little shrine by the winter wheat that we planted in the back last year. It is about a quarter mile up from the acequia madre. I go there to pray for *la labor,* the harvest. So we can have a good crop. The land needs this blessing. . . . When I was younger, I already cut and baled the hay. I helped plant potatoes. I also had a big garden and I irrigated the garden and sometimes the bigger field crops. I was a good mechanic and fixed the tractor when it broke down. . . . Farming is the best thing of my life.[9]

Sister Teresa Jaramillo, another San Luis native, describes a local sense of place that weaves her body and spirituality into the land, La Sierra (The Mountain):

I know the name of every snowfield and all the *cañoncitos.* Each is a special place for the wild plants I collect: the berries, medicine herbs, and mushrooms. Each with its special place. I know the names of the springs and waterfalls. I know the names of the creeks and the lakes and ponds with the beautiful fish. I know the names of the hills where the trees can be found with piñon nuts or resin. I know the valleys and meadows and the names of the grasses and trees that grow here. I know the animals and the plants that live here in the mountain. They are my spiritual brothers and sisters, my teachers. I know the places where the animal trails take you, and the beaver ponds, and the places where my uncle took sheep to graze. I know La Sierra because she is my home.[10]

La Identidad: Place, Identity, and Resistance

The loss of ancestral land and water rights or the destruction of the local environment by developers or polluters leads to strong visceral responses from land-based Chicanas/os. When the common lands of the community were clear-cut, Adelmo Kaber felt *susto* (fright so intense it may result in the loss of the soul):

> *Me dio susto ver como cambio La Sierra.* I suffered fright-illness seeing how the Mountain changed. *Siento que perdí mi alma.* I feel I lost my soul. *Cortaron los árboles, y por eso el agua ya no viene mas que con mal.* They cut the trees, and for that the water does not come except with bad things.[11]

Mujeres en Acción: Chicanas and Environmental Justice

Chicanas continue to play a leading role in the EJM. Lorraine Granado and Rocky Martínez outline a critique of the dominant culture:

> All women, it doesn't matter what their color or culture, they all had a mother, and a grandmother, and a great grandmother. . . . [I]t goes all the way back to the mother of the earth. . . . Every human should defend the earth because whether they believe that she's a living spirit or not isn't the point. The point is, without her, nobody could live . . . when you defend Mother Earth you're defending your air, water, all the rock, green, vegetation, all the relatives, the swim, creep, crawl peoples, four-leggeds, two-leggeds, winged persons, star nations, cloud nations, thunder beings. You're defending the universe when you defend the earth.
>
> I think it's about . . . Western European thinking . . . and the whole notion that things are to be conquered, subdued, used for the benefit of the folks doing the conquering and subduing. . . . Everything is objectified. . . . The earth is not living; it is an object to be used. The Indians were not people, blacks were not people; they were objects to be used. So it's a whole "conquer for my own benefit". . . notion that people . . . should accrue as much wealth as they could. In order to do that, all other things had to be devalued . . . and destroyed. That I think is the cause of it, and really is a way of looking at life. . . . [W]e can call it progress, we call it development . . . but it's not about that, it's about exploitation.[12]

La Juventud: Generations for Environmental Justice

The youth are emerging to lead environmental justice struggles in rural and urban communities. Edwin Sánchez, a fifth-generation farmer, described his passion for acequias, while Aubin Maestas, a teenager from the acequia farming community of San Luis, expressed his motives for joining the anti-logging protests in 1996:

> My dad's father showed him how to build compuertas (irrigation head-gates) and my father showed me. . . . I have learned a lot about acequias. I started learning when I was very young, like ten or twelve years old. The first thing I did was to help clean the ditch. Later, I learned how to irrigate. The first field I irrigated was sweet peas, beans, and corn. . . . I also learned how to plant the crops and to cultivate. . . . I like making the wooden compuertas because they are a puzzle you have to put together. The compuerta is like the history of our farm, a puzzle that you put together. You start off with just a little piece and in the end it all fits together very well. A good farm is like that. It fits together very well with the land and water around it. It fits together well with all the neighbors.[13]

> I came here with my mother and grandmother because the loggers are taking all the trees. They are hurting the mountain and I want to help stop that.[14]

Mexican Americans face a daunting range of environmental threats to their well-being. These ecological problems have deep roots in the status of a national-origin community that has suffered systematic economic and political oppression.[15] Today we all live in a world made seemingly smaller by global markets and mass media, the Internet, and our constant movement across the planet. Most people still experience everyday life in a locality, in a specific place, however. Our attachment to place—our neighborhood, our hometown or village, the land around us if you will—is as important to our sense of who we are as the common cultural bonds of language, religion, history, food, music, and dress. The same attachment to place comes under attack whenever we directly experience environmental threats in our neighborhoods and workplaces. Many of the people whose voices grace this book became activists only after their home space, their place, was threatened with environmental and social harm. Resistance to ecological degradation often springs from people's place-based identities and lived experiences.

■ Overview of the Book

Mexican Americans and the Environment is divided into the principal themes of ecology, history and culture, and politics. Chapters 1 and 2 provide a general introduction to ecology from classical scientific ecology to contemporary political ecology. Chapters 3 and 4 present an environmental history that spans the border, incorporating present-day Mexico and the U.S. Southwest in an area I call **Mega-Mexico.** Chapters 5, 6, and 7 critique the principal schools of American environmentalism and then introduce the organizations and struggles of Mexican Americans in contemporary ecological politics.

From Scientific to Political Ecology

I consider ecology both a field of scientific research and a political **discourse.** Chapters 1 and 2 introduce the central themes and concepts that have guided the scientific study of ecology. The objective in these two chapters is to provide a basic understanding of the methods, concepts, and models used in the remaining chapters, where I present environmental issues in the context of the culture, history, and politics of the Mexican American experience. Chapter 1 covers the first half of the twentieth century, which is the classical period of American scientific ecology. Chapter 2 addresses more recent developments since the 1970s and focuses on what I call the "ecologies of chaos."

Chapter 1 introduces classical ecology, which is the study of living organisms and their surrounding physical environment. This **paradigm** eventually resulted in the concept of the **ecosystem,** one of the most profound ideas of the twentieth century because it reveals the interconnection of living organisms and their surrounding environment. The classical model emphasized order and stability in nature. By the 1950s, the ecosystem concept had taken the form of models to measure the flow of energy in an interconnected web of organisms. Ecosystems came to be defined in terms of an ideal state of dynamic **equilibrium,** or **homeostasis.**

Chapter 1 introduces the main thinkers who developed the concepts of ecology, including Ellen Swallow, Frederic Clements, Herbert Gleason, Arthur Tansley, Aldo Leopold, and Eugene Odum. These thinkers developed concepts crucial to the study of ecosystems, including biodiversity, homeostasis, the **food web,** and the **land ethic.** Under their guidance, ecology evolved from the first fairly simple models of plant communities into increasingly complex theories of self-regulating ecosystems. The chapter ends with a brief discussion of the dominant cybernetic model of the ecosystem, which emphasized order and stability in nature and has been criticized as biased in favor of capitalist managerial values. The dominance of this model was to prove a pivotal factor in the rise of the EJM.

By the early 1970s, ecologists were focusing more on processes of environmental change instead of order and stability. Chapter 2 introduces these more recent trends, all of which share a concern with **chaos** and **uncertainty** in ecosystems. Humans were suddenly in the picture, and the study of the uncertainty produced by human modification of ecosystems became much more important. This chapter presents five distinct approaches to the **ecology of disturbance,** which is defined as the study of natural and human-induced uncertainty and change in ecosystems. These five fields include conservation biology, restoration ecology, environmental history, **ethnoecology,** and political ecology.

México Desconocido: Environmental History of Greater Mexico

Chapters 3 and 4 present the environmental history of the Mexican-origin people across a broad swath of space and time, focusing on both cultural and ecological change. Many books have been written about the social, political and cultural history of the Mexican-origin people. Most are written as if human action can unfold in a world where the environment is no more significant than a stage prop in the theater of human drama. By failing to consider the interrelations of place and culture in history, these works ignore important forces that have actively shaped our historical experiences. They thereby miss making connections between processes of cultural, social, and environmental change, and forsake a chance to understand human relationships through the lens of our relationship to the earth.

Because the environmental history of Greater Mexico is largely untold, my approach to history focuses on the overlooked stories of the place itself—Mega-Mexico's changing biophysical character in relation to its species, landscapes, ecosystems, and cultures. Ecological history shifts attention away from the exploits of explorers, military generals, pioneers, first settlers, and industrialists to the land itself. It redirects the focus to the less well-known stories of the aboriginal civilizations and local cultures that have inhabited this province.

Biologists have perhaps arrived sooner than historians at a clear vision of México desconocido (unknown Mexico). Wildlife biologists use the term

Mega-Mexico to refer to a biogeographic province of North America defined by the territorial spread of Mexican flora and fauna.[16] This large province extends from the Lacandón rain forest in southeastern Chiapas to the headwaters of the Río Bravo del Norte (Rio Grande) in the San Juan Mountains of south central Colorado, and from the Yucatán Peninsula to the coasts of Baja and Alta California. Biologists' maps teach us that tropical songbirds from Mexico's Lacandón rain forest migrate during the spring and summer to the eastern United States and Canada. Songbirds that breed in the Colorado Rockies winter in the highlands of central Mexico through Chiapas. Monarch butterflies migrate from their nesting **habitat** in the montane pine forests of Michoacán as far north as Canada. To study wildlife and its habitat, biologists do not narrow their scope to the limits imposed by political borders.

Chapters 3 and 4 are based on the idea that the same wisdom about borders might apply to the study of human cultures and communities. Like songbirds and butterflies, Mexicans inhabit places across borders. Their migration and settlement of Mega-Mexico is much older than the border. Therefore, I use the terms Greater Mexico, a term from history and cultural anthropology, and Mega-Mexico interchangeably to refer to a province of North America that includes the Republic of Mexico and the areas north of the border annexed by the United States after the Mexican War of 1846–1848 and now known as the U.S. Southwest (Texas, New Mexico, Colorado, Arizona, California, and parts of Utah and Nevada).

The sources of ecological knowledge in contemporary Mexican-origin communities run the gamut from *A* to *Z*—literally from Aztec to Zapotec. From ancient Mayan cities in the heart of Mexico's tropical jungles to the transnational suburbs of Zapotec Indians in twenty-first-century Los Angeles, Mexican-origin people have created a cultural and ecological Mega-Mexico. They have long-established historical and cultural ties across the border from Chiapas to Seattle.

Chapter 3 describes human-induced processes of ecological and cultural change in Mexico, south of the current U.S.–Mexico border—El Sur. This environmental history starts with two **ecological revolutions** involving different **modes of production.** The first is the aboriginal mode of production (from before Spanish contact to 1519), which was based on a more or less sustainable relationship between local cultures and the natural world. Mexico's indigenous cultures saw nature as the sacred source of all livelihood. This mode of production led to profound ecological changes, including the domestication of an extraordinary variety of native wild plants. Aboriginal Mexicans developed the **land race** cultivars of maize, beans, and squash from wild relatives more than five thousand years ago. The second ecological revolution was the Spanish colonial mode of production (1519–1821), a long period of turbulent ecological and cultural change. Invasion and colonization by Europeans and their horses, cattle, hogs, wheat, and other biological and cultural baggage created a new ecology in postconquest Mexico.

In Chapter 4, the focus shifts to the area north of the present border—El Norte. The chapter starts with an overview of biological diversity in a landscape of "mountain islands and desert seas." It examines the myth of a pristine wilderness and introduces the ancestral indigenous civilizations. A third ecological revolution is associated with the unique **Norteña/o** mode of production (1598–1848). This mode of production emphasized communal property and cooperative labor in a frontier environment. It allowed the peoples of El Norte to inhabit most places from Texas to California without causing significant harm to the environment. A fourth ecological revolution is tied to the rise of the industrial-capitalist mode of production (1848–1950), which promoted the exploitation of labor and nature as **commodities.** This most recent ecological revolution unleashed a second grand episode of environmental disturbance and cultural change, resulting in the extinction of numerous native species and the disruption of local cultures and landscapes.

Mexican Americans and Ecological Politics

Chapters 5, 6, and 7 deal with the history of American ecological politics in light of the Mexican American experience. The chapters cover three major waves of environmentalism, a social movement based on the science or philosophy of ecology. Chapter 5 covers the first wave of environmentalism, which occurred around the turn of the twentieth century (the 1890s and 1900s). It involved disputes between two opposing philosophies originally proposed by Gifford Pinchot and John Muir. Pinchot was a champion of scientific management of forests and embraced a philosophy of **natural resource conservation** for the sake of economic development. Muir was an impassioned defender of **wilderness preservation** who worked to prevent ecological damage by placing limits on the economic uses of intact native forests and other so-called wild landscapes. Muir thought nature should exist as much as possible in a pristine, undisturbed state. Wilderness was a place where humans were only visitors and nature could evolve without human interference. These two movements shaped U.S. environmental policy and law over the entire course of the twentieth century.

There are sharp differences between Chicana/o concepts of the environment and the natural resource and wilderness schools of thought in mainstream environmentalism. Mexican Americans tend to define nature as homeland, not natural resources or wilderness. These differences have important political and ecological consequences, which I critique throughout chapter 5. Chapter 5 also describes the second wave of environmentalism involving the rise of the Group of Ten (G10) in the 1970s. The G10 consists of financially well-endowed national environmental organizations that have played critical roles in American ecological politics since about the late 1970s. These corporate-style organizations reinvented the ecology movement by making it more professional. They relied on an army of competent legal, scientific, and political experts to pressure Congress to enact federal laws supporting a clearly defined national environmental agenda. Chapter 5 closes with a discussion of Rachel Carson, a scientist who occupies a unique place in the history of environmentalism because of the bridges she built between science and the public interest.

Chapter 6 focuses on a third wave of environmentalism involving post-1980 radical ecological movements. In the United States they include movements for **deep ecology, social ecology, ecosocialism, ecofeminism,** bioregionalism, and environmental justice. I discuss the common ground, philosophical differences, and political conflicts between Chicana/o communities and the various radical environmental movements. The chapter ends with an overview of the EJM, which effected changes in contemporary environmental policies by bridging the concepts of nature/environment, culture, and social justice.

Finally, chapter 7 reviews the Mexican American EJM since the 1980s. It follows the central themes of the grassroots voices quoted earlier. I present the struggles of different Mexican American communities, including farmworkers, urban residents, farmers and ranchers in land grant villages, factory workers, and rural colonia residents. The struggles of these various communities have contributed to the rise of a powerful social movement that is reinventing the science and politics of ecology. Through the EJM, they have sought to promote economic and political equality and self-determination, and they have often integrated environmental protection into these struggles.

The Mexican American people have borne a disproportionate share of the burden of environmental risks. They have endured pollution and other forms of environmental degradation compounded by social problems like poverty and lack of education. In both rural and urban communities, Mexican-origin people are the first to be affected by development projects that uproot them from their homes; pollute their land, water, and air; and force them into menial jobs and wretched poverty. The efforts to clean up and protect Mexican American communities from further harm are everywhere met by unresponsive bureaucracies and legal red tape. These injustices are examples of environmental racism, and they are important aspects of the Chicana/o experience that resulted in organizing struggles and movements for environmental and economic justice.

The conclusion examines the future of ecology and environmental politics in relation to the activism of the Mexican-origin people on both sides of the border. The **globalization** of the economy through so-called free trade agreements like the **North American Free Trade Agreement (NAFTA)** is affecting the course of environmental problems across borders. These changes have provoked an international grassroots environmental and economic justice movement. Mexican-origin communities are developing sustainable and equitable alternatives to global capitalism. Mexican-origin people are a diverse set of indigenous and **mestiza/o** ethnic communities ranging from those of the Maya in the autonomous Zapatista zones of the Lacandón jungle in Chiapas, the transnational community of Zapotec Indians who maintain places in the mountains of Oaxaca and in the Los Angeles basin (Oaxacalifornia), and the acequia farmers in San Luis, Colorado. These communities of resistance offer hope for social justice, democracy, and ecology in a world torn apart by inequality, greed, and power, and the selfish destruction of our home, the earth.

■ **Notes**

1. R. García, "Notes on (Home)Land Ethics: Ideas, Values, and the Land," in *Chicano Culture, Ecology, Politics: Subversive Kin,* ed. D. G. Peña (Tucson: University of Arizona Press, 1998), 79–120. García uses the term Indo-Hispano to refer to the indigenous Mexican people of northern New Mexico and southern Colorado.

2. D. G. Peña, "The 'Brown' and the 'Green': Chicanos and Environmental Politics in the Upper Rio Grande, *Capitalism, Nature, Socialism* 3 (1992): 79–109; quotation on pp. 91–92.

3. D. A. Alston, ed., *We Speak for Ourselves: Social Justice, Race, and Environment* (Washington, DC: Panos Institute, 1990).

4. C. Chávez, "Farmworkers at Risk," in *Toxic Struggles: The Theory and Practice of Environmental Justice,* ed. R. Hofrichter (Philadelphia: New Society Publishers, 1993), 163–64.

5. Quoted in E. Mann and the Watchdog Organizing Committee, *L.A.'s Lethal Air: New Strategies for Policy, Organizing, and Action* (Los Angeles: Labor/Community Strategy Center, 1991), 8.

6. R. Moore and L. Head, "Building a Net That Works," in *Unequal Protection: Environmental Justice and Communities of Color,* ed. R. D. Bullard (San Francisco: Sierra Club Books, 1994), 195.

7. Moore and Head, "Acknowledging the Past, Confronting the Present: Environmental Justice in the 1990s," in Hofrichter, *Toxic Struggles,* 120–21.

8. J. C. Gallegos, "El futuro," in *Sangre de Tierra: The Life and Works of an Acequia Farming Family,* 37–39 (original book manuscript by J. Gallegos, April 2001, San Luis, Colorado; in the author's collection).

9. A. Kaber, V. Sánchez, and E. Sánchez, "Acequias, Generaciones y Compuertas," in *Voces de la Tierra: Five Hundred Years of Acequia Farms in the Rio Arriba, 1598–1998,* ed. D. G. Peña and R. O. Martínez (Tucson: University of Arizona Press, forthcoming).

10. T. Jaramillo, interview by D. G. Peña, June 1998, El Poso, Sierra Culebra, Colorado (in the author's collection at the Rio Grande Bioregions Project, University of Washington, Seattle).

11. Quoted in D. G. Peña, "Endangered Landscapes and Disappearing People? Identity, Place, and Community in Ecological Struggles," in *The Environmental Justice Reader: Politics, Poetics, Pedagogy,* ed. J. Adamson, M. M. Evans, and R. Stein (Tucson: University of Arizona Press, 2002).

12. Quoted in M. Davis, "Philosophy Meets Practice: A Critique of Ecofeminism through the Voices of Three Chicana Activists," in Peña, *Chicano Culture, Ecology, Politics,* 223, 222.

13. Kaber, Sanchez, and Sanchez, "Acequias," 9.

14. Aubin Maestas, responding to a reporter's question about his participation in an anti-logging protest at the Taylor Ranch in San Luis, Colorado (June 1995).

15. See Rodolfo Acuña, *Occupied America: A History of Chicanos* (New York: Harper and Row, 1988) for an introduction to the history of Chicana/o struggles and social movements.

16. J. Rzedowski, "Diversity and Origins of the Phanerogamic Flora of Mexico," in *Biological Diversity of Mexico: Origins and Distribution,* ed. T. P. Ramamoorthy, R. Bye, A. Lot, and J. Fa (Oxford: Oxford University Press, 1993), 134–35.

Mexican Americans

& the Environment

Principles of Scientific Ecology

The ecosystem concept provides a way to interpret the idea of the whole . . . and the organization of nature in space and time.
—Frank B. Golley (1993)

Ernst Haeckel, a prominent German zoologist and follower of Charles Darwin, proposed the concept of **ecology** in 1866. *Oekologie* was the name he gave to the scientific study of "the relations of living organisms to the external world, their **habitat,** customs, energies, [and] parasites."[1] The early classical ecologists focused their research on local environments, but by the end of the twentieth century, the various approaches to scientific ecology shared a fundamental idea: that the field of study, the **ecosystem,** includes both living organisms (the **biota**) and the extended physical world surrounding and permeating life (the abiota). Even the stable range of temperature and the oxygen content of the atmosphere are created and maintained by the biota. In terms of planetary history, it took a billion years for bacterial life-forms to create the mix of oxygen and nitrogen we breathe today.[2] Whereas classical ecologists viewed ecosystems as existing in ideal steady states, now we believe that the web of interactions between biotic and abiotic factors creates a constant process of pulse, flux, and disturbance.

Humans have historically been overlooked as a part of this complex web of ecological relationships. People are part of the environment, and our economic and social activities have wide-ranging effects on ecosystems. Arguably, all areas of the earth have been inhabited or managed in some way by people for some time. Human inhabitation has often resulted in ecological damage, but important exceptions are discussed later. The **globalization** of modern development practices over the past five hundred years has led to environmental degradation and social and economic displacement. Global warming, ozone depletion, deforestation, desertification, and the contamination and depletion of clean air and water all appear to reduce the ability of planetary ecosystems to support human and nonhuman life. Perhaps the most profound lessons of ecology are to be found in

Topic Highlight 1. Environmental Threats to Ecosystems, Biodiversity, and Human Health

Scientific ecologists have shown how environmental damage to eco-systems destroys habitat, reduces the diversity of species of flora and fauna, and impairs human health. Some estimates place the annual cost of damage to ecosystems at more than $800 billion in lost productivity of nature and similar billions in health and social costs. Some environmental threats, like global warming, have the potential to disrupt planetary eco-systems on such a large scale that life as we know it today would likely cease to exist.

Environmental Threat	Examples of Effects on Ecosystems and Humans
Global warming	Shifts in distribution of vegetation, including domes-ticated crops; loss of habitat; displacement and ex-tinction of species; human hunger and displacement
Ozone depletion	Loss of protective ozone layer leading to damage to all plant and animal life; higher rates of skin cancer, cataracts, and other diseases among humans
Deforestation	Loss of habitat leading to extinction of flora and fauna; displacement or extermination of local, land-based cultures
Desertification	Reduction in soil fertility and disruption of nutrient cycles leading to decline of agriculture; loss of hab-itat leading to extinction of flora and fauna
Air pollution	Acid rain damage to boreal forests and natural wa-ter bodies; increases in cardiopulmonary and other human diseases due to smog
Water pollution	Pollution or loss of habitat leading to extinction of aquatic life; increased human health problems due to contaminated water

Biodiversity is the variety of living organisms on the planet, including all species of plants, animals, fungi, algae, bacteria, and other micro-organisms. Biodiversity also includes the variety of life patterns and processes (ecosystem structures and functions) and biosphere diversity. The biodiversity of living organisms encompasses the following known and estimated total species:

LIFE-FORM	KNOWN SPECIES	ESTIMATED SPECIES
Insects, arthropods	874,161	30 million
Higher plants	248,400	275,000–400,000
Other invertebrates	116,873	millions
Fungi, algae	73,900	—
Fish	19,056	21,000
Birds	9,040	9,200
Reptiles, amphibians	8,962	9,400
Mammals	4,000	4,200

Habitat refers to the ecological living space of species. Many different species typically live in and use the same habitat, and the specific role each species plays in the habitat is called its **ecological niche.** The principle of the interconnection of species is an important concept in ecosystems ecology. If human activity eliminates a niche, there are often cascading effects that harm other species. Destruction of habitat is the primary cause of species extinctions in the world today. ■

the growing evidence linking environmental damage with harmful effects on the health of humans and other organisms. The rise of a synthetic and highly toxic environment has led to widespread reduction of biodiversity (see topic highlight 1). These and numerous other forms of ecological change have been criticized as direct hits on the planet's life-support systems, biodiversity, and cultural diversity. People's direct lived experience of ecological degradation and social injustice has led to powerful **new social movements** to protect the environment. Ecology is thus not only a set of scientific methods and theoretical models for the study of the interrelations of biota and abiota. It is also a set of political practices and **discourses** tied to **social movements** seeking to protect the environment.

In this chapter I introduce the principles of classical scientific ecology as developed by ecologists over the first half of the twentieth century. I start with the grand classical themes of interconnection, holism, climax, association, community, and the search for **equilibrium** models of nature. The classical school championed the ideal of the ecosystem as a superorganism created by the cumulative effects of plants moving toward a harmonious climax state. These concepts were further developed amid mid-twentieth-century debates over the predominant models that treated the environment as an integrated whole, a collection of interconnected plant and animal communities that existed in a state of equilibrium.

An American chemist, Ellen Swallow Richards, was the first to popularize the concept of ecology in the United States in the early 1900s.[3] Swallow defined ecology as the study of the relations of living organisms with their organic and nonorganic surroundings. She proposed that this study should always be connected to *human ecology,* "the study of the surroundings of human beings in the effects they produce on the lives of men [*sic*]." Included are the natural environment (land, water, air), other natural conditions of existence (like climate and light), and the "artificial," or **built environment,** produced by human activity along with "noise, dust, poisonous vapors, vitiated air, dirty water, and unclean food."[4]

Swallow's integration of early classical ecology with human ecology is noteworthy. With the exception of Aldo Leopold and Eugene Odum, most thinkers during the classical period of ecology focused on the "pure" scientific study of the natural environment. They proceeded as if the environment could be examined separate from human cultures and societies. Unfortunately, for much of the twentieth century, scientific ecologists largely lost sight of Swallow's case for integrating human interactions with environmental conditions.[5] Instead, scientific ecologists focused on natural plant and animal species and their habitats. It would take the better part of the twentieth century for ecologists to bring humans back into the study of ecology.

 ## Succession to Climax or Accidental Associations?

Frederic Clements ushered in the classical American school of ecology with its focus on the study of the evolution of plant communities. He is best known for the principles of plant succession and the concept of the vegetational climax. Clements believed that every region of the earth experienced ecological change in a manner that led to a *climax successional community.* In other words, he saw plant communities in a given area evolving from less to more complexity and diversity, leading to a mature and complex equilibrium state, which he called the climax.[6] The particular climax state of vegetation in a given area was largely determined by the climate there. Clements's model of natural plant evolution included three basic ideas: (1) interconnection, or the interdependency of a community of species; (2) holism, or how the community of species forms a whole organism complex that is greater than the sum of its parts; and (3) climax, or an ideal endpoint state of maturity, complexity, and stability.

Herbert Gleason criticized the idea that plants progressed toward an inevitable climax. He discerned a more open and less predictable pattern of dynamic plant associations. While recognizing the existence of plant communities, he rejected the idea that these came into existence by sheer force of collective action as if by some sort of superorganism. Instead, he proposed that plant communities were accidental associations and at least partly the outcome of adaptations by individual species that produced a shifting mosaic of plants. These more or less random associations were outcomes of the competition for **ecological niches** (the roles of species in a set of overlapping habitats):

> Plant associations exist. . . . [But when we] attempt to classify associations, as individual examples of vegetation, into broader groups . . . [w]e enter the domain of philosophy, and speculate on the fundamental nature of the association, regard[ing] it as the basic unit of vegetation. . . . An area of vegetation which one ecologist regards as a single association may by another be considered as a mosaic or mixture of several . . . associations.[7]

There were sharp disputes between the followers of Clements, who believed that plant communities behaved like organisms (organismic school), and anticlimax thinkers like Gleason, who envisioned more random associations driven largely by the adaptive responses of individual members of species to environmental conditions (individualist school). Subsequent work in ecology led to the development of the concept of the ecosystem as a way to bridge the organismic and individualist schools of thought.

■ Nature as Ecosystem

Arthur Tansley, a British botanist, introduced the concept of the ecosystem in an article published in 1935. Critical of the successional climax school, Tansley developed the ecosystem concept in order to overcome the idea that natural species form a type of superorganism that is a "self-willing" biotic community. Instead, "the more fundamental conception is . . . the whole *system* (in the sense of physics), including not only the organism-complex, but also the whole complex of physical factors forming what we call the environment of the **biome**—the habitat factors in the widest sense."[8]

Tansley explained the concept of the ecosystem in three principles: (1) a hierarchy of physical systems, (2) a tendency toward relatively stable states of equilibrium, and (3) the interconnection between an organism-complex and a physical-environmental complex.[9] He placed the concept of species interconnectedness in a new context by envisioning the ecosystem as a pyramid-like structure. This hierarchical structure included living organisms in a complex web of relationships with the physical-environmental complex, that is, the abiota. Thus, biotic organisms and the "physical-chemical environment" in which they lived acted together to form an ecosystem. This physical-environmental complex included inorganic environmental factors like air, sunlight, and moisture as well as the universal laws of physics, like gravity, magnetism, and especially entropy (the degradation of matter and energy into a state of decay).

■ The Web of Life

Inspired by the work of Charles Elton, American ecologist Raymond Lindeman published in 1942 the first paper outlining a model of the ecosystem as a **food web.**[10] This was one of the first attempts to chart energy flows in a biological system. Lindeman was interested in the nature of the food cycle because it represented an excellent biological example of the Second Law of Thermodynamics (the tendency of energy to dissipate toward a state of entropy). He described the food cycle as an energy circuit or web of relationships among different organisms. He differentiated organisms into four types called producers, consumers, decomposers, and transformers (see figure 1). The producers, also known as *autotrophs,* generate their own nourishment. Consumers, known as *heterotrophs,* must consume other organisms to survive, and *transformers* include certain bacteria that can convert organic into inorganic compounds.

In this web of life, plants are the primary producers because they fix carbon by transforming sunlight (a source of energy) through photosynthesis. This process converts inorganic substances such as carbon dioxide and

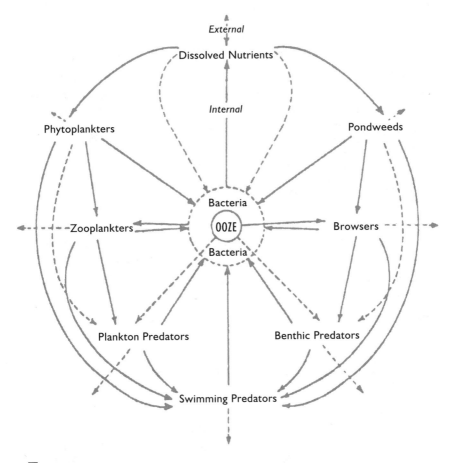

External

Dissolved Nutrients

Internal

Phytoplankters

Pondweeds

Bacteria

OOZE

Bacteria

Zooplankters

Browsers

Plankton Predators

Benthic Predators

Swimming Predators

■ I. Lindeman's food web.

water into complex organic substances. Animals are the primary consumers because they utilize vegetation, or other smaller animals that feed on plants, as their source of energy. Certain bacteria and fungi are classic decomposers because they use the chemical substances in dead organisms for their energy. In this web of life, the consumer is eventually consumed because death is a form of energy recycling. Lindeman saw the food web as organized in the structure of a pyramid or hierarchy: "The organisms within an ecosystem may be grouped into a series of more or less discrete trophic levels . . . as producers, primary consumers, secondary consumers, etc., each successively dependent upon the preceding level as a source of energy."[11]

Lindeman supported individualist ecology by appealing to the competitive hierarchy of the food web. He also supported the organism-complex school by arguing for the interconnection of species through the energy circuits of the food web. Living organisms were seen as delicately interconnected through various successively dependent trophic (energy transfer) levels. It would take another important thinker to fully develop philosophical and especially ethical concepts that resonated with the principles of scientific ecology in the mid-twentieth century.

■ The Land Ethic

In 1949, Aldo Leopold's book, *A Sand County Almanac*, was published posthumously. This beautifully written and thoughtful little book is arguably the most enduring and influential contribution to American **environmental ethics.** Beginning from the concept of community, Leopold argued that the **land ethic** "simply enlarges the boundaries of the community to include soils, water, plants, and animals, or collectively: the land." Leopold's land ethic "changes the role of *Homo sapiens* from conqueror of the land-community to plain member and citizen of it."[12] Leopold had a scientific background as a game and wildlife manager, but he seemed more willing than other scientists to discuss the social, cultural, and political-economic implications of ecology. Leopold strongly objected to economic imperatives, which he believed reduced the prospects for conservation of the **land organism.** He spelled out this concern in clear and eloquent terms: "Conservation is getting nowhere because it is incompatible with our Abrahamic concept of the land. We abuse the land because we regard it as a **commodity** belonging to us. When we see the land as a community to which we belong, we may begin to use it with love and respect."[13]

Leopold popularized the principles of scientific ecology, making them available to a wider audience. But he never resolved certain limitations in his work. Leopold was critical of the commodification of the land, of the way in which capitalism treated land, water, and even living organisms as things to be bought and sold on the market for a profit. However, he never offered a direct critique of capitalism. Leopold consistently avoided a direct and frank critique of the problematic role of capitalist production values in the exploitation and degradation of the land. This aversion to addressing political-economic contradictions became embedded in much of American environmental ethics for several decades.

Leopold remained more or less wed to an economic view of nature. He never fully escaped his background in game management, as reflected in his view of the land in terms of its "biological productivity," which he took as a sign of organismic health. Leopold also never abandoned the use of old and mixed metaphors. At one moment he calls the land an organism, and at another likens it to an "ecological mechanism."[14] A key point about Leopold is that his writings were not just a watershed in the development of the ethical dimensions of scientific ecology; they informed the work of many important environmental organizations such as the Wilderness Society, which he cofounded to advocate for public policies based on the land ethic. He helped move scientific ecology toward a more open and practical engagement with ecological politics.

■ Stability and Change in Ecosystems

By the 1950s, Eugene P. Odum had synthesized ecology in his treatise *Fundamentals of Ecology* (1953).[15] His grand synthesis resulted in a set of conceptual innovations on old themes. His ecosystems model focused on both stability and change. Odum creatively brought together the classic concerns of structure and function with an emergent focus on processes of change. For Odum, the structure and function of the ecosystem, while hierarchical, was also integrated across different spatial and temporal levels. He conceptualized the structure of life as a hierarchical "biological spectrum," ranging from the smallest organized bits of matter to the largest geophysical structures that constituted the **biosphere.** Moving from the micro level to the macro scale, the biological spectrum encompassed protoplasm, cells, tissues, organs, organ systems, organisms, populations, communities, ecosystems, and the biosphere. Odum also clarified the **biome** types in the world, identifying six major terrestrial biomes, or climate-based divisions: coniferous forest, deciduous forest, desert, grassland, mountain, tropical rain forest, and tundra.

Odum's most significant contribution was the concept of **homeostasis,** or dynamic balance. This effort to reconcile the principles of order and change in ecosystems proposed that the biological spectrum is integrated and interdependent. The ecosystem is also subject to perturbations, which are localized disturbances expressed in the breakdown of the feedback loops of the ecosystem (see figure 2). The biotic structure (community of life-forms) of the ecosystem creates biochemical feedback loops that

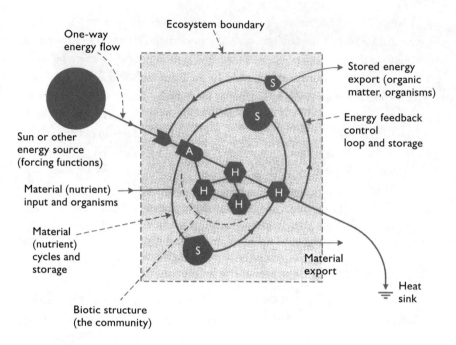

One-way
energy flow

Ecosystem boundary

Stored energy
export (organic
matter, organisms)

Energy feedback
control
loop and storage

Sun or other
energy source
(forcing functions)

Material (nutrient)
input and organisms

Material
(nutrient)
cycles and
storage

Material
export

Heat
sink

Biotic structure
(the community)

■ 2. Functional diagram of an ecosystem by Eugene Odum.

function as a system of checks and balances. These energy feedback loops in the ecosystem are created by the cycling and storage of materials and nutrients. These feedback loops can "dampen oscillations," or minimize the changes, caused by fluctuations in environmental conditions.

Odum proposed that homeostasis accounts for the resilience of the ecosystem in the face of environmental disturbance and change. He further proposed that scale (in time and space) is a factor of some importance in determining differences in ecosystem resilience.[16] At smaller scales and shorter time frames, the feedback loops of the ecosystem function as **set-point controls** to prevent the system from slipping into chaos then collapsing in a state of entropy. At larger scales, however, set-point controls are unpredictable. Odum believed ecosystem complexity was evidence that the energy produced by nature was at its highest state of efficiency and productivity.

Odum warned that human activities, if not properly managed by ecosystem engineers, could result in serious damage to nature's elegant balance. For example, agricultural runoff and industrial point source pollution can alter nutrient cycling and the availability of energy to living organisms. Human disturbances can provoke *cascading effects* that permeate through the different levels of the ecosystem. For example, a breakdown of natural chemical balances in a lake contaminated by pollution cause fish to begin dying; algal blooms and other single-species dominant niches appear. The biochemical feedback loops can no longer maintain a fully habitable environment under such conditions. In Odum's ecosystems ecology, the extended biophysical environment is a source of adaptation because the life-forms of the biological spectrum have had to develop "strategies" to deal with processes of ecosystemic change. The resulting dynamic balance is what Odum defined as homeostasis. This complex model became known as **cybernetic,** or ecosystems, ecology. Odum's work, funded by the Atomic Energy Commission, was important because it rendered biological concepts compatible with the framework of information theory (and therefore eventually computer simulations). Energy was conceptualized as bits of information. Natural ecosystems processed this information through multiply redundant self-regulating feedback loops to maintain a homeostatic state of dynamic equilibrium, in which the whole maintains stability despite fluctuations in its parts.

Critiques of Cybernetic Ecology

By 1960, the cybernetic ecosystems model had become the dominant **paradigm** in American environmental science. In universities it was championed as the "New Ecology" that promised to deliver a science of **sustainable ecosystem management** to a nation stung by widespread air and water pollution. It was not without its critics, however. Some criticized its mechanistic depiction of nature, top-down engineering ethos, and reflection of managerial capitalist values.[17] Odum's ties to military research agencies and the Atomic Energy Commission reinforced this view of a technocratic approach to ecology. Greg Mitman expressed concern that Odum's cybernetic ecosystems theory treated nature as "a system of components that could be managed, manipulated, and controlled. The ecologist's task increasingly became that of environmental engineer; ecologists were to be professional managers who could monitor and fix the environmental problems created by human society."[18]

Donald Worster notes that the managerial ethos of cybernetic ecosystems theory translated into bureaucratic practices that privileged scientific experts as responsible for managing a hitherto mismanaged environment.[19] Worster also notes that modern capitalist organization had a broad role in shaping New Ecology by making it "conform . . . neatly to modern society and its expectation of nature." He claimed Odum's model of the ecosystem was merely imitating the logic of the "modernized economic system":

> [N]ature now becomes a corporate state, a chain of factories, an assembly line. Conflict can have little place in such a well-regulated economy. . . . In this age of computer-run organizations, it was probably inevitable that ecology too would come to emphasize the flow of goods and services— or of energy—in a kind of automated, robotized, pacified nature.[20]

Other ecologists emphasized how cybernetic ecology provided an alternative set of values derived from the model's elegant articulation of interconnection and interdependency: "[A] finely sustained balance appeared to be at the center of nature's complexity, not individualism, waste, selfish competition, and brutish power," observed one of Odum's more eloquent defenders.[21] On numerous public occasions Odum took a position against environmental destruction stemming from the abuses of the military-industrial complex, saying, "Humans ignored the circular causality inherent in nature at their own peril; they risked making their own environments uninhabitable, their own future unsustainable." Other eco-activists defended Odum's ecosystems model because they associated it with alternative values of self-restraint, stability, cooperation, humility, and moderation.[22]

Despite these controversies, the development of scientific ecology over the course of the first half of the twentieth century set the stage for the rise of new approaches to the study of human interactions with the environment. The emergence of **chaotic ecology** in the 1970s and 1980s is the focus of the next chapter. This new paradigm focuses on human and natural disturbances as sources of ecological change. In other words, it focuses on conflict instead of order and on change instead of stability.

■ Discussion Questions

1. Discuss the key points of disagreement between the organismic and individualist schools of scientific ecology.

2. What are some examples of the interrelationships between biotic and abiotic factors that illustrate the idea of homeostasis?

3. Identify and discuss the range of biome types in your locality.

4. Name at least three species in your area that are extinct or endangered. What caused their extinction or endangerment?

5. Discuss the refinements to classical ecology proposed by later theorists. Did Tansley resolve the conflict between the organismic and individualist schools? Did Lindeman? Odum?

6. The Atomic Energy Commission funded Odum's work. In what ways could this have influenced the development of ecosystems ecology?

■ Suggested Readings

Bramwell, Anna. 1980. *Ecology in the Twentieth Century: A History.* New Haven: Yale University Press.

Clarke, Robert. 1974. *Ellen Swallow: The Woman Who Founded Ecology.* New York: Follett.

Golley, Frank B. 1993. *A History of the Ecosystem Concept in Ecology: More Than the Sum of the Parts.* New Haven: Yale University Press.

Leopold, Aldo. 1949. *A Sand County Almanac.* Oxford: Oxford University Press.

Merchant, Carolyn. 1993. "The Emergence of Ecology in the Twentieth Century." In *Major Problems in American Environmental History,* ed. Carolyn Merchant. Lexington: D. C. Heath and Co.

Odum, Eugene P. 1953. *Fundamentals of Ecology.* Philadelphia: Saunders.

———. 1997. *Ecology: A Bridge between Science and Society.* Sunderland, MA: Sinauer Associates.

Worster, Donald. 1977. *Nature's Economy: A History of Ecological Ideas.* Cambridge: Cambridge University Press.

———. 1993. *The Wealth of Nature: Environmental History and the Ecological Imagination.* New York: Oxford University Press.

■ Notes

1. Haeckel derived *ecology* from the Greek root *oikos,* "the daily maintenance and operation of the family household." *Oikos* is also the root for the older term *Oekonomie,* and Haeckel used the second meaning of the root word to suggest that "the living organisms of the earth constitute a single economic unit resembling a household

or family dwelling intimately together, in conflict as well as in mutual aid"; quoted in D. Worster, *Nature's Economy: A History of Ecological Ideas* (Cambridge: Cambridge University Press, 1994), 192.

2. J. Lovelock, *Gaia* (New York: Oxford University Press, 1979); L. Margulis, "Gaia, The Living Earth: A Dialogue with Fritjof Capra," *The Elmwood Newsletter* 5, no. 2 (1989); L. Margulis and D. Sagan, *Microcosmos* (New York: Summit, 1986), and *What Is Life?* (New York: Simon and Schuster, 1995); S. H. Schneider and P. J. Boston, eds., *Scientists on Gaia* (Cambridge, MA: MIT Press, 1993).

3. C. Merchant, *Major Problems in American Environmental History* (Lexington: D. C. Heath and Co., 1993), 444; see also R. Clarke, *Ellen Swallow: The Woman Who Founded Ecology* (New York: Follett, 1973).

4. Merchant, *Major Problems,* 445.

5. D. G. Peña, "The 'Brown' and the 'Green': Chicanos and Environmental Politics in the Upper Rio Grande," *Capitalism, Nature, Socialism* 3, no. 1 (1992): 79–103.

6. Worster, *Nature's Economy,* 2, and "Nature and the Disorder of History," in *Reinventing Nature? Responses to Postmodern Deconstruction,* ed. M. J. Soulé and G. Lease (Washington, DC: Island Press, 1995), 65–85.

7. H. A. Gleason, *Plant Associations and Their Classification: A Reply to Dr. Nichols* (Ithaca: International Congress of Plant Science, 1926). Quoted in Merchant, *Major Problems,* 448.

8. A. G. Tansley, "The Use and Abuse of Vegetational Concepts and Terms," *Ecology* 16, no 3 (1935): 284–307; quotation on p. 299.

9. F. B. Golley, *A History of the Ecosystem Concept: More Than the Sum of the Parts.* (New Haven: Yale University Press, 1993), 8–9.

10. R. L. Lindeman, "The Trophic-Dynamic Aspect of Ecology," *Ecology* 23, no. 4 (1942): 399–418.

11. Quoted in Merchant, *Major Problems,* 453–54.

12. A. Leopold, *A Sand County Almanac* (New York: Oxford University Press, 1949), 204.

13. Quoted in Worster, *Nature's Economy,* 287.

14. Ibid.

15. E. P. Odum, *Fundamentals of Ecology* (Philadelphia: Saunders, 1953).

16. E. P. Odum, *Ecology: A Bridge between Science and Society* (Sunderland, MA: Sinauer Associates, 1997), 44–45.

17. B. Bryant, "Nature and Culture in the Age of Cybernetic Systems" (paper presented at the Annual Meeting of the American Sociological Association, August 2000), available from http://epsilon3.georgetown.edu/~coventrm/asa2000/panel3/bryant.html; also see G. Mitman, *The State of Nature: Ecology, Community, and American Social Thought, 1900–1950* (Chicago: University of Chicago Press, 1992); Worster, *Nature's Economy.*

18. Mitman, *State of Nature,* 210.

19. Worster, *Nature's Economy,* 313.

20. Quoted in Ibid.

21. Bryant, "Nature and Culture," 5.

22. Ibid., 5–6; quotation on p. 5.

Ecologies of Chaos

Most of nature is very, very complicated. How could one describe a cloud? A cloud is not a sphere. . . . It is like a ball but very irregular. A mountain? A mountain is not a cone. . . . If you want to speak of clouds, of mountains, of rivers, of lightning, the geometric language of school is inadequate.
—Mandelbrot (1990)

Culture is what one must know to act effectively in one's environment.
—Eugene Hunn (1989)

As children we quickly learn that the weather can be unpredictable. The forecast calls for sunny skies but instead we are deluged by a heavy rainstorm. The idea that the natural world is so complex as to be virtually unpredictable underlies **chaos theory** (also called *complexity theory*). This does not mean that attempts to understand **ecosystems** are futile. It does mean that ecosystems are extraordinarily complex and not readily managed to serve human aims without causing unanticipated consequences. The original source of chaos theory is a legendary story told in 1961 by meteorologist Edward Lorenz of the butterfly effect: A butterfly flaps its wings in Brazil and Texas gets a tornado.[1] His point was that tiny differences in the initial conditions of a given system can result in unpredictable consequences at higher levels. Chaos theory offered a new view of ecosystems that emphasized disturbance and the **uncertainty** at all levels of life from the gene and the individual organism to the **biosphere.**

Chaotic ecologists forego the idea that ecosystems strive toward some ultimate natural balance (Odum's **homeostasis**). To them the cybernetic ecosystem model more closely describes the operation of an orderly factory assembly line than the shifting pulses of a lake, pond, marsh, forest, or desert. The cybernetic model assumes that every action and reaction in nature can be known, observed, and controlled. It further assumes that, all ecological conditions and relationships can be regulated (and managed) in accordance with their function in a whole greater than the sum of its parts.

In fact, Howard T. Odum's classic flowchart of the ecosystem looks oddly like clusters of automated factories connected by information superhighways of energy pathways (see figure 3). By the 1970s, chaotic ecologists were realizing that ecosystems seldom follow such orderly, predictable, or manageable patterns.

The **ecology** of chaos focused on humans as principal agents of ecological change. Ecological scientists were beginning to understand the importance of studying plants, animals, **habitats,** landscapes, and the biosphere in light of the environmental changes induced by human activities. They focused on a broad range of changes occurring in a global environment wracked by **anthropogenic** (human-caused) problems such as the ozone hole, climate change, tropical rain forest destruction, and the decline of coral reefs, mangroves, wetlands, and other ecosystems. These changes were increasingly pegged to the uncertainty induced by human activities, especially those associated with industrialization and urbanization.[2]

To appreciate the **Chicana/o** experience from ecological vantage points one must understand the new approaches to ecosystem science. Here I present five distinct subfields of ecosystem science that contribute to an elaboration of ecological perspectives on the Mexican American experience:

- *Conservation biology,* which focuses on the ecological effects of natural and human disturbances on the diversity of species, genetic materials, habitat, and processes of evolutionary change.

- *Restoration ecology,* which focuses on the rehabilitation and restoration of habitats, ecosystems, and regional landscapes. This approach values the benefits that humans can provide to both urban and rural environments.

- *Environmental history,* which studies the influences over time of human societies on the environment. Environmental history also focuses on ideas about nature and how these have shaped human uses of the environment.

- *Ethnoecology,* which is the study of **traditional environmental knowledge (TEK).** Subfields of ethnoecology range from ethnobiology (local knowledge of plants and animals) to ethnohydrology (local knowledge of watersheds). An important subfield is agroecology, which is the study of agriculture as an ecosystem, with a distinct focus on traditional and indigenous farming practices.

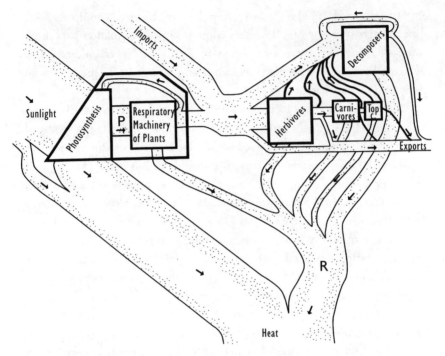

Labels in figure: Imports, Sunlight, Photosynthesis, P, Respiratory Machinery of Plants, Herbivores, Carni-vores, Top, Decomposers, Exports, R, Heat

■ 3. Diagram of the cybernetic ecosystem by Howard Odum, 1957. Notice how energy paths are depicted as freeways and ecological niches as factories.

- *Political ecology,* which focuses on the study of power relations in the production, distribution, and management of **environmental risks** and benefits. Political ecology studies the rise of **social movements** and conflicts related to the environment.

■ The Ecology of Disturbance

A new **paradigm** emerges whenever a shift occurs in the underlying model that defines the methods and theories widely accepted and used by scientists. An important example of this shift involves the influence of chaos theory on the **ecology of disturbance.** Disturbance ecology rejects the classical ideals of a stable climax and **equilibrium.** It focuses instead on a shifting, patchy mosaic pattern of landscapes. The so-called patchy mosaic is the by-product of *nonlinear dynamics*—the fluctuating, pulsating, and even catastrophic quality of ecological processes.

Disturbance ecology sees homeostasis (dynamic balance) as an ideological construct based on a narrow economic, technocratic, and managerial view of nature. Although disturbing things and creating chaos is all part of nature's grand design, this fact does not mean that humans are free to recklessly exploit the earth. Instead, ecologists must regard anthropogenic effects as particularly important because humans, uniquely among all species, have the technological capacity to alter ecosystems in unpredictable ways and at very large spatial (even global) scales. An additional complication is that the "inherent unpredictability of ecosystems plays havoc with conventional resource management." Efforts to manage ecosystems often cause more harm than good to the environment, especially when managers act with disregard for the ecological knowledge and livelihoods of local people.[3]

Conservation Biology

After the passage of the Endangered Species Act of 1973, the conservation of biodiversity became a major concern of citizens, the state, and scientific researchers. Conservation biology uncovered evidence that disturbance is a major factor affecting the evolution of ecosystems, landscapes, and species. Some natural disturbances are not noticeable in a human life span because they occur over vast stretches of time and space. As continents drift over millions of years, titanic forces push and fold mountains, carve out valleys, alter the course of rivers and other waterways, and open or close entire ocean basins. On the other hand, humans can directly observe natural disturbances at smaller temporal and spatial scales, such as volcanoes, earthquakes, landslides, tsunamis, tornados, hurricanes, floods, droughts, El Niño and La Niña, and wildfires.

These disturbances may alter ecosystems across the spatial scale, from individual habitat patches to regional landscapes and the biosphere. At the regional scale, the **landscape mosaic** is altered by natural cycles of disturbance and regeneration. Wildfires follow the contours and limits imposed by terrain and water. Fire returns nutrients to the soil and creates conditions for new plant growth. Some tree species, such as lodgepole pine (*Pinus contorta Dougl.*), even require fire to reproduce. This is why conservation biologists tend to think of natural disturbances as forces that shape the earth's biodiversity. But human modifications have altered the role of such natural processes of environmental change, with potential effects on biodiversity.[4]

Conservation biologists have documented the historical deterioration of ecosystems and the extinction of plant and animal species. They have connected the decline of biodiversity directly to human **fragmentation** of the natural landscape and disturbance of wildlife habitat. They also found that extinction rates were increased by natural changes such as the migration of new species to island environments and by the migration of **invasive species** brought from Europe to nearly every nook and cranny of the planet.[5]

Conservation biologists found that most of the native forests of North America had been transformed over a relatively short period of just two hundred years. The clearing of vegetation by European American settlers had transformed native habitats and ecosystems. Extensive forests, which had been intensively managed for millennia by native peoples through fire and other practices, were converted into isolated patches and remnants. Conservation biologists have described these remaining forest patches as habitat islands isolated from each other in a sea of tree plantations, clear-cuts, **monoculture** farms, and other unnatural openings. Habitat fragmentation is a major anthropogenic force contributing to the extinction of species and loss of biodiversity.[6] For example, deforestation permanently withdraws carbon and other vital nutrients out of the ecosystem; it simplifies the diversity of forest structure and eliminates habitat for forest interior species; and it reduces the pool of genetic diversity available to species for reproduction. Conservation biologists link human activities to the extinction of endangered species every year.[7]

Some conservation biologists focus on the connectivity of landscapes. To optimize reproductive success and maintain genetic diversity, plant and animal species need habitat connected across the landscape. By connecting habitat islands, **biological corridors** allow plants and animals to move around. The connectivity of landscapes is necessary to sustain the full range of biodiversity across the biosphere. It is especially important to reconnect and protect the remaining habitat islands in today's highly fragmented landscapes. Anthropogenic changes in landscape connectivity and habitat integrity increase uncertainty at all levels—genes, individual species and populations, ecosystems, landscapes, regions, and the biosphere.[8]

Conservation biologists have been frank in their appraisal that human activities are principal sources of harmful ecological change. They have tended to view anthropogenesis in largely negative terms, almost invariably seeing human activities as a threat to **ecosystem integrity.** Conservation biologists may however have overgeneralized the destructive influences of human societies by failing to distinguish among the range of land ethics and management practices embraced by the world's diverse **cultures.**

From Disturbance to Restoration Ecology

The rediscovery of anthropogenesis led to applied research in restoration ecology. This field involves the study of anthropogenic changes at the landscape ecology level to determine their implications for the design of strategies to restore and manage ecosystems. Restoration ecology recognizes the significance of disturbance in producing the typical shifting and patchy landscape mosaic. A fundamental focus in restoration ecology is the assessment of the potential role of humans in restoring ecological integrity. Human activities may contribute **ecological services** to the local environment and assist in recovery through active regeneration of degraded places.[9]

Restoration ecologists seek to reconcile human **inhabitation** and livelihood uses with ecosystem protection. One approach involves the establishment of protected core reserves of biodiversity (see figure 4). The core reserve model for **ecosystem management,** used by the United Nations Man in the Biosphere program, is designed to balance the needs for **traditional use areas** with the preservation of wildlife habitat undisturbed by human activities. The process of biodiversity protection operates by setting aside an inviolate core zone of wildlife habitat surrounded by multiple-use buffer zones. Human use increases outward and ecological protection increases inward (see figure 5). Each protected area is ideally linked to other core reserve areas by means of biological corridors. These corridors can connect the highly fragmented and isolated habitat islands that are the predominant landscape pattern in most regions of the world today (see figure 6). This model has been praised as a strategy for balancing the needs of ecosystem integrity (connectivity, biodiversity) with human sustenance and well-being. However, use of this model has led to uncertain results. The Sian Ka'an Biosphere Reserve in Quintana Roo, Mexico, is an example of the limitations and problems facing restoration ecologists seeking to implement conservation theory on the ground.[10] Attempts to establish a protected core zone with surrounding buffer zones are being undermined by conflicts among stakeholders, including indigenous people continuing traditional uses, mestizos displaced from other areas of Mexico relocating there, tourism boosters lobbying for more use of the area, and organized crime illegally harvesting tropical hardwoods.

Restoration ecology has created greater awareness of human limits in

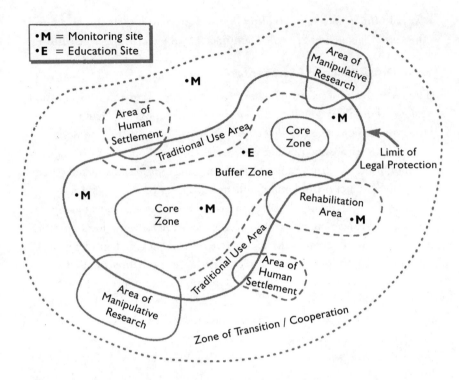

•**M**

Area of
Manipulative
Research

Area of
Human
Settlement

Traditional Use Area

Core
Zone

•**M**

•**E**

Buffer Zone

Limit of
Legal Protection

•**M**

Core
Zone

•**M**

Rehabilitation
Area

•**M**

Traditional Use Area

Area of
Human
Settlement

Area of
Manipulative
Research

Zone of Transition / Cooperation

4. Ideal biosphere reserve design.

ecosystem management.[11] It poses unresolved questions: For example, what is the nature of a pristine environment? How can we know what an environment looked like before it was disturbed by human activities? Is the objective of restoration ecology to re-create pristine environments, or is it to restore ecosystems that can provide habitat for wildlife and areas for **sustainable** human use? Restoration ecology alerts us to the unpredictable and ambiguous results produced by the active role humans have undertaken in constantly reinventing ecosystems.

■ Anthropogenesis: Placing People in the Environment

Environmental history and environmental anthropology study the ways in which concepts like nature, ecosystem, and wilderness are socially constructed and culturally produced. (This does not negate the existence of a biophysical world that surrounds and permeates life independent of the

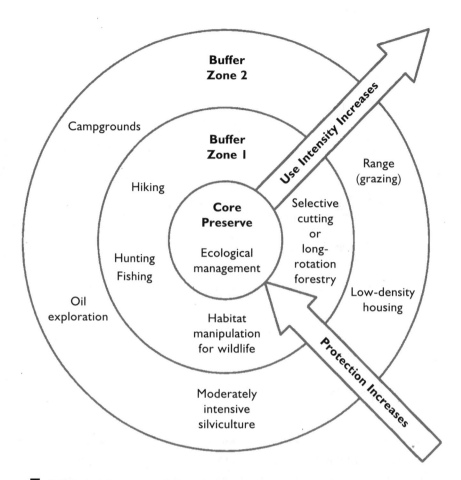

Buffer
Zone 2

Campgrounds

Buffer
Zone 1

Hiking

Use Intensity Increases

Range
(grazing)

Core
Preserve

Selective
cutting
or
long-
rotation
forestry

Hunting
Fishing

Ecological
management

Oil
exploration

Low-density
housing

Habitat
manipulation
for wildlife

Protection Increases

Moderately
intensive
silviculture

■ 5. Biological core reserve design principles.

human imagination.) Historians and anthropologists have emphasized the significance of the contested ways that different human groups define nature in light of conflicting economic, political, and social objectives. Nature becomes that which is perceived through the lens of the world-views and ideologies of given cultures and social classes. Nature is contested terrain wherever different human groups make competing claims to specific places.[12]

Environmental History and the Social Construction of Nature

Environmental history emerged in the 1970s amid studies of the historical patterns of ecological change associated with human inhabitation of the

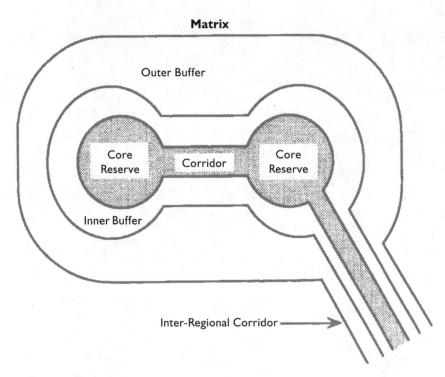

Matrix

Outer Buffer

Core Reserve

Corridor

Core Reserve

Inner Buffer

Inter-Regional Corridor ⟶

■ 6. Design of corridors and core reserves.

earth. The historical study of ecosystems often revolves around the concept of **modes of production.** This refers to the social relations of production, the technology, and the labor processes that human societies use to transform natural resources into sustenance and livelihood. Environmental historians study the changing conditions of ecosystems to better understand processes of ecological transformation under different modes of production that exhibit specific patterns of settlement and resource use.

Some writers see the modern roots of ecological crisis in the spread of *colonialism* (military and political domination in which a territory or nation is invaded, conquered, and administered for the benefit of the invaders) and *imperialism* (the global spread of European and American capitalist military dominance and exploitation of the resources and labor of the Third World).[13] Alfred Crosby's history of ecological imperialism highlights the biological dimensions of conquest, namely the plants, animals, and microorganisms that accompanied the invaders. Colonialism involved catastrophic biological invasions in addition to the political and military suppression of native peoples.[14] For example, the British Empire has been dubbed the "Empire of the Dandelion." The hardy European weed took hold in every nook and cranny of the British Empire. The biological baggage of the European expansion—its weeds, crops, wild and domesticated animals, and microscopic organisms—swept across the empire in wave after relentless wave of invasion that displaced numerous native species and landscapes.

Donald Worster proposes using three factors to guide environmental history: The first is the history of the biophysical landscape itself, that is, the "natural history" of places.[15] Recovering this history may involve reconstructing past or extinct ecosystems that existed before anthropogenic change. The second is the history of human modes of production and reproduction and their effects on the biophysical environment over time. The third involves the history of ecological ideas—of ideologies, belief systems, and ethics—that have shaped human concepts of nature. Political and legal institutions are important in the histories of the socio-spatial organization of places. Worster urges historians to focus on how whole cultures, not just exceptional individuals, perceive and value nature. He believes environmental historians should examine "ideas as ecological agents" because they have transformed the human relationship with nature and account for the rise of modern environmentalism.

Carolyn Merchant proposes a similar approach combining ecology, political economy, and human consciousness. She uses the framework of **ecological revolutions.** These are historical "processes through which different societies change their relationship to nature . . . [and that] arise from tensions between production and ecology and between production and reproduction."[16] Ecological revolutions involve shifts in human consciousness, including human ideologies of nature. Colonialism and capitalism were accompanied by shifts in the modes of economic production and social and cultural reproduction. The colonial and industrial-capitalist ecological revolutions created a split between humans and nature. Merchant believes the subsequent redefinition of nature as a natural resource and **commodity** accelerated its exploitation.

Some scholars focus on shifting historical patterns in class, culture, race/ethnicity, and gender identities in the **discourses** related to the social construction of nature. Theories of difference (of the "Other") in the social construction of nature hold that nature does not exist independent of the texts, narratives, and discourses that humans produce to construct ways of articulating power, meaning, and living in the world. Human experience of the biophysical environment proceeds alongside the development of language, customs, laws, and economies. Culture and social position shape the construction of ideologies of nature, affecting people in their direct lived and material experience of places. For example, the "empty wilderness" that was so strange and threatening to colonial pioneers was a "familiar homeland" filled with memories and place-names for the native inhabitants.[17] Nature is contested terrain in a double sense: It is the site where different human cultures clash over their mythical and legal claims to make use of the environment. It is also the site for contested meanings of place in the battle for political control among contesting value systems that differ in their scientific or economic definitions of nature (for example, as resource, wilderness, ecosystem, or homeland **commons**).

Environmental history places humans back in the field of ecological studies through a variety of methods for the study of anthropogenesis. Insights about ecological change in historically evolving landscapes enhance the scientific study of ecosystem change. Environmental history focuses attention on ideological dimensions of scientific ecology and related discourses. It examines how intellectual models of ecosystems are historically situated; defined by culture, race, class, gender, geography and social position; and constrained by existing political and economic regimes.[18]

Ethnoecology: From Chaos to Reinhabitation

Environmental anthropology focuses on **cultural adaptation** across a wide variety of ecosystems. Research in environmental anthropology encompasses mountain, temperate lowland, tropical rain forest, cold desert, and marine ecosystems, among other settings. It focuses on cultural forms ranging from the earliest small-scale human societies to the contemporary global system. Environmental anthropologists study nature-culture interactions across the social scale from small villages and communities to large associations including states, markets, and other social formations. One approach offers the view that it is not so much individuals but cultures and the institutions of collective action that are the principal agents of ecological change.[19]

Much of the research in environmental anthropology focuses on ecological knowledge beyond the limited Western scientific standpoint—this is the field of *ethnoecology*. It focuses on the diverse place-based knowledge of local cultures, often including ethnic or indigenous communities. The focus of environmental anthropologists on the loss of cultural diversity resonates with the concern of conservation biologists for the loss of biodiversity. Some environmental anthropologists make explicit links between the destruction of biological diversity and the extirpation of cultural diversity. Many see local cultures as stewards of biodiversity and their displacement as a factor tied to the loss of habitat for wild and domesticated species of flora and fauna.[20]

Environmental anthropology developed out of several important intellectual traditions. One is the approach represented by Julian Steward and his students, who developed the principles of **cultural ecology** in the 1950s.[21] Steward proposed a culture core consisting of the strategies and technologies that local human communities develop for subsistence in a given environmental setting. Subsistence technologies and survival strategies are shaped by the limits of local ecological conditions. **Cultural ecology** demonstrates a close connection between the environment and the organization of culture in that place. Local cultures require knowledge of the ecosystem to develop the technology and social organization to effectively inhabit a given place.

Ethnobiology is the study of people's knowledge of plants and animals. In one approach, ethnobiologists study the taxonomies, or cognitive maps, local cultures use to classify plants and animals. Generations of accumulated observations map the environment through specific memories of place. For example, mental maps may identify the location of habitat for particular wild plants useful in the preparation of herbal remedies. Local place-names may define localities by marking sites with names that allude to the ecological qualities of the plants and animals that live there. Place-names may refer to sites of ritual significance, hunting and gathering zones, or places imbued with shared historical meaning. Place-based knowledge is transmitted via the oral tradition, rituals, apprenticeships, and other practices that involve intimate and sustained exchange of local knowledge of the biophysical environment. Local cultures may use such mental maps to organize subsistence strategies or set aside areas for protection. The study of such place-based knowledge illustrates the profound connections between environmental conditions and local livelihoods.[22]

Ethnoecology involves the study of TEK, a particular form of place-based knowledge of the diversity and interactions among plant and animal species, landforms, watercourses, and other qualities of the biophysical environment in a given place. Ethnoecology encompasses a variety of subfields, including ethnobotany (peoples' knowledge of plants), ethnozoology (peoples' knowledge of animals), ethnoentomology (peoples' knowledge of insects), ethnohydrology (peoples' knowledge of watersheds), and agroecology (peoples' knowledge of ecological dynamics in agriculture).[23] The study of ethnoecology demonstrates the depth and sophistication of TEK and the scientific qualities of such local knowledge. Many anthropologists emphasize the idea that TEK is a form of science. Ethnoecology often plays a critical supportive role in intercultural conflicts related to the political, legal, and scientific construction of nature, place, and culture. Ethnoecology can legitimate aboriginal land and water rights and strengthen local participation in environmental management.[24]

Many ethnoecologists focus on structured inequalities that induce displacement of local cultures. In this view, ethnoecology requires an engagement with political ecology. *Structured inequalities*—such as differences in income, poverty, education, access to health care, or political enfranchisement—result from economic and political changes that displace and marginalize local cultures and threaten their livelihoods under the pressures of the global capitalist economic system. These inequalities involve blatant disregard of local knowledge and dismissal of TEK in risk assessment, planning, policy, and legal discourse. In the legal realm, inequities are expressed in the contempt that lawyers and judges often have for **customary law** and normative self-rule by indigenous cultures.[25]

Conservation biologists have too often expressed misanthropic (antihuman) views and have privileged a one-sided story about the human menace to ecosystem integrity. Humans are viewed as bad—an invariably destructive force in nature. I believe ecosystem scientists, including conservation biologists, have drawn too hard a line between people and nature. They have been slow to recognize that numerous local cultures inhabit places without causing significant damage to the ecosystem. Sympathetic ecosystem scientists may select a few fabled indigenous communities to serve as rare examples of a vanishing humanity that once coexisted in harmony with nature. One leading figure in conservation biology notes that "[t]he only success stories in real multiple-use conservation are a handful of indigenous peoples who have somehow been able to co-exist with their environments for long periods without impoverishing them" and suggests that these rare examples show that "humans have the potential to act as a keystone species in the most positive sense."[26] A **keystone species** is an organism that other species rely on for habitat and food. An example of such a species are beavers, which fell trees to build dams and lodges. Their activity creates wetlands and changes the vegetation so that many new species come to inhabit the newly disturbed area.

In fact, ethnoecology documents more than a "handful" of human keystone communities. Ethnoecologists use *keystone community* to denote a place-based or local culture that protects and extends native biodiversity and habitats through customary land and water use practices. Numerous place-based cultures, not all of them indigenous, in many parts of the world assume a keystone role in the ecosystems they inhabit.[27]

Many land-based local cultures produce landscape modifications such as wetlands and agroforestry mosaics that serve as habitat for wild plants and animals. Such keystone communities have found ways to produce sustainable **cultural landscapes**—mosaic-like environments that integrate human use areas with native habitat. Anthropogenic modifications can provide ecological services like connectivity and habitat.[28] This is why keystone communities are also called *ecosystem people* or *cultures of habitat.*[29]

Local cultures can provide these benefits without possessing any explicit set of rules for protecting and managing ecosystems. Some scholars argue that conservation effects are unintended consequences of the small scale of such societies. Others emphasize the idea that place-based cultures intentionally protect some ecosystems simply because they rely on the maintenance of biodiversity for their livelihoods.[30] Over time some place-based cultures develop explicit conservation ethics, or moral principles, and even adopt the language of ecosystem management to describe longstanding customary practices for the protection of habitat and biodiversity.[31] Others draw attention to the difference between the Western value placed on nature conservation and **wilderness preservation** and the indigenous local culture emphasis on sustainable inhabitation and right livelihood (the right to follow traditional practices in production and reproduction).[32] Natural assets like clean water, deep soil horizons, wildlife habitat, and open space are products of the beneficial services provided by place-based cultures.[33] These findings are sure to provoke debate on the implications of TEK for conservation theory and practice.

A final subfield affiliated with environmental anthropology is agroecology, which is the scientific study of alternative and traditional agriculture. Agroecology first emerged in the 1970s as part of a widening critique of the Green Revolution (GR). The GR was a global effort initiated in the 1950s to modernize and Westernize agriculture by developing and introducing high-yield, high-input varieties of hybrid crops to Third World farmers.

Table 1   Ecological processes in contrasting agroecosystems

AGROECOSYSTEM	CROP DIVERSITY	TEMPORAL PERMANENCE	ISOLATION	STABILITY	GENETIC DIVERSITY	HUMAN CONTROL	NATURAL PEST CONTROL
Modern monoculture	Low	Low	Low	Low	Low	High	Low
Modern orchard	Low	High	Low	Moderate	Moderate	Moderate	Moderate
Organic farm	Moderate	Moderate	Low to moderate	Moderate	Moderate	Moderate	Moderate
Traditional polyculture	High	High	High	High	Very high	Low	High

Source: Adapted from Miguel Altieri, Agroecology: The Scientific Basis of Alternative Agriculture (Boulder: Westview Press, 1995), Figure 3.6, p. 59.

This thrust toward modernized agriculture had numerous harmful effects on the land, water, wildlife, farmers, and communities. The GR exported the American model of highly engineered and chemically oriented mechanized agriculture. It imposed high-level inputs of modern industrial agrochemicals, use of large-scale machinery, and reliance on heavily subsidized investments in large-scale irrigation systems supported by the construction of large dams and reservoirs. These policies and technologies favored industrial monocultures over smaller and more sustainable traditional **polycultures** (farms that grow a diversity of native **land race** crops). Local farmers everywhere were displaced by the appropriation of their lands for industrial agriculture or the construction of dams, reservoirs, highways, and other infrastructure.

The architects of the GR misunderstood TEK-based local farming systems, reducing complex agroecosystems to simple and vulgar stereotypes.[34] The crude and racist trope of the slash-and-burn model of **shifting cultivation,** or swidden, is legendary. For a long time, traditional farming practices were depicted as primitive, inefficient, and environmentally destructive. So-called backward peasants mindlessly cut and burned the trees to grow meager food crops, all the while unknowingly devastating the forests. Then, in 1954 Harold Conklin published his famous treatise on Hanunuo agroecosystems in the Philippines. This work led other anthropologists to "dismantle the dominant view of shifting cultivation as a haphazard, destructive, and primitive way of making a living." Conklin's research set a tone that inspired subsequent generations of ethnoecologists and agroecologists to document the "logic, complexity, and sophistication of local knowledge."[35]

In contrast to the stereotype of primitive, inefficient, and destructive farming practices, indigenous agroecosystems are characterized by high crop diversity, optimal use of space and available resources, recycling of nutrients and other inputs, effective and communal water and soil conservation and management, natural control of weeds and pests, and sustainable income and subsistence for the farmer and local community.[36] Traditional farming systems are more sustainable and equitable than are the industrial monocultures promoted by the proponents of the GR. Comparative study of agroecosystems reveals that traditional polyculture farms are more stable, diverse, and productive compared to modern monocultures because they are better adapted to the uncertainties of climate, moisture, and insect predation (see table 1).

Political Ecology: Power, Institutions, Social Movements, and the Environment

Earth's ecosystems and biosphere are clearly being affected by the political and economic activities of human societies. But how are those activities organized and explained? The many varieties of political ecology provide an important set of approaches to answer that question. For purposes of this book, I will define political ecology as the study of power dynamics in social conflicts over environmental policy, law, and regulation. This often involves the study of social movements engaged with environmental issues. Political ecology also implies the study of the role of science in this process, since environmental science is often woven into the discourses that define ecological problems and their solutions. It is through the exercise of political and economic power that different human groups try to assert control over the environmental conditions in place.[37]

An issue in political ecology is the critique of **sustainable development** (SD) discourses, which may involve ethnographies of the state and nongovernmental organizations (NGOs). This concept became a fixture in modern environmental discourse after the 1972 United Nations Stockholm conference on the world environment and development. By 1987, the United Nations World Commission on Environment and Development (UNCED) had formulated a framework for SD to address the global nature of environmental problems. The commission defined SD as "development that meets the needs of the present without compromising the ability of future generations to meet their own needs."[38] Multilateral planning for SD continued between the 1992 Rio Earth Summit and the 2002 World Summit on Sustainable Development held in South Africa. UNCED proposed that economic growth is necessary to create jobs, reduce poverty, meet the social needs of a growing population, and generate the wealth to invest in environmental protection. Development is important because poverty is seen as the principal cause of environmental degradation: Poor people do bad things to the environment in order to survive. Scientific experts would be called on to guide management of the so-called global commons, those areas of the earth, such as the atmosphere and deep oceans, that are neither owned nor claimed by any nation. These experts, many of them ecologists, tend to view Third World cultures as ignorant and backward.[39]

The UNCED strategy of SD is based on the idea that Third World countries are exceeding the **carrying capacity** of the land because they cannot manage the demands placed on the environment by the growing number of poor people. This thinking follows Garrett Hardin's influential theory of the tragedy of the commons.[40] Hardin was interested in showing how scientific ecologists could provide a framework to maintain the carrying capacity of the land and protect it from overexploitation. According to Hardin, the tragedy of the commons occurs because "free-riders" inevitably try to maximize their own benefits without regard for the effects on others and the environment. If no one owns a resource, then there is no way to compel users not to exceed its carrying capacity. Therefore, Hardin championed the management of resources by enlightened private owners and scientific experts to prevent the tragedy of the commons.

Political ecologists point out that what Hardin is describing is an *open-access system*. In such a system, public lands are open to all users, who may extract as many resources as they want without restriction. This does not accurately describe the historical use of common lands, however. Many political ecologists are concerned that the survival of TEK may depend on the ability of local cultures to protect their common pool resources (CPRs), or communally owned and managed traditional use areas. Throughout history, CPRs have been ruled and managed by local communities and were not open to use by outsiders. Such closed-access systems are probably the oldest and perhaps most sustainable forms of resource tenure in the world. Before **enclosure** and privatization of these **commons,** local cultures collectively managed them as traditional use areas.

Political ecologists are critical of UNCED's top-down, managerialist approach to SD. They point to its lack of concern for unequal political and economic power relations in the creation of poverty. Some argue that the fundamental cause of poverty is not overpopulation but rather colonialism and imperialism—the conquest and domination of Third World countries by foreign powers. Others have challenged the very concept of poverty. According to Vandana Shiva, there are two kinds of poverty; one is the "imagined poverty" of a subsistence lifestyle, and the other is the poverty of deprivation.[41] A subsistence lifestyle is not true poverty, even if development experts and planners call it so. It is imagined because it is not material in nature. Instead, it is based on cultural assumptions and myths rooted in Western models of consumerism, in which continually increasing consumption of goods is desirable. A subsistence lifestyle is really just a form of right livelihood. Local people may defend it as a low-consumption lifestyle based on respect for the local environment, which they often view as sacred ground or homeland.

Western-style development leads to the second type of poverty, the poverty of deprivation. Shiva and others see this as the real poverty because people experience it in the form of material effects such as malnutrition, hunger, illness, and higher mortality. They are robbed of their immediate means of subsistence and experience this as direct poverty. With barriers of traditional local control removed, capitalism can exploit resources through extraction of raw materials. A new type of territory is invented—the extractive resource colony. Places like India, Mexico, Brazil, and Indonesia attracted colonial powers precisely because of their "coveted natural resources." These places were colonized and plundered to support the expansion of the global consumer mass cultures of modern Western nations.[42]

Many local cultures experience their encounters with development as ecological impoverishment. Goldman calls this displacement of locals by private speculation, colonial authority, or commercial exploitation the "tragedy of the commoner."[43] Enclosure deprives local people of access to their means of subsistence and undermines their ability to engage in independent livelihoods. Displacement from the commons erodes the TEK of local cultures and deprives the world of indigenous models for sustainable inhabitation of ecosystems.[44]

Political ecologists have focused attention on grassroots participation in ecosystem management. Michael Redclift proposed and contrasted two important models of ecosystem management: top-down **environmental managerialism** versus bottom-up *collaborative environmental management*.[45] Environmental managerialism, the dominant model of ecosystem management, privileges the expert knowledge of development planners and environmental scientists. Collaborative environmental management privileges place-based knowledge and TEK. A fundamental difference is in the definition of governance and participation: The environmental managerialism model limits local participation to needs identification in project scoping and design; it also privileges implementation of project objectives by planning experts. The collaborative environmental management model privileges local mobilizing around "self-identified needs" and works through collaborative partnerships with external allies in project scoping, design, and implementation.

These differences are more than a simple matter of semantics and pose serious questions that go to the core assumptions of environmental planning and management. In the conventional managerialist paradigm, environmental planners impose land-use planning techniques on environmental users to define their space; the same applies in the privileging of expert control over environmental risk analysis. The planners engage in technology appraisal to define the production (or mitigation) system for the targeted users. The planners assume the a priori legitimacy of structural policies to define for users their market and state links.[46]

In collaborative environmental management, environmental users define the geographical and cultural boundaries of place to define land-use planning. Indigenous knowledge and patterns of ecological adaptation define the process of technology appraisal, and externally imposed and technically inappropriate methods are rejected. An underlying assumption of collaborative environmental management is that household livelihood requirements define the basic structural policies. Market-steered and state-defined imperatives typical of hierarchical managerialism are rigorously rejected. A critical political ecology of sustainable development reveals how an increasing number of local communities are challenging the privileges accorded expert planners and their assumptions. They are elaborating—often in collaboration with the non-governmental sector—thousands of independent (non–state-sponsored) projects to mobilize resources and implement their own initiatives in restoration ecology, cultural resource and heritage landscape management, community-based economic development, and other similar grassroots-oriented programs.[47]

Critical political ecology is concerned with the role of science in the **legitimation** of public policies.[48] When they serve as experts in court cases involving environmental disputes, scientists often legitimize resource use and development policies that favor the interests of powerful corporations.[49] Scientists are "servants of power" when they align with the political and economic interests that harm local communities. Scientific testimony justifies exploitation and destruction of local environments for a legal system that treats ecological degradation as a "tradable development damage permit."[50] Studies have also shown how the legitimation of destructive practices occurs in the context of hegemonic legal and administrative discourses. These discursive practices disqualify local knowledge and privilege expert knowledge. The law has generally failed to trust or value the claims of local knowledge when deciding environmental disputes.[51] On the other hand, scientists do not always act as servants of power. They may also play supportive roles by working with local and indigenous communities to document TEK and defend them against environmental harm.

Political ecologists are making important contributions to the study of **new social movements (NSMs).** Some use theories of NSMs that consider kinship, local groups, and informal civic associations as potent sources of new ecological movements. Melucci and others argue that NSMs arise out of the "submerged networks of everyday life."[52] NSMs presumably emerge from civil society rather than from formal organizations with vested interests in maintaining the status quo, such as labor unions and political parties. Another idea is that NSMs involve new forms of *identity politics*. NSMs arise from the articulation of collective identities by individuals from cultures and other social groups (e.g., those based on race, class, gender, or sexual orientation) that have been excluded, exploited, or subordinated by the dominant institutions of society. Many researchers see NSMs as focused on quality of life and cultural demands instead of more traditional bread-and-butter issues. NSMs seek alternatives to the dominant institutions and may work to reclaim the autonomy of the civil society by liberating local places from encroachment by market and state forces.

Political ecology, together with conservation biology, restoration ecology, environmental history, and ethnoecology, compose the ecologies of chaos. These fields are important domains of knowledge and scientific discourse because they focus on processes and patterns of change and disturbance in ecosystems. They also couple natural systems with human social and economic systems. The study of anthropogenesis, of human-effected changes in and disturbance of ecosystems, thus becomes an interdisciplinary problem subject to insights from the biological and social sciences alike. The integration of these various fields is necessary if we are to approach the study of human impacts on natural environments as biological and social (power-laden) problems. In the next two chapters, I apply some of these concepts to the environmental history of Mega-Mexico what is now Mexico and the southwestern United States.

■ Discussion Questions

1. What are the main differences between the cybernetic ecosystems model and the ecology of chaos and disturbance? What do these differences tell us about the social and cultural assumptions that underlie scientific knowledge?

2. List and discuss some everyday examples of the principle that tiny differences in initial conditions may lead to unpredictable results. What implications does this uncertainty have for understanding anthropogenesis?

3. Can you name some examples of traditional environmental knowledge that have been incorporated into Western science and technology?

4. Organize yourselves into research groups of four or five members. Research as a group (in libraries, on the Web, etc.) a particular culture and its TEK. Debate the implications of this TEK for the theory and practice of ecosystem management and nature conservation.

■ Suggested Readings

Altieri, Miguel. 1995. *Agroecology: The Science of Sustainable Agriculture*. Boulder: Westview Press.

Cronon, William, ed. 1995. *Uncommon Ground: Toward Reinventing Nature*. New York: W. W. Norton.

Merchant, Carolyn. 1989. *Ecological Revolutions: Nature, Gender, and Science in New England*. Chapel Hill: University of North Carolina Press.

Nazarea, Virginia, ed. 1999. *Ethnoecology: Situated Knowledge/Located Lives*. Tucson: University of Arizona Press.

Noss, Reed F., and Allen Y. Cooperrider. 1994. *Saving Nature's Legacy: Protecting and Restoring Biodiversity*. Washington, DC: Island Press.

Townsend, Patricia K. 2000. *Environmental Anthropology: From Pigs to Politics*. Long Grove, IL: Waveland Press.

■ Notes

1. For chaos theory, see E. Tenner, *Why Things Bite Back: Technology and the Revenge of Unintended Consequences* (New York: Vintage Books, 1997); and C. S. Holling, F. Berkes, and C. Folke, "Science, Sustainability and Resource Management," in *Linking Social and Ecological Systems: Management Practices and Social Mechanisms for Building Resilience,* ed. F. Berkes and C. Folke (Cambridge: Cambridge University Press, 1998), 342–62. On the butterfly effect, see E. Lorenz, "Deterministic Nonperiodic Flow," *Journal of the Atmospheric Sciences* 20, no. 1 (1963): 130–41; also see J. Gleick, *Chaos: The Making of a New Science* (New York: Viking, 1987); and F. Capra, *The Web of Life: A New Scientific Understanding of Living Systems* (New York: Anchor Books, 1990), 134–35.

2. A. Goudie, ed., *The Human Impact Reader: Readings and Case Studies* (London: Blackwell Publishers, 1997).

3. Holling, Berkes, and Folke, "Science, Sustainability and Resource Manage-

ment," 353; T. Forsyth, *Critical Political Ecology: The Politics of Environmental Science* (London: Routledge, 2003).

4. S. J. Pyne, *Fire: A Brief History* (Seattle: University of Washington Press, 2001); and *Fire in America: A Cultural History of Wildland and Rural Fire* (Seattle: University of Washington Press, 1997).

5. R. H. MacArthur and E. O. Wilson, *The Theory of Island Biogeography* (Princeton: Princeton University Press, 1967); A. Crosby, *Ecological Imperialism: The Biological Expansion of Europe, 900–1900* (Cambridge: Cambridge University Press, 1986).

6. R. F. Noss and A. Y. Cooperrider, *Saving Nature's Legacy: Protecting and Restoring Biodiversity* (Washington, DC: Island Press, 1994).

7. E. O. Wilson, "Threats to Biodiversity," *Scientific American* 9 (1989): 108–16. Wilson estimates that plant and animal species extinctions are occurring at a pace 10,000 times faster than before the appearance of humans.

8. Noss and Cooperrider, *Saving Nature's Legacy,* esp. 150–56, 336; R. E. Grumbine, *Ghost Bears: Exploring the Biodiversity Crisis* (Washington, DC: Island Press, 1992).

9. J. J. Berger, ed., *Environmental Restoration* (Washington, DC: Island Press, 1990); W. E. Hudson, ed., *Landscape Linkages and Biodiversity* (Washington DC: Island Press, 1991); A. D. Baldwin, J. De Luce, and C. Pletsch, eds., *Beyond Preservation: Restoring and Inventing Landscapes* (Minneapolis: University of Minnesota Press, 1994); P. H. Gobster and R. B. Hull, eds., *Restoring Nature: Perspectives from the Social Sciences and Humanities* (Washington, DC: Island Press, 2000).

10. Noss and Cooperrider, *Saving Nature's Legacy;* I thank Eugene Hunn for pointing out the problems in Quintana Roo. On this biosphere reserve, see A. López Ornat, *Sian Ka'an Coastal Biosphere Reserve and Surrounding Forests,* available online at http://www.ramsar.org/cop7181cs14.doc. Man and the Biosphere program information is available at the United Nations World Heritage Sites program Web site: http://www.wcmc.org.uk/protected_areas/data/wh/sianka'a.html.

11. Noss and Cooperrider, *Saving Nature's Legacy;* M. Boyce and A. Haney, *Ecosystem Management: Applications for Sustainable Forest and Wildlife Resources* (New Haven: Yale University Press, 1999); K. A. Kohm and J. Franklin, *Creating a Forestry for the 21st Century: The Science of Ecosystem Management* (Washington DC: Island Press, 1996). A survey of ecosystem management models that value "nature's services" is in G. Healy, *Nature and the Marketplace: Capturing the Value of Ecosystem Services* (Washington DC: Island Press, 2001). The classic contribution to the study of common pool resources and ecosystem management is E. Ostrum, *Governing the Commons: The Evolution of Institutions for Collective Action* (Cambridge: Cambridge University Press, 1991).

12. W. Cronon, *Uncommon Ground: Toward Reinventing Nature* (New York: W. W. Norton, 1995), 51.

13. R. Guha, *Environmentalism: A Global History* (Boston: Addison-Wesley, 1999).

14. A. Crosby, *Ecological Imperialism: The Biological Expansion of Europe, 900–1900*

(Cambridge: Cambridge University Press, 1986); and *The Columbian Exchange: Biological and Cultural Consequences of 1492* (Westport, CT: Greenwood Press, 1972).

15. D. Worster, appendix to *The Ends of the Earth: Perspectives on Modern Environmental History*, ed. D. Worster (Cambridge: Cambridge University Press, 1977), 289–307.

16. C. Merchant, *Ecological Revolutions: Nature, Gender, and Science in New England* (Chapel Hill: University of North Carolina Press, 1989), 23.

17. R. Guha, "Radical Environmentalism and Wilderness Preservation: A Third World Critique," *Environmental Ethics* 11, no. 1 (1989): 71–80; D. G. Peña, "The 'Brown' and the 'Green': Chicanos and Environmental Politics in the Upper Rio Grande," *Capitalism, Nature, Socialism*, 3, no. 1 (1992): 79–103. Cronon presents an important set of essays that interrogate the foundational concepts of ecology, including ecosystem, nature, and wilderness. This growing body of knowledge yields "abundant evidence that 'nature' is not nearly so natural as it seems. Instead, it is a profoundly human construction." Cronon, *Uncommon Ground*, 25.

18. D. G. Peña, ed., *Chicano Culture, Ecology, Politics: Subversive Kin* (Tucson: University of Arizona Press, 1998).

19. P. K. Townsend, *Environmental Anthropology: From Pigs to Politics* (Prospect Heights: Waveland Press, 2000).

20. Peña, "'Brown' and the 'Green'" and *Chicano Culture, Ecology, Politics*; E. Hunn, "The Value of Subsistence to the World," in *Ethnoecology: Situated Knowledge/Located Lives*, ed. V. Nazarea (Tucson: University of Arizona Press, 1999).

21. J. H. Steward, *Theory of Cultural Change: The Methodology of Multilinear Evolution* (Urbana: University of Illinois Press, 1955).

22. E. Hunn, "Ethnoecology: The Relevance of Cognitive Anthropology for Human Ecology," in M. Freilich, ed., *Relevance of Culture* (New York: Bergin and Garvey, 1989).

23. F. Berkes, *Sacred Ecology: Traditional Ecological Knowledge and Resource Management* (Philadelphia: Taylor and Francis, 1999); Nazarea, *Ethnoecology;* E. Hunn, "Value of Subsistence"; and G. Cajete, ed., *A People's Ecology: Explorations in Sustainable Living* (Santa Fe: Clear Light, 1999).

24. For TEK as science, see Hunn, "Value of Subsistence," 24–25. On the role of ethnoecology in intercultural conflict, see E. Hunn, *Nch'I-Wana, the Big River: Mid-Colombia Indians and Their Land* (Seattle: University of Washington Press, 1991); D. Peña, "Identity and Place in Communities of Resistance," in *Just Sustainabilities: Environmental Justice in an Unequal World*, ed. J. Agyeman, R. D. Bullard, and B. Evans (London: Earthscan; Cambridge: MIT Books, 2003); G. A. Hicks and D. Peña, "Community Acequias in Colorado's Rio Culebra Watershed," *University of Colorado Law Review* 74 (2003): 387–486.

25. D. G. Peña, "Autonomy, Equity, and Environmental Justice" (paper prepared for the Provost's Lecture Series on Race, Poverty, and the Environment, Brown University, Providence, RI, April 2003).

26. R. F. Noss, "A Sustainable Forest Is a Diverse and Natural Forest," in: *Clearcut: The Tragedy of Industrial Forestry,* ed. B. DeVall (San Francisco: Sierra Club Books, 1994), 37.

27. Brien Meilleur has used the concept of keystone societies. See B. Meilleur, *Eating on the Wild Side: The Pharmacologic, Ecologic, and Social Implications of Using Non-cultigens* (Tucson: University of Arizona Press, 1994); also see D. Ghai and J. Vivian, eds., *Grassroots Environmental Action: People's Participation in Sustainable Development* (London: Routledge, 1996); V. Nazarea, *Ethnoecology;* Peña, *Chicano Culture, Ecology, Politics;* G. Nabhan, *Cultures of Habitat: On Nature, Culture, and Story* (Washington, DC: Counterpoint, 1997); F. J. Pinchón, J. Uquillas, and J. Frechione, eds., *Traditional and Modern Natural Resource Management in Latin America* (Pittsburgh: University of Pittsburgh Press, 1999); R. Peet and M. Watts, eds., *Liberation Ecologies: Environment, Development, and Social Movements* (London: Routledge, 1997); and R. J. González, *Zapotec Science: Farming and Food in the Northern Sierra of Oaxaca* (Austin: University of Texas Press, 2001).

28. D. Peña, "Cultural Landscapes and Biodiversity: The Ethnoecology of an Upper Rio Grande Watershed Commons," in Nazarea, *Ethnoecology,* 107–32; and "The Watershed Commonwealth of the Upper Rio Grande," in *Natural Assets: Democratizing Environmental Ownership,* ed. J. K. Boyce and B. Shelley (Washington, DC: Island Press, 2003), 169–86; also see Hicks and Peña, "Community Acequias," 172–76.

29. R. F. Dasman, "The Importance of Cultural and Biological Diversity," in *Biodiversity: Culture, Conservation, Ecodevelopment,* ed. M. L. Oldfield and J. B. Acorn (Boulder: Westview Press, 1991), 7–15. On cultures of habitat, see Nabhan, *Cultures of Habitat.* On local cultures and environmental change, see C. H. Redman, *Human Impact on Ancient Environments* (Tucson: University of Arizona Press, 1999). On cultures' intentional maintenance of biodiversity, see E. A. Smith and M. Wishnie, "Conservation and Subsistence in Small-Scale Societies," *Annual Review of Anthropology* 29 (2001): 493–524.

30. Hunn, "Value of Subsistence."

31. Peña, "Watershed Commonwealth"; Hicks and Peña, "Community Acequias."

32. Guha, "Radical Environmentalism."

33. Boyce and Shelley, *Natural Assets.* See also Peña, "Cultural Landscapes and Biodiversity" and "Watershed Commonwealth."

34. V. Shiva, *The Violence of the Green Revolution: Third World Agriculture, Ecology, and Politics* (London: Zed Books, 1993).

35. H. Conklin, "The Relation of Hanunuo Culture to the Plant World" (Ph.D. diss., Yale University, 1954). Also see H. Conklin, "The Study of Shifting Cultivation," *Current Anthropology* 2, no. 1 (1961): 27–61. Both quotations from Nazarea, *Ethnoecology,* 3.

36. M. Altieri, *Agroecology: The Science of Sustainable Agriculture* (Boulder: Westview Press, 1995).

37. T. Forsyth, *Critical Political Ecology: The Politics of Environmental Science* (London: Routledge, 2003); Peet and Watts, *Liberation Ecologies.*

38. UNCED, *Our Common Future* (New York: Oxford University Press, 1987), 43.

39. Ibid. For a critical view, see *Whose Common Future? Reclaiming the Commons.* The Ecologist (Philadelphia: New Society Publishers, 1993); M. Redclift, *Sustainable Development: Exploring the Contradictions* (London: Routledge, 1987).

40. G. Hardin, "The Tragedy of the Commons," *Science* 162 (1968): 1243–48.

41. *Whose Common Future?* addresses the role of colonialism and imperialism in creating poverty. On imagined poverty, see V. Shiva, *Staying Alive: Women, Ecology, Development* (London: Zed Books, 1988), 10–13.

42. *Whose Common Future?* 21–73; R. L. Bryant and S. Bailey, *Third World Political Ecology* (London: Routledge, 1997), 105–6.

43. A. Escobar, *Encountering Development: The Making and Unmaking of the Third World* (Princeton: Princeton University Press, 1995); M. Goldman, "Tragedy of the Commons or the Commoner's Tragedy?" *Capitalism, Nature, Socialism* 4 (1994): 49–68; also see M. Goldman, ed., *Privatizing Nature: Political Struggles for the Global Commons* (London: Routledge Press, 1998).

44. Hunn, "Value of Subsistence."

45. Redclift, *Sustainable Development,* 133–70 and chap. 7. For a more recent iteration of these ideas, see D. G. Peña, "Environmental Anthropology and the Restoration of Local Systems of Commons Management" (paper presented to the superintendent and staff, Taroko National Park, Taiwan, September 2001).

46. Redclift, *Sustainable Development,* 158.

47. For examples, see Ghai and Vivian, *Grassroots Environmental Action,* 41; Peet and Watts, *Liberation Ecologies,* 41; Bryant and Bailey, *Third World Political Ecology,* 41.

48. Forsyth, *Critical Political Ecology.*

49. D. Peña and J. Gallegos, "Local Knowledge and Collaborative Environmental Action Research," in *Building Community: Social Science in Action,* ed. P. Nyden et al. (Thousand Oaks, CA: Pine Forge Press, 1997), 85–91.

50. L. Levidow, "The Eleventh Annual Meeting of the International Association for Impact Assessment," *Capitalism, Nature, Socialism* 3, no. 1 (1992): 117–24.

51. Peña and Gallegos, "Local Knowledge and Collaborative Environmental Action Research"; also see D. G. Peña, "A Gold Mine, an Orchard, and an Eleventh Commandment," in *Chicano Culture, Ecology, Politics,* 249–77.

52. A. Melucci, J. Keene, and P. Mier, eds., *Nomads of the Present: Social Movements and Individual Needs in Contemporary Society* (Philadelphia: Temple University Press, 1988). Also see J. L. Cohen, "Strategy or Identity: New Theoretical Paradigms and Social Movements," *Social Research* 52, no. 4 (1985): 663–716. In the Third World context, some leading exponents of NSM theory include Peet and Watts, *Liberation Ecologies;* and Bryant and Bailey, *Third World Political Ecology.*

3

Environmental History of Mega-Mexico, El Sur

Even though we only have our little beans, they are legitimate, and we can eat them with pleasure because we know they are clean.
—Heard among the Zapotecs of Talea

Hernán Cortés and the conquistadors left behind a detailed record of the conquest of Mexico. These conquest narratives include accounts of the first European visit to the Mexica twin island cities of Tenochtitlan and Tlatelolco. Bernal Díaz del Castillo, an officer in Cortés's invading force, kept a journal of the visit to the Aztec capital on Lake Texcoco at the start of a series of brutal encounters that culminated in conquest. Díaz described his first impressions on arriving at the Mexica capital city on November 8, 1519:

> I was never tired of noticing the diversity of trees and the various scents given off by each, and the paths choked with roses and other flowers, and the many local fruit trees and rose bushes, and the ponds of fresh water. We must not forget the gardens . . . and their ponds and tanks of fresh water . . . and the baths that [Motecozumah] had there, and the varieties of small birds that nested in the branches, and the medicinal and useful herbs that grew there.[1]

Changing Biological and Cultural Diversity of Mega-Mexico

The conquistadors were in awe of the metropolitan Lake Texcoco district, home to a million people, intact forests, clear rivers, and numerous species of birds, fish, deer, and other wildlife. The Díaz chronicle includes one of the first recorded cases of public restrooms in the world at that time. The integration of reed and grass shelters into a sewage recycling system protected the freshwater supplies of the Mexica island city. The waste was stowed away in one of the thousands of canoes that filled the lakes to be recycled as fertilizer in the famous floating gardens or *xinampas* (also *chinampas*). This system of raised-bed agriculture built on lattices floating on the surface of the lakes and lagoons was originally developed by Maya Indians and later adopted by the Mexica (Aztecs).

Four hundred years later, the **ecology** of twenty-first-century Mexico City is an urban hell on earth. Slum hovels are shrouded by sinister smog. The floating gardens, arboretums, waterfalls, wetlands, lagoons, lakes, forests, and islands of the native landscape have been erased. One of the great environmental problems of modern-day Mexico City is on display: the fecal dust that blows every day from the dried-up beds of ancient Lake Texcoco.

Diaz's account of Motecozumah's gardens resonates of a little known Mexico, *México desconocido,* one of the world's great centers of biological and cultural diversity. Mexico has six terrestrial ecological and three aquatic **ecological life zones** (see table 2). It ranks first in the world in the number of marine mammal species (33), pine tree species (55), oak tree species (138), and cactus species (834). It ranks second behind Brazil in the number of reptile species, fourth in the number of amphibian species, and fifth in the number of mammalian species. Mexico accounts for 10 to 12 percent of all the species of flora and fauna on the earth and ranks as one of the world's most biologically diverse countries along with Brazil, Colombia, Ecuador, and the Indonesian archipelago (see table 3).[2]

The major ethno-linguistic families in Mexico include the Chinanteca, Chontil, Huasteco, Huichol, Maya, Mayo, Mazahua, Mixe, Mixteca, Nahuatl (Aztec or Mexica), Hña Hñu, Tarahumara, Tojolobal, Totonaca, Zapoteca, and Zoque. Around 54 of the 120 language groups that existed in 1521 survive today, and more than eight million individuals speak indigenous languages. Each of the surviving language family groups in Mexico contains dozens of distinct dialects and local vernaculars. For example, Mexican linguists have defined fifty-seven different Zapotec dialects alone, so the number of native languages spoken in Mexico is much higher than is usually assumed.[3] These indigenous groups have developed an incredible base of ethnobotanical and other **traditional environmental knowledge (TEK).** For example, the Tzeltal can name and use more than a thousand different plants for medicinal and other purposes (see table 4).

Humans and plants coevolved in **Mega-Mexico** across a great span of time and space to produce an exceptional variety of domesticated crops and

Table 2   Terrestrial and aquatic ecological zones of Mexico

ECOLOGICAL ZONE	ESTIMATED AREA (in million ha)	TYPICAL VEGETATION
Humid tropic	22	High and medium evergreen forests and savannahs
Subhumid tropic	40	Deciduous forests
Humid temperate	1	Mixed evergreen-deciduous forests
Subhumid temperate	33	Pine, oak, and mixed forest
Arid and semiarid	39	Scrub and grassland
Alpine	0.3	High, wide, barren plains and tundra
Aquatic (saline)	—	Mangroves, salt marshes
Aquatic (lacustrine)	—	Lake reeds and grasses
Aquatic (riparian)	—	Mixed forests

Source: T. P. Ramamoorthy, R. Bye, A. Lot, and J. Fa, eds. *Biological Diversity of Mexico: Origins and Distribution* (Oxford: Oxford University Press, 1993).

to conserve many wild relatives of cultivars.[4] Biologists note that a "large portion of a critically important 'gene belt' that circles the world between the Tropics of Cancer and Capricorn lies in Mexico. This coincides with the distribution of centers of agricultural origins. . . . Mexico's uniqueness [lies] in that it is the only nation where a megadiversity country and a center of agricultural origin coincide within the 'gene belt.' "[5] Biologists regard Mega-Mexico as a *Vavilov Center*—a biogeographic area that has played a principal role in the domestication of wild plants and the conservation of the wild relatives of cultivars.[6]

The ancient alimentary trinity of *maíz* (maize, or corn, *Zea mays L.*), *frijol* (beans, *Phaseolus* spp.), and *calabacita* (squash, *Cucurbita* spp.) was among the first wild plants domesticated by aboriginal Mexicans some five thousand years ago. Numerous aboriginal crops and herbal remedies are still produced and consumed in contemporary Mexican American communities. The ubiquitous *huertos familiares* (kitchen gardens) are splendid in their preconquest mixture of maíz, frijol, calabacita, chile, *aguacate,* and *limón.* The domesticated plants of Mega-Mexico were major contributions to the global ecology of food. These aboriginal crops transformed global diets and contributed to the demographic and colonial expansion of Europe after the conquest and settlement of the Americas.[7]

This crop diversity is important because it is the source pool for gene

Table 3 Selected indicators of Mexico's biodiversity

SPECIES	TOTAL NUMBER OF SPECIES (1990)	RANK AMONG WORLD'S BIODIVERSITY HOT SPOTS	NUMBER EXTINCT SPECIES (1990)	NUMBER THREATENED/ ENDANGERED SPECIES (1990)
Birds	769 (breeding) 257 (migrants, accidentals)	6 (after Brazil, Indonesia, Colombia, Venezuela, Ecuador, Peru, and Bolivia)	18	155
Butterflies	25,000 est. 1,200 identified (7 percent of known world total)	2 (after Brazil)	30 (?)	220
Reptiles	717	2 (after Brazil)	8	110
Marine mammals	33	1	11	20
Pine trees	55	1	2	10
Oak trees	138	1	4	32
Cactus	834	1	12	143

Sources: F. O. Monasterio et al., *Tierra profanada: Historia ambiental de México* (Mexico City: Instituto Nacional de Antropología y Historia and Secretaría de Desarrollo Urbano y Ecología, 1987), T. P. Ramamoorthy, R. Bye, A. Lot, and J. Fa, *Biological Diversity of Mexico: Origins and Distribution* (Oxford: Oxford University Press, 1993).

Notes: Mexico accounts for 10 to 12 percent of all the species of flora and fauna on earth and ranks high among all nations in overall biodiversity. It ranks fourth in the number of amphibian species and fifth in mammals. Mexico counts 18,000 to 30,000 vascular plants (of which 10,000 to 15,000 are endemic).

Table 4 Plant knowledge among selected indigenous groups of Mexico

ETHNIC GROUP	STATE	NUMBER OF SPECIES USED	ECOLOGICAL ZONE
Seri	Sonora	516	Arid
Tarahumara	Chihuahua	398	Subhumid temperate
Pu'rhépecha	Michoacán	230	Subhumid temperate
Tzeltal	Chiapas	1,040	Subhumid and humid temperate
Maya	Yucatán	909	Subhumid tropical
Huasteco	San Luis Potosí	657	Humid tropical

Source: Centres of Plant Diversity, Smithsonian Institution, available online at http://www .nmnh.si.edu/botany/projects/cpd/ma/table26.htm. Data and additional resources are available online at http://www.nmnh.si.edu/botany/projects/cpd/.

Table 5 Threatened and endangered animal species in Mexico

GROUP	NUMBER OF THREATENED OR ENDANGERED SPECIES	NUMBER THAT ARE ENDEMIC SPECIES
Mammals	92	1
Birds	155	16[a]
Reptiles	11	3
Amphibians	48	7
Fish	52	12
Invertebrates	21	17
Total	**379**	**56**

Source: Secretaría de Desarrollo Urbano y Ecología (SEDUE), *Informe sobre el estado del medio ambiente en México* (Mexico City: SEDUE, 1986).
[a] Most of these were species endemic to tiny offshore Pacific islands.

traits that confer disease, blight, or drought resistance on traditional indigenous crops. This coevolution results in ongoing gene transfers between domesticated and wild varieties. For example, *Zea diploperennis,* a wild relative of domesticated white maize, contains genes that resist seven diseases afflicting cultivars. It is **endemic** to a small area in the state of Jalisco, where local indigenous people name it *madre de maíz* (mother of maize). This is an example of a local **culture** protecting a native wild plant related

Table 6 Threatened plant species of Mexico

PLANT GROUP	EX	EX/V	EN	EN/V	V	R	I	TOTAL
Lichens	I		I					2
Ferns	I		I		4	19	4	29
Gymnosperms	2		18		8	18	I	47
Monocotyledons	2		42	I	126	169	29	369
Dicotyledons	8	4	82	2	179	471	54	800
Total	**14**	**4**	**144**	**3**	**317**	**677**	**88**	**1,247**

Source: World Conservation Monitoring Center (1993).
Notes: Ex = extinct, En = endangered, V = vulnerable, R = rare, I = indeterminate (E, V, or R).

Table 7 Deforestation rates in Mexico by type of closed forest

FOREST TYPE	ESTIMATED AREA (km²)	DEFORESTATION (km²/yr)	DEFORESTATION RATE (%/yr)
Temperate coniferous	169,000	1,630	0.96
Temperate broadleaved	88,000	820	0.93
Tropical evergreen	97,000	2,370	2.44
Tropical deciduous	161,000	3,220	2.00
Total	**515,000**	**8,040**	**1.56**

Source: O. Masera, M. de J. Ordóñez, and R. Dirzo. "Emisiones de carbono a partir de la deforestación en México." *Ciencia* 43 (1992): 151–53.

to a **land race** cultivar.[8] Such local grassroots conservation of seeds is common for the wild relatives of *Phaseolus* ssp. (beans), *Cucurbita* ssp. (squash), *Amaranthus* ssp. (amaranth), and countless other species.

Much of this biological diversity is endangered. There are 379 animal species on Mexico's endangered and threatened lists, and 56 of those are endemic (they are found nowhere else, see table 5). More than 1,240 plant species in Mexico are currently listed as threatened, endangered, or vulnerable. At least 14 plants are listed as extinct, but this is likely an underestimate (see table 6). Mexico also has one of the highest rates of deforestation in the world (see table 7).

Threats to cultural diversity are equally serious. Conventional estimates are that more than half the languages that existed in Mexico at the time of contact are now extinct. The extinction of a language implies the loss of the local knowledge, customs, and practices associated with the devastated culture. The loss of language undermines the ability of local cultures to manage land, water, and wildlife according to their own customs for the protection of their sources of livelihood. This loss also results in environmental degradation. The erosion of soil and culture go together. The demise of TEK is a net loss to humanity in the reduced diversity of cultural heritage.

Pre-contact Civilizations

How did the state of biological and cultural diversity in Mexico change so dramatically over the past five hundred years? Environmental changes were well underway long before Cortés arrived in Tenochtitlan in 1519. For more than three thousand years, the Olmec, Maya, Toltec, Mexica, and other civilizations transformed and managed local and regional environments. Greater Mexico's ecological transformation predated the arrival of the Spaniards, but it was conquest and its aftermath that unleashed the forces of large-scale environmental degradation: widespread destruction of native vegetation and **habitat,** extinction of species, soil erosion, worsening air and water pollution, displacement of indigenous communities, and extirpation of cultures.

The Maya Managed Mosaic

For a very long time, Maya agricultural systems were poorly understood and widely stereotyped as primitive, unchanging, and unproductive. The classic stereotype of **shifting cultivation** is expressed in the following quotation: "The modern Maya method of raising maize is the same as it has been for the past three thousand years or more—a simple process of felling the trees, of burning the dried trees and brush, of planting, and of changing the location of the cornfields every few years."[9] The stereotypical image of an overpopulation of Indians indiscriminately felling trees persists in popular and scientific **discourses.**

In contrast, Arturo Gómez-Pompa and Andrea Kaus argue that "the root causes of deforestation are not population growth or shifting cultivation. . . . Instead, tropical deforestation in Mexico is due to neglect of traditional people's vast experience with resource management."[10] Gómez-

Pompa and Kaus suggest that protecting cultural diversity is a precondition for the conservation of biological diversity, since local indigenous cultures have substantial "libraries" of TEK related to native flora and fauna. The loss of TEK may lessen the prospects for biodiversity conservation.

More recent studies of Maya forest-based agriculture and traditional land use and management practices have led to the model of the managed mosaic. Maya agroecosystems followed a pattern of shifting mosaics. They created a **mode of production** that allowed the forest to alternate between domesticated and wild (self-willing) states. Forest users maintained a shifting balance between subsistence production and biodiversity. Maya farmers developed impressive knowledge of horticulture and agroforestry. Their agroecosystems included the famous milpas (forest maize gardens) and the equally impressive huertos familiares. Traditional milpas are a **sustainable** model for cultivation of crops in the humid tropical **biome** of Mexico's southeast. Although rarer today, these methods are based on the principle of *biomimicry,* in which the biological system of the farm plot, kitchen garden, or managed forest mosaic imitates the diversity and layers of the local native flora and fauna and their habitat.[11]

Maya **polyculture** milpas and kitchen gardens had multiple layers of crops that imitated the diversity of the surrounding rain forest (see figure 7). Multilayered kitchen gardens might contain root crops and tubers (cassava, *camote*) that anchor the soil and prevent surface erosion. They might have a groundcover layer, like pumpkin or squash, that suppresses weeds and provides habitat for beneficial insects. Other groundcover might include the plants for the *hortaliza,* or herb patch. There would surely be a middle layer of principal staple crops, like maize and beans, which grow well together because of their chemical (or **allelopathic**) relationships that prevent overcrowding. Finally, there might be a lower canopy layer consisting of fruit-bearing trees and bushes, and an upper canopy layer of the most common large trees in the rain forest. These layers create diversity, making the gardens less susceptible to damage from pests and pathogens.

The Maya distinguished between *chichluum* (dark, organically rich soil with limestone gravels) and *kankab* (dark red soils with or without gravel). They preferred chichluum for cultivation, as it retained moisture better and was more fertile.[12] Complex terrace and check-dam structures controlled soil erosion. The Maya raised-bed agroecosystems were the direct predecessors of the xinampas of Xochimilco and Chalco that Cortés

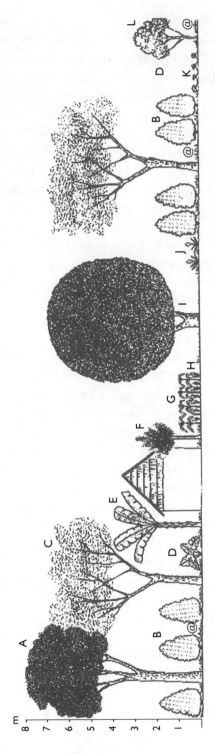

■ 7. Sketch of a Maya kitchen garden. **A.** *Persea americana* Miller (aguacate); **B.** *Coffea arabica* L. (café); **C.** *Inga leptoloba* Schlechter (chalahuite); **D.** *Xanthosoma* sp. (makal); **E.** *Musa sapientum* L. (plátano); **F.** *Citrus aurantium* L. (naranja); **G.** *Zea mays* L. (maíz); **H.** *Phaseolus vulgaris* L. (frijol); **I.** *Mangifera indica* L. (mango); **J.** *Ananas comossus* (L.) Merril (piña); **K.** *Psidium guajava* L. (guayaba); @. *Vicia faba* L., *Capsicum annuum* L., *Cucurbita pepo* L., *Sida rhombifolia* L., *Paspalum conjugatum* Bergius, *Phytolacca icosandra* L., *Commelina diffusa* Burm F., *Solanum nigrum* L., *Saracha procumbens* (Cav.) Ruiz & Pavón, *Acalypha* sp.

saw in the Valley of Mexico. Maya farmers exploited ecological zones in lowland and upland areas. They were adept at occupying localized **ecological niches** such as those found in *bajadas* and *rejolladas*. Bajadas, or natural limestone depressions filled with dense wetlands, are perfect for the construction of raised cultivation beds because they capture rainfall. The bajada wetlands were an important part of the managed mosaic and were integrated into a wide range of agricultural and ethnobotanical activities (both cultivation and gathering). Rejolladas are dry sinkholes (Maya *k'oopob*) used by the Maya forest gardeners to grow cacao and other specialized fruit trees. Rejolladas were also planted with maize, beans, and squash in the summer and jicama, *amole* (yucca), camote, and *macatl* in winter.[13]

Maya contributions to ethnobotany are legendary. Their ethnobotany (knowledge of the properties and uses of wild flora) included more than a thousand plants collected in the rain forest. These plants were valued for their medicinal properties and were encouraged as companion plants in the multilayered mosaic of the forest and kitchen gardens. Maya ethnobotany relied on a managed mosaic of domesticated and wild (or random) plant associations. This managed mosaic was simply a pattern of *cultural agroforestry*, that is, a mixture of species across the intensively managed **cultural landscapes** and the relatively undisturbed natural landscapes.

The Maya mosaic merged domesticated or cultural landscapes with "wild" (self-willing) natural landscapes.[14] The managed mosaic worked within the limits of the **carrying capacity** of the land and caused little long-term damage to rain forest **ecosystems.** There is some evidence of localized environmental degradation, which likely resulted from the pressures imposed on local cultivators by elites who periodically sought excessive tribute in times of war or political conflict.[15]

The Maya worldview prohibited excessive exploitation and hoarding by individuals. Forests and other large landscapes were off-limits to individual owners. The invocation of nature in the Maya concept of *in lak ech* (*tu eres mi otro yo,* "you are my other self") is an important example of this philosophy.[16] In this conception, nature is contemporary in age with humans. The interconnectedness of species is evident to the self. Maya consciousness is rooted in communal expressions of identity, and knowledge is transmitted across the generations through ritual and imitation. The Maya imitate nature in their patterns of farming and mythmaking, if not always in their political arrangements and palace intrigue.

The Mexica Lake Metropolis

Joel Simon writes that the Mexica (Aztecs) lacked scientific knowledge of ecology and were ignorant of the effect of humans on the environment. He acknowledges their vast knowledge of nature but emphasizes its "mythical" and "unscientific" character: "The Aztecs had no idea that the same great tectonic forces that raised the land from the sea also created the mountains. . . . [They] knew nothing about high-pressure systems or tropical depressions or prevailing westerlies or . . . about the environmental basis for the Mayan collapse."[17] Simon's take on México desconocido includes the usual misreading of Maya ecology as a pathway to ecological catastrophe. He mistakenly assumes Mexica knowledge of nature was shrouded in superstition and magic. It seems disingenuous to characterize the Mexica as unscientific simply because they lacked knowledge of plate tectonics. This type of knowledge was not produced anywhere in the world until the development, over the course of the twentieth century, of remote-sensing technologies to gather data on geomorphology, meteorology, oceanography, and seismology.

The Mexica classified soil in the Central Plateau into more than sixty types according to qualities like color, coarseness, permeability, density of organic material, and moisture retention.[18] Simon acknowledges that the Mexica had a term, *tepetate,* for hardpan—a soil that has been compacted by overcultivation or other careless farming practices. The Mexica awareness of hardpan belies the notion that they lacked scientific knowledge of ecological principles. They may not have had a theory of plate tectonics, but they understood their soils.

On their arrival in the Valley of Mexico, the Mexica were forced by the inhabitants of the land-side cities to settle on an undesirable island in the middle of Lake Texcoco. They responded to a shortage of arable land by constructing xinampas. They dredged mud from the shallow lake bottom and placed it on floating platforms of reeds, grasses, and aquatic plants. Soil was built over time through the addition of more mud, recycled waste, and the detritus of cover crops. These artificial islands were planted with maize, beans, squash, tomatoes, avocados, and numerous other crops.

Over time these artificial islands covered much of the Lake Texcoco district, especially the twin lakes of Chalco and Xochimilco. The floating gardens created a raised-bed **polyculture** of astonishing productivity: In 1519, they produced 100 million pounds of maize.[19] The xinampas pro-

vided most of the food required by the lacustrine metropolis of Tenochtitlan. In addition to basic staple crops, xinampas produced cassava (a starchy
root crop) and amaranth (a sacred grain later banned by the Spaniards for
politico-religious reasons). The floating gardens and royal orchards were
planted with fruit-bearing trees, shrubs, and vines. Rooftop and patio
kitchen gardens were also common. Every available square meter was
planted with vegetables, fruits, herbs, and decorative plants. The Mexica
also cultivated companion plants that aided soil fertility and provided
natural weed control. Mexica farming systems were ecologically sustainable and even regenerative.[20]

The Mexica maintained botanical and zoological gardens and arboretums. Plant collections had practical uses and the arboretums provided
habitat for some wild animals. Aviaries (bird enclosures) were common-
place. Wild animals including deer, parrots, eagles, and hawks were kept
for ritual purposes; they were considered spiritual companions or paragons
of behavior that humans should emulate. Legends told of the importance
of animals as teachers of the art of rightful living on the land and water.

The Mexica developed an extensive ethnobotany. Traditional healers
and physicians (Nahuatl *ticitl*, Spanish *curanderas/os* and *médicas/os*, re-
spectively) were familiar with thousands of wild and domesticated plants
used in medicinal practice. Mexica *remedios* (natural remedies) are still
widely used today. The ethnobotany of the Mexica was not limited to
herbal remedies; the formal study and classification of cultivated food
crops was also important.[21] Experimentation with crop selection and inter-
cropping likely resulted in the diffusion of practices such as the use of
companion plants (e.g., the use of beans and other legumes for their
nitrogen-fixing properties).

Mexica knowledge of hydrology and civil engineering was evident in
their construction of the canals, dikes, causeways, drainage ditches, aque-
ducts, and anthropogenic islands and wetlands that dissected the lake
district. The mosaic of anthropogenic islands, wetlands, and hydraulic
infrastructure prevented the brackish waters of Lake Texcoco from in-
truding into the sweet waters of Lakes Chalco and Xochimilco where most
of the xinampas were located. The main freshwater for Tenochtitlan was
delivered by aqueduct from a locale on the mainland known as Chapulte-
pec (Hill of Grasshoppers). This watershed was protected to conserve
freshwater quality and quantity. Tree cutting and hunting were prohibited
in the headwaters zone.[22] Traditional land, water, and forest conservation

practices allowed for a reasonably sustainable supply of freshwater, protected fish and wildlife habitat, recycled wastes without polluting watercourses, and controlled agricultural ecosystems. On the eve of the Cortés *entrada* (first entry), the Mexica had a semblance of ecological balance with their lacustrine environment.

The Mexica metropolis had a visible and esteemed cadre of women healers and midwives (Nahuatl *tetlacuicuilique;*[23] Spanish *curanderas* and *parteras*). Midwifery was one of the few professions that Tenocha women were allowed to pursue. These caregivers provided most Mexica women with access to at least a modicum of health and medical care during pregnancy, childbearing, and postpartum recovery. Tenocha midwives and healers may have had their own *calmecac* (a royally sanctioned, semi-religious institute of higher learning) to educate new practitioners. Midwifes had their own patroness, the goddess of fertility and health, Teteo-innan, also called Temazcalteci, "the grandmother of the steam bath." Midwives took control of the household and used the home's *temazcalli* (steam bath) to comfort the mother and encourage a soothing labor during childbirth.[24] The institution of midwifery may have prolonged the longevity of infants and reduced the incidence of postpartum morbidity among women and newborns.

Royalty (*pilli*) and commoners (*macehualtin*) found distinction in civil engineering, hydrology, and agriculture.[25] The Mexica produced knowledge in fields of ethnoscience that had practical implications for urban planning and land and water use management. These included agro-ecology, botany, hydrology, and edaphology (from the Greek *edaphos,* floor, ground, soil, the scientific study of soils).

The Mexica did not significantly degrade the environment over the two hundred–year period between the founding of Tenochtitlan (1325) and the conquest (1521). The five lakes of the Texcoco district were well managed. Forests were largely intact, and farming occupied special ecological niches in the cultural **landscape mosaic** without spilling out willy-nilly into the rest of the biophysical landscape. The Mexica managed to protect ecosystems and biodiversity through active land and water use management practices they valued to protect the clean, plentiful, and renewable supplies of water and food. The Mexica saw nature as a whole greater than the sum of its parts. The natural world implied an intricate web of relationships among all living and supernatural beings. The Mexica recognized plants, animals, landforms, watercourses, and seasonal changes as evidence of nature operating as an independent, active force in the world. Nature was imbued with the powers of creation and chaos. The Mexica believed human actions could often have unintended consequences. Catastrophe was always lurking beneath the chaos of human activity, especially when people abused the land, water, and wildlife or neglected their obligations to the community.

■ The Spanish Colonial Ecological Revolution

The Spanish conquest and colonization of Greater Mexico brought dramatic ecological and cultural changes. The most profound was the decimation of the indigenous population. Reliable estimates are that the indigenous population in the Central Plateau declined from ten to one million in little more than a century. The principal causes of this demographic catastrophe were disease, forced labor under oppressive working conditions, and malnutrition. Spaniards brought diseases such as smallpox, measles, and scarlet fever, exotic pathogens for which the native population lacked natural defenses.[26] Cortés did not conquer the Mexica with superior military strategy and weaponry. Mexica warriors initially expelled the conquistadors from Tenochtitlan, but then were decimated by measles and smallpox epidemics that raged through the Lake Texcoco district between 1519 and 1521. The uncertainties of human biological evolution allowed Cortés to take advantage of an unintended but no less lethal form of germ warfare.

Many natives died from disease, overwork, and malnutrition in the mines and plantations, where they were subject to the brutal law of **encomienda,** under which the crown conveyed to individual conquistadors the right to exploit aboriginal labor in designated territories encompassing native communities. Throughout the sixteenth and seventeenth centuries, *encomenderos* (Spaniards with rights to forced labor) perpetrated waves of dispossession, relocation, and exploitation of aboriginal communities. Combined with epidemic diseases, these practices resulted in the extinction of more than half of Mexico's aboriginal ethnic groups during the first century and a half of colonization.[27]

The exploitative conditions of forced labor had direct ecological consequences. The excessive demands and burdens of forced labor meant that indigenous farmers could not maintain the xinampas, terraces, check dams, irrigation ditches, and other erosion and runoff control structures they had perfected over generations. The maintenance of these complex and ubiquitous structures required regular and intensive periods of communal labor. These monumental works of communal infrastructure had been constructed under the guidance of a body of village-level **customary law** that dictated the amount of labor and organization of construction, maintenance, and operation community members would provide. The advent of forced labor under the encomienda system prevented aboriginals from maintaining these communal landscapes. This accelerated the process of ecological change as the native agroecological landscapes gradually fell into disrepair and neglect.[28]

The introduction of new cultigens, agricultural practices, and domesticated animals also produced radical changes in Mexico's ecology. Between 1518 and 1559, the colonists introduced a wide variety of domesticated plants and animals that had originally been imported to Spain from other parts of the world, including Mediterranean Europe, the Middle East, Africa, and India (see table 8). Aboriginal communities readily adopted many of these new plants and animals. For example, many Nahua, Mixtec, and Zapotec farmers acquired and raised goats and pigs for subsistence.

The introduction of livestock was almost singular as a cause of land degradation. Rancheros overstocked many rangelands, leading to loss of vegetative cover, soil erosion, and destruction of watercourses. Overgrazing is associated with the decline of native plant species in many of Greater Mexico's grasslands, especially in the arid regions of the near northern frontier in Durango, Sonora, Chihuahua, and Coahuila. Many native species of flora were driven into extinction as a result of the degradation of habitat by livestock. The effects of overgrazing were for a time concentrated in areas of early mining development (Zacatecas and Guanajuato) where ranchers provided food to the mine owners, supervisors, and their families. But livestock production soon spread throughout the expanding colony as urban populations grew and the demand for beef, mutton, and other meat increased.

Weeds displaced native flora, which had the additional effect of reducing the habitat available to certain fauna (e.g., small mammals and reptiles). Spanish-introduced livestock spread weeds by carrying seeds on their hooves or droppings. Weeds grew wherever livestock destroyed native vegetation, and the invasion of exotic weeds inhibited recovery of

Table 8   Domesticated plants and animals introduced to Mexico by the Spanish

PLANT/ANIMAL	DATE OF INTRODUCTION	HISTORICAL NOTES
Oranges	1518	Planted by Bernal Díaz del Castillo in Veracruz
Horses	1519	Brought by Cortés and his captains
Wheat	1521	Planted by an African slave by the name of Juan Garrido
Beef, milk cows	1522	Imported by Cortés from the Greater Antilles
Pigs	1522	Imported by Cortés from the Greater Antilles
Goats	1522	Imported by Cortés from the Greater Antilles
Donkeys	1522	Imported by Cortés from the Greater Antilles
Sheep	1522	Imported by Gonzalo de Ordaz from Cuba
Oxen	1522	Imported by Gonzalo de Ordaz from Cuba
Sugarcane	1522	Imported by Cortés; established in Morelos by 1530
Silkworms	1529	Brought by Francisco de Santa Cruz and cultivated by Delgadillo and Martín Cortés
Date palms	1529	First grown by Motolinia at the Cuernavaca Monastery
Flax	1532	First planted by Don Sebastián Ramírez de Fuenleal
Hemp	1532	First planted by Don Sebastián Ramírez de Fuenleal
Bananas	1537	Introduced by Don Vasco de Quiroga at a plantation near Uruapan, Michoacán
Mangoes	1550	Origin unknown
Wine grapes	?	Cortés requested wine grapes in 1522, but they arrived much later
Olives	?	Cortés requested olives in 1522, but they arrived much later
Coffee	?	Introduced from the Antilles by Antonio Gómez de Guevara and first planted in Córdova

Source: A. Cue, *Historia social y económica de México, 1521–1854* (Mexico City: Editorial Trillas, 1983); F. Ortiz Monasterio, et al., *Tierra profanada: historia ambiental de México* (Mexico City: Instituto Nacional de Antropología e Historia and Secretaría de Desarrollo Urbano y Ecología, 1987).

native grasses, herbaceous forbs, and other flowering plants. The composition of plant **communities** in the grasslands changed in favor of Eurasian species in overgrazed areas.

Conquest did not mean immediate or total surrender. Active and passive aboriginal resistance was present from the beginning. Many aboriginal elites and commoners maintained control over some of the land. In some places they maintained a monopoly over certain crops (e.g., cacao and henequen).[29] The loss of land to the conquistadors was initially limited to an area that stretched west to east from Mexico City to Veracruz, where Cortés had made landfall on the coast of the Gulf of Mexico. This area, which became known as the Mexico City–Veracruz corridor, included the first European-designed townsites in the area of Puebla. This was the first zone in Mexico dedicated to the production of wheat and other Old World cultivars. The official policy of the viceroy was that the cultivation of wheat would be encouraged over that of maize in the plantations at Atlixco founded in 1580.

Initially, the conquistadors relied on aboriginal knowledge of the land, water, and agriculture for their own survival. By 1580, aboriginal milpas were growing maize, beans, and other customary land race crops, as well as Spanish-introduced Old World cultivars. These included lettuce, cauliflower, cucumbers, garbanzos, fava beans, radishes, and onions, as well as medicinal herbs like mint and aromatics like cilantro.[30] It was only later, over the course of the late seventeenth and early eighteenth centuries, after the hacienda (landed estate) system was firmly established, that Mexico witnessed the decline of aboriginal agroecosystems and the transformation of their associated cultural and natural landscapes.

One of the most revealing events of the colonial period was the ill-advised destruction of Lake Texcoco. This occurred under the direction of Enrico Martínez, a German Spaniard from Seville who had worked for the Inquisition as a translator of the testimony of heretics.[31] The original plan, proposed by Cortés, called for the dismantling of Tenochtitlan and the construction of a new Spanish city of Mexico on the ruins of the aboriginal metropolis. This episode involved the destruction of the major temples, apartment buildings and courtyards, zoological gardens, aviaries, arboretums, and floating gardens. All traces of Mexica vernacular architecture and **cultural landscapes** were completely erased. The finest masonry stones used in the construction of the Cathedral of Mexico came from the Mexica's Templo Mayor. The Mexica temples and other royal buildings were demolished and recycled in the construction of many important Spanish religious and governmental edifices. Martínez also called for the destruction of the anthropogenic lake ecosystem that had sustained the Mexica civilization for more than two hundred years. The obstinate Martínez called this plan *El desagüe general,* or "the general dewatering."

The draining of Lake Texcoco took place between 1608 and 1609 and involved the forced labor of more than sixty thousand Indians. It destroyed the vestiges of aboriginal agriculture and appropriated water for the nascent Spanish haciendas around Atlixco. By 1629, Mexico City had flooded again. For five years, until 1634, the city was inundated. Canoes replaced horses, houses collapsed, thirty thousand indigenous people died, all but four hundred of twenty thousand Spanish residents retreated, a third of the city was destroyed by floodwaters, and Martínez was jailed for treachery.[32] Mexico City never recovered from this unfortunate ecological miscue. *La cuenca* (watershed) was diverted into the Río Tula and out of the floodplain of Lake Texcoco. Instead of the sought-after new farmland, the drainage of Lake Texcoco revealed a hardpan of dry salt flats. Similar arrogant disregard, even contempt, for existing cultural and natural landscapes was repeated throughout the course of the colonial **ecological revolution** in other regions of México desconocido.

A critical turning point was reached during the late seventeenth century. The decimation of aboriginal peoples had exhausted the principal source of forced labor. The encomienda was no longer functioning as intended, and the Spanish royalty and clergy increasingly condemned its reprehensible brutality and dehumanization. The pre-Hispanic agroecosystems were collapsing. Aboriginal peoples had faced more than 150 years of forced labor, relocation, epidemics, war, famine, and land loss. They could no longer sustain the ancient agroecosystems and their mosaic-like landscapes.

The demographic collapse strengthened the case against the old encomienda system and set the stage for a transition to the hacienda, a system of large private landed estates.[33] There were two main types of haciendas: **monoculture** plantations (Spanish *fincas* or *sembrados de monocultivo mayor*) and livestock ranches (**ranchos**). The first plantation haciendas were established in new towns near Atlixco in the Mexico City–Veracruz corridor. By 1700, *hacendados* (private landowners) had taken control of some of the best farmlands in this corridor. They created a new landscape consisting of Old World monoculture crop fields dominated by wheat and other grains. Wheat was as important to the Spanish way of life as maize was to the

Mexican aboriginals. As haciendas expanded, the remaining natives were forced on to marginal lands deemed unsuitable for agriculture. Campesinos (farmworkers) were forced to grow maize on rocky mountain soils without the benefit of the old communally maintained terraces and check dams. Under these ecological and social conditions, the campesinos eroded the fragile *laderas* (mountainsides). They also lacked space for their *hortalizas* (herb patches), huertos familiares (kitchen gardens), and *huertas familiares* (home orchards). Their agroecology was reduced to the use of neglected *sembrados,* which refers to ground that has been sown with seed or a small subsistence plot of maize.

The haciendas slowly flourished and their fate was linked to the growth of the cities and mining centers. The first great discovery of silver was in Zacatecas in 1746. Throughout the mid-1700s the Spaniards exploited new silver mines at Taxco (Guerrero), Zumpango (Guerrero), and Sultepec (estado de México). The opening of silver mines in Guanajuato, Real del Monte, and Pachuca quickly followed. The haciendas serving the mining centers at Zacatecas and Guanajuato counted five thousand Indian laborers and several hundred Spaniards and **mestizas/os** during their heydays in the mid to late 1700s.

Urban growth resulting partly from the rise of manufacturers and small industry supported the plantation-style haciendas. In 1571, there were more than 80 large *obrajes* (manufactories) in Mexico that produced a variety of textiles. By 1604, there were more than 114 obrajes in urban centers like Mexico, Puebla, Tlaxcala, Tepeyac, Celaya, Querétaro, and Valladolid. By the early 1700s the number had more than doubled, to about 230 establishments. These preindustrial handicraft workshops contributed to the development of a small middle class of shop owners and skilled artisans affiliated with *gremios* (guilds), stimulating a small internal market for hacienda products. Throughout the 1700s the obrajes and gremios continued to grow as the demand for textile products increased.[34]

In the colonial near northern frontier of Mexico, the hacienda assumed the quintessential form of *ranchos de ganado* (livestock ranches), remaking the landscape ecology of these areas. Livestock ranching drove the growth and consolidation of landholdings. In the Valley of Mexico and other regions of the Central Plateau, the conversion of communal aboriginal lands to private ownership had been constrained by the demographic crisis, geographic conditions, economic necessities, legal doctrines, and political affairs. The northern provinces were free of these limitations because the crown allowed colonizers to treat aboriginal peoples as nomadic and semi-nomadic savages, or *chichimecas* (an ethnocentric Nahuatl term that means "sons of the dogs"). The racist policies of *reducción* (reduction, referring to conversion to Christianity and missionization) and *congregación* (congregation in towns) were used to eliminate the threat to northward expansion posed by aboriginal communities. The congregaciones, or *congregas,* were essentially population resettlement centers where formerly nomadic tribes were forced to become sedentary captive labor for the missions and ranchos. The congregas were always associated with a complex of missions, forts and garrisons, and the ephemeral plantation or ranch. Reducción and congregación set the stage for the rapid expansion of the haciendas in the northern frontier zones. The ranchos of Durango, Coahuila, Chihuahua, and Sonora became the largest haciendas in Mexico, with private estates of a million acres and more.[35]

By the end of the colonial period, Mexico's aboriginal cultures and ecosystems had experienced radical changes. Mining, logging, and monoculture farming and ranching reduced biodiversity by altering and fragmenting the landscape of habitats and movement corridors. There is scant documented evidence on the extinction of species during the colonial period. It is generally known, however, that at least a dozen mammals were extirpated from their historic Mexican ranges. For example, as early as 1700, the tapir (*Tapirella bairdii*) was extirpated from more than half of its historic range in Mexico. The grizzly bear (*Ursus arctos horribilis*) was extirpated from all of Mexico by 1792 and the Michoacán bear (Spanish *Oso michoacano*) was extinct by 1800.[36] Many extinct species may have been unclassified. Many native species of flora and fauna were lost as a consequence of the degradation of habitat, primarily from the effects of livestock ranching and timbering. The most severely affected species were also the most easily overlooked: small herbaceous plants (forbs) and grasses. Alejandro von Humboldt, a sympathetic and astute observer of Mega-Mexico's natural and cultural diversity, was the first naturalist to note the decline of numerous native plant species under the onslaught of the large cattle ranchos.[37]

The most profound changes were a direct result of the brutal decimation of aboriginal cultures. Native cultural landscapes, the fabled managed mosaics, were abandoned or deteriorated from neglect as a consequence of colonial land tenure and forced labor policies. The collapse of aboriginal agroecosystems and their associated cultural landscapes damaged habitat for many native species of flora and fauna. Yet the most dramatic changes were still to come in the nineteenth and twentieth centuries. New waves of ecological and cultural change followed the transition to a modern industrial-capitalist mode of production, resulting in a new transborder Mexico that is still taking shape today.

■ Discussion Questions

1. What led to the dispersal (or collapse) of the classic Maya civilization?

2. Can a complicated classification system like the edaphic (soil) models of the Maya and Mexica exist without an understanding of scientific principles of observation and experimentation? Are there alternative paths to scientific knowledge?

3. Discuss the scientific knowledge of the Mexica in the fields of agroecology, edaphology, and hydrology. Compare their knowledge to the status of European science in these fields in 1519. What do these differences tell us about the role of culture in contrasting worldviews of nature?

4. What caused the demographic collapse of the indigenous population after the Spanish conquest and colonization?

5. What is the significance of the introduction of exotic plants and animals to Mexico by Europeans? Consult the list in table 8 and explore the implications of each introduced species for changes in the ecology, flora, and fauna of Mega-Mexico.

■ Suggested Readings

Crosby, Alfred. 1972. *The Columbian Exchange: Biological and Cultural Consequences of 1492.* Westport, CT: Greenwood Press.

Fedick, Scott C., ed. 1996. *The Managed Mosaic: Ancient Maya Agriculture and Resource Use.* Salt Lake City: University of Utah Press.

Ortiz Monasterio, Fernando, et al., eds. 1987. *Tierra profanada: Historia ambiental de México.* Mexico City: Instituto Nacional de Antropología y Historia, Secretaría de Desarrollo Urbano y Ecología.

Ramamoorthy, T. P., Robert Bye, Antonio Lot, and John Fa, eds. 1993. *Biological Diversity of Mexico: Origins and Distribution.* Oxford: Oxford University Press.

Rojas, Teresa, ed. 1991. *La agricultura en tierras mexicanas desde sus orígenes hasta nuestros días*. Mexico City: Grijalbo.

Simon, Julian. 1999. *Endangered Mexico: An Environment on the Edge*. San Francisco: Sierra Club Books.

■ Notes

1. Motecozumah was the spelling commonly used by Mexica informants to Spanish missionaries. Spanish translators may have mispronounced, and therefore misspelled, the name of the Mexica king as Montezuma. See J. Kandell, *La Capital: The Biography of Mexico City* (New York: Random House, 1988), 6. Quotation from B. Díaz del Castillo, *The Conquest of New Spain* (London: Penguin Books, 1963), 214, 228.

2. R. A. Mittermeier, "Primate Diversity and the Tropical Forest: Case Studies from Brazil and Madagascar and the Importance of Megadiversity Countries," in *Biodiversity*, ed. E. O. Wilson (Washington, DC: National Academy Press, 1988); also see T. P. Ramamoorthy, R. Bye, A. Lot, and J. Fa, eds., *Biological Diversity of Mexico: Origins and Distribution* (Oxford: Oxford University Press, 1993), xxxiii.

3. Eugene Hunn, personal note to the author. Linguists from the Summer Institute for Linguistics have documented the Zapotec dialects. Also see the online bibliography of the *International Journal of American Linguistics* at http://www.ethnologue.com.

4. R. Bye, "The Role of Humans in the Diversification of Plants in Mexico," in Ramamoorthy et al., *Biological Diversity of Mexico*, 708.

5. Ramamoorthy, introduction to *Biological Diversity of Mexico*, xxxiii.

6. Mexico is a major center for the origin of such cultigens as maize, beans, squash, chiles, avocados, peanuts, and amaranth. See J. Rzedowski and M. Equihua, *Atlas cultural de México: Flora* (Mexico City: SEP, 1987), 168–95.

7. A. Crosby, *The Columbian Exchange: Biological and Cultural Consequences of 1492* (Westport, CT: Greenwood Press, 1972).

8. Ramamoorthy, introduction to *Biological Diversity of Mexico*, xxxiii.

9. S. Morley, *The Ancient Maya* (Stanford: Stanford University Press, 1946), 141.

10. A. Gómez-Pompa and A. Kaus, "Traditional Management of Tropical Forests in Mexico," in *Alternatives to Deforestation: Steps toward Sustainable Use of the Amazon Rain Forest*, ed. A. B. Anderson (New York: Columbia University Press, 1990), 46.

11. On the sustainability of milpas, see ibid.; also see M. Altieri, *Agroecology: The Science of Sustainable Agriculture* (Boulder, CO: Westview Press, 1995). The idea that the milpa mimics the rain forest is probably attributable originally to C. Geertz, *Agricultural Involution* (Berkeley: University of California Press, 1969); see also J. M. Benyus, *Biomimicry: Innovation Inspired by Nature* (New York: Quill/William Morrow, 1997).

12. S. Kepecs and S. Boucher, "The Pre-Hispanic Cultivation of *Rejolladas* and Stone-Lands: New Evidence from Northeast Yucatán," in *The Managed Mosaic:*

Ancient Maya Agriculture and Resource Use, ed. S. Fedick (Salt Lake City: University of Utah Press, 1996), 77.

13. Ibid, 71–72, 77.

14. See generally, Fedick, *Managed Mosaic.*

15. The collapse of elite-controlled Maya city-states may have been precipitated by the withdrawal of the labor of independent farmers who abandoned royal mono-culture plantations and returned to milpas deep in the rain forest mosaic. See Kepecs and Boucher, "Pre-Hispanic Cultivation"; K. A. Pyburn, "The Political Economy of Ancient Maya Land Use: The Road to Ruin," in Fedick, *Managed Mosaic,* 236–50.

16. R. Garcia, "Notes on (Home)Land Ethics: Ideas, Values, and the Land," in *Chicano Culture, Ecology, Politics: Subversive Kin,* ed. D. G. Peña (Tucson: University of Arizona Press, 1998), 80.

17. J. Simon, *Endangered Mexico: An Environment on the Edge* (San Francisco: Sierra Club Books, 1999), 7–10.

18. N. Barrera Bassols and J. A. Zinck, eds., *Ethnopedology in a World Wide Perspective: An Annotated Bibliography,* ITC Publication No 77 (Enschede, The Netherlands: International Institute for Aerospace Survey and Earth Sciences, 2000); also see J. L. de Rojas, *México Tenochtitlan: economía y sociedad en el siglo XVI* (Mexico City: Fondo de Cultura Económica, 1986); B. J. Williams and C. Ortiz-Solario, "Middle American Folk Soil Taxonomy," *Annals of the Association of American Geographers* 71 (1981): 335–58.

19. Simon, *Endangered Mexico,* 11.

20. Altieri, *Agroecology,* 143; also see M. Altieri, M. K. Anderson, and L. C. Merrick, "Peasant Agriculture and the Conservation of Crop and Wild Plant Resources," in *Readings from Conservation Biology: Plant Conservation,* ed. D. Ehrenfeld (London: Society for Conservation Biology and Blackwell Science, 1993), 82–91.

21. For lists of popular Mexican ethnobotanicals, see J. Atzin, *Antiguo recetario medicinal Azteca* (Mexico City: Gómez Gómez Hermanos, Editores, 1988); and H. Gali, *Las hierbas del indio* (Mexico City: Gómez Gómez Hermanos, Editores, 1984). For Mexican remedios in what is now the U.S. Southwest, see M. Moore, *Medicinal Plants of the Mountain West* (Albuquerque: Museum of New Mexico Press, 1979); G. Cajete, *A People's Ecology, Explorations in Sustainable Living: Health, Environment, Agriculture, Native Traditions* (Santa Fe: Clear Light Publishers, 1999); R. Ford, ed., *The Nature and Status of Ethnobotany,* Anthropological Papers No. 67, Museum of Anthropology, University of Michigan (Ann Arbor: University of Michigan Press, 1994), esp. 51–80, 137–63. For scientific taxonomies, see R. Bye, "The Role of Humans in the Diversification of Plants in Mexico," in Ramamoorthy, *Biological Diversity of Mexico,* 707–32; E. H. Hernández Xolocotzi, "Aspects of Plant Domestication in Mexico: A Personal View," in ibid., 733–56.

22. In the fifteenth century, the ruler of nearby Texcoco, Nezahualcóyotl (Hungry Coyote), gave permission for the area to be made a forest reserve to protect the Mexica

water supply; F. O. Monasterio et al., *Tierra profanada: Historia ambiental de México* (Mexico City: INAH/SEP, 1988), 108.

23. The translation is "those who draw out stones from the body." Other names for healers were *tetlanocuilanque,* "those who draw out worms from the teeth" and *texiocuilanque,* "those who draw out worms from the eyes." J. Soustelle, *Daily Life of the Aztecs on the Eve of the Spanish Conquest* (Stanford: Stanford University Press, 1961), 92.

24. On the calmecac, see Rojas, *México Tenochtitlan,* 25; on Mexica midwifery, see Soustelle, *Daily Life of the Aztecs,* 188–89.

25. Rojas, *México Tenochtitlan.* Calmecacs hosted students dedicated to the study of two ancient classical cultures, the Toltec and Maya. The Mexica provided Spanish missionaries with codicil diagrams and narratives explaining aspects of Maya ethnobotany. In the sixteenth century, Mexica sources noted the Maya lexicon referring to different parts of flowering plants; see J. S. Flores and W. Ucan Ek, *Nombres usados por los Mayas para designar a la vegetación,* Cuadernos de Divulgación 10 (Xalapa, Veracruz: Instituto Nacional de Investigaciones sobre Recursos Bióticos, 1983), 11–12.

26. Population estimates in S. Cook and W. Borah, *The Indian Population of Central Mexico, 1531–1610* (Berkeley: University of California Press, 1960); on disease, see Crosby, *Columbian Exchange,* 35–63.

27. E. Wolf, *Sons of the Shaking Earth* (Chicago: University of Chicago Press, 1959).

28. Simon, *Endangered Mexico,* 49; M. Romero-Frizzi, "La agricultura en la época colonial," in *La agricultura en tierras mexicanas desde sus orígenes hasta nuestros días,* ed. T. Rojas (Mexico City: Editorial Grijalbo, 1991), 168, 185.

29. Romero-Frizzi, "Agricultura en la época colonial."

30. Ibid, 160.

31. Simon, *Endangered Mexico,* 66.

32. Ibid.

33. See M. C. Meyer, W. L. Sherman, and S. M. Deeds, *The Course of Mexican History* (Oxford: Oxford University Press, 1998).

34. F. O. Monasterio et al., *Tierra profanada,* 153.

35. Meyer, Sherman, and Deeds, *Course of Mexican History.*

36. Eugene Hunn reports that the tapir is still found in Oaxaca, Quintana Roo, Campeche, and Chiapas (personal note to the author). Monasterio et al., *Tierra profanada;* also see A. S. Leopold, *Fauna silvestre de México* (Mexico City: Instituto Mexicano de Recursos Renovables, 1982).

37. A. Humboldt, *Ensayo político sobre el Reino de la Nueva España* (Mexico City: Editorial Porrúa, 1966).

4

Environmental History of Mega-Mexico, El Norte

Oh, our mother, the earth; oh, our father, the sky,
May the fringes be the falling rain,
May the border be the standing rainbow.
—Tewa Indian chant

Sin agua, no hay vida.
(Without water, there is no life).
—Traditional saying from Rio Arriba

When we were a new nation with the wilderness before us, we were two million Americans with a toehold on the continent. We needed to multiply and develop the land and we did. We tapped the wilderness for its resources, passed a billion acres of public lands into private ownership, and plowed the hillsides to plant our crops.
—George M. Leonard (1988)

El Norte (the North) roughly comprises that part of the Republic of Mexico that, after 1848, became the states of Texas, New Mexico, Colorado, Arizona, and California. Diverse **Mexican-origin peoples** inhabit El Norte, and they have developed distinct regional **cultures.** By 1769, there were well-established **Norteña/o** communities in the major watersheds of Texas, New Mexico, Colorado, Arizona, and California.[1] This chapter presents an environmental history of El Norte by focusing on two **ecological revolutions:** first the Norteña/o ecological revolution (1598–1848) and second the Anglo-American industrial capitalist ecological revolution (1848–1950).

Ecological Worldviews

The epigrams represent three distinct worldviews of nature: Native, Mexican or Norteña/o, and Anglo-American. The Tewa are among the first nations of the northern Pueblos.[2] They have inhabited New Mexico's Rio Grande corridor since the early fourteenth century. They trace their ancestral roots to the Anasazi, a pueblo-dwelling culture who over many more millennia inhabited the Colorado Plateau.[3] The Tewa do not view nature as a **commodity,** natural resource, or wilderness. The earth is home and is a wild (self-willing) and familiar land.

In the Tewa worldview, animal and plant spirits handed down sacred place-names infused with ecological meaning.[4] Thus, the Tewa might name a spot in the forest where they find herbs and medicinal plants "Bear Root Springs Beneath the Red Rock Wall." Back in the pueblo, the children memorize the name and location of the spot by age ten. The Tewa know which plants are most suitable for cultivation in different environments and are meticulous seed savers. They are deeply committed to cooperative irrigation.[5] Nature provides analogs for appropriate human behavior, lessons that are remembered and taught in legends and origin stories. In Coyote stories among many Native American communities, humans learn the rules of living in place from animal teachers. The animal guides constantly remind humans to avoid being greedy and self-centered.[6]

Other worldviews emerged after 1598 and the first Spanish-Mexican settlements in New Mexico. The one usually mentioned is the worldview of the conquistadors, said to spring from a thirst for gold. In this worldview, nature is a dangerous wilderness inhabited by so-called *indios bárbaros.* To the conquistadors, nature was something to be tamed and exploited to create wealth and empire. Redemption lay in saving Indian souls. However, Spanish and later Mexican laws, customs, and governance institutions eventually evolved to create opportunities for mutual Mexican–Native American aid and coexistence in geographically isolated **bioregions.** Institutions for settlement, agriculture, and land and water use were well adapted to the aridity of the region. The **customary law** of the **acequia** system is a good example of an institution that proved valuable to the welfare of Native and Mexican American communities. The fact of elite exploitation of native labor does not lessen the importance of Spanish and Mexican land and water laws as **sustainable** institutions for human adaptation in an arid environment.

The Norteña/o worldview emerged as Mexican-origin people intermarried with Native Americans and learned to coinhabit the watersheds of the north. Over generations Norteñas/os "became native" to place. The quotation from Teresa Jaramillo in the introduction to this book describes plants and animals as spiritual kin, as teachers. This ecological worldview rejects the conquistador-like desire to dominate nature and conquer natives. It resonates with Native American philosophies of nature, in which nature is home and animals are teachers. This worldview is expressed in the saying, Sin agua, no hay vida. Mexican-origin cultures in El Norte drew from the confluence of multiple civilizations.[7] Vital elements came from contact and engagement with the first nations of El Norte, including the Pueblo, Navajo, Apache, Tohono O'odham, Ute, and Cahuilla.

A third ecological worldview represents the frontier attitude of Anglo-American expansionism and is similar to the subjugate-and-conquer ideology of the conquistadors.[8] Anglo-Americans viewed El Norte as an uninhabited wasteland to be conquered and developed. The quote from Leonard illustrates this dominant worldview. Anglo-Americans saw an immensity of wilderness and sought to clear-cut their way to a more civilized space. Labor and nature were seen as expendable resources, commodities to be bought and sold in the marketplace. The white settlers also embraced the ideology of Manifest Destiny: They believed they were predestined, chosen by God, to subdue the wilderness, remove the savages, and bring the shining light of reason and law to backward cultures and untamed landscapes. They were to use their versions of science, technology, and economic power in the conquest of nature and dominion over the ostensibly primitive cultures standing in their way across the so-called western frontier.

◼ Ecological Revolutions in El Norte

The Norteña/o ecological revolution (1598–1848) was characterized by adaptation of Mexican-origin people to the biophysical conditions of regions defined by the scarcity of water. With the exception of upland areas, moisture in El Norte from Texas to California is generally meager. The Rio Grande, Arkansas River, and Colorado River are the principal watercourses. Sustainable adaptation to the conditions of aridity is an overlooked hallmark of the earliest Spanish-Mexican settlements.[9]

In most Norteña/o communities, land tenure was egalitarian. Whereas some communities had a minority of rich landowning elites (*ricos*), the great majority of Mexican-origin settlers were smallholding farmers, independent artisans, or workers. Inhabitants typically had rights of usufruct (rights to use that belonging to another, in this case the sovereign governments of Spain and Mexico).

These rights were exercised on **traditional use areas** (*ejidos*) and were subject to customary rules and social obligations of tightly knit communities.[10] **Commons** rules prohibited massive removal of natural vegetation, curtailed monopoly control over resources, discouraged overgrazing by livestock, and promoted **mutual aid** and cooperative labor in local economies based on subsistence, barter, and some regional trade. Local customary laws were painstakingly adapted over generations to the unique circumstances of each place. Under customary law, Mexican-origin communities developed their own local rules for the management and allocation of commonly held resources.[11]

The industrial-capitalist ecological revolution followed the Anglo-American conquest and colonization of El Norte after 1848. Between 1870 and 1970, the capitalist ecological revolution accelerated the pace of and expanded the areas subject to economic exploitation. Exploitation of land, water, and labor led to dramatic ecological transformations accompanied by a radical shift in property rights. The privatization and federal expropriation of Spanish- and Mexican-period land grants (*mercedes*) were principal forces underlying this shift. Native American tribes, *mexicano* rancheros, and Hispano acequia farmers were displaced from their ancestral common and family lands. **Enclosure** disrupted the stability of Native American and Mexican-origin communities. The expropriation of these lands by private and governmental interests in many places undermined the commons and weakened traditions of local democracy via customary law.

Displaced farmers and workers entered the flow of domestic and international migration and joined existing Mexican-origin communities in urban centers, agricultural districts, and rural areas. Massive displacement from their lands, north and south of the border, set the stage for the processes that defined the experience of the Mexican-origin people throughout the course of nineteenth and twentieth centuries. **Chicana/o** historians have traced the evolution of five interrelated processes in the encounter between Mexican-origin and Anglo-American civilizations:

1. industrialization and forced urbanization of the Mexican-origin population;
2. imposition of a racially stratified labor market and exploitative system of administered labor migration;
3. systematic political disenfranchisement;

4. external administration of local institutions; and
5. a racist ideology that defines Mexicans as an inferior race of "half-breed Indians."[12]

Mexican-origin people resisted racial and class domination, responding with fierce labor and **social movements** rooted in a deeply embedded sense of lost lands and injustice. This chapter ends with stories of early resistance to environmental injustice. From El Paso to northern New Mexico, and from Arizona to California, Mexicans resisted domination, the loss of common lands, and the degradation of the environment.

■ Biological Diversity in El Norte

The native flora and fauna of El Norte inhabit a broad ecological spectrum, ranging from subtropical jungles to alpine tundra. El Norte has been described as a landscape of "mountain islands and desert seas."[13] This description refers to a biogeographical quality of the area: With the exception of south Texas, much of El Norte is characterized by north-south running mountain ranges separated, and isolated from one another like islands, by wide desert valleys and plains. The mountain islands are relatively wet and cold, whereas the "desert seas" are drier and hotter. This pattern is typical of all the major *cordillera* **biomes,** including the southern Rocky Mountains, the Sierra Nevada, and the coastal ranges of Alta California (more or less the modern U.S. state of California). The mountainsides are mosaics of plant and animal **communities** that shift in composition and density according to elevation, moisture, soil type, and solar orientation.

A person can walk through multiple **ecological life zones,** that is, distinct communities of vegetation, by climbing from the floor of a desert valley to the highest nearby mountain peak. In the Rio Arriba, for example, as one walks out of the Upper Sonoran, or cold desert, environment in the valley bottoms to ever-higher elevations, one passes through piñon-juniper woodland (an *ecotone,* or transition between two zones), montane ponderosa and other conifer forests, subalpine spruce-fir forests, Krummholz transition (the "twisted tree" or tree line ecotone), and alpine tundra (see figure 8). Along the way, from lower to higher elevations, one passes through different types of the riparian life zone, the most biologically diverse **ecosystem** type in El Norte, which occurs along watercourses.

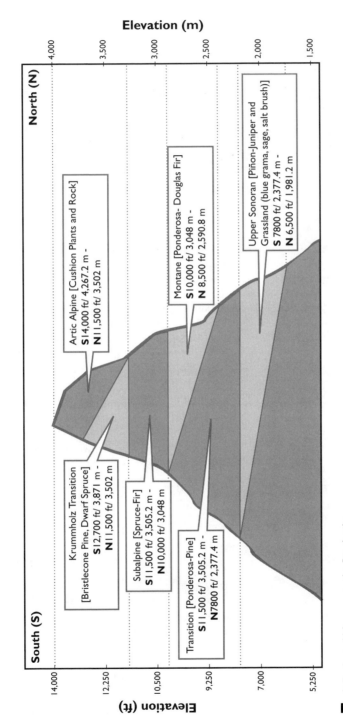

Elevation (m)

North (N)

Arctic Alpine [Cushion Plants and Rock]
S 14,000 ft/ 4,267.2 m -
N 11,500 ft/ 3,502 m

Montane [Ponderosa- Douglas Fir]
S 10,000 ft/ 3,048 m -
N 8,500 ft/ 2,590.8 m

Upper Sonoran [Piñon-Juniper and
Grassland (blue grama, sage, salt brush)]
S 7800 ft/ 2,377.4 m -
N 6,500 ft/ 1,981.2 m

South (S)

Krummholz Transition
[Bristlecone Pine, Dwarf Spruce]
S 12,700 ft/ 3,871 m -
N 11,500 ft/ 3,502 m

Subalpine [Spruce-Fir]
S 11,500 ft/ 3,505.2 m -
N 10,000 ft/ 3,048 m

Transition [Ponderosa-Pine]
S 11,500 ft/ 3,505.2 m -
N 7800 ft/ 2,377.4 m

Elevation (ft)

■ 8. Ecological life zones in the Rio Arriba.

Table 9   Biological diversity of El Norte

STATE	NUMBER OF PLANT SPECIES	NUMBER OF VERTEBRATE[a] ANIMAL SPECIES
Arizona	3,370	862
California	8,375	650
Colorado	4,100	597
New Mexico	3,900	275
Texas	5,500	1,245

Sources: For plant species see T. H. Kearney and R. H. Peebles, Arizona Flora (Berkeley: University of California Press, 1960); M. J. Mac, P. A. Opler, C. E. P. Hacker, and P. D. Doran, eds., Status and Trends of the Nation's Biological Resources (Reston, VA: U.S. Geological Survey, 1998); W. C. Martin and C. R. Hutchins, A Flora of New Mexico, 2 vols. (Hirschberg, Germany: Cramer, 1980); W. A. Weber and R. C. Wittman, Catalog of the Flora of Colorado (Norman: University of Oklahoma Press, 1987); Audubon Society Texas (available online at http://www .audubon.org/chapter/tx/tx/abttas.html); CalFlora Database (available online at http://www .calflora.org). For animal species see C. H. Lowe Jr., Vertebrates of Arizona (Tucson: University of Arizona Press, 1964); California Department of Fish and Game, Habitat Conservation Planning Branch (available online at http://www.dfg.ca.gov/hcpb/species/p_a_rglr/genplants animals.shtml); Colorado Division of Wildlife (available online at http://wildlife.state.co.us/); Colorado Natural Heritage Program (available online at http://cnhp.colostate.edu/); New Mexico Natural Heritage Project (available online at http://nmnhp.unm.edu/tracking/ tracking_general.php); Audubon Society Texas Web site.
[a] Vertebrate species include amphibians, birds, fish, mammals, and reptiles.

El Norte shares numerous species of native wild flora and fauna with the rest of **Mega-Mexico.** The mountain lion, bobcat, coyote, Mexican gray wolf, brown bear, grizzly bear, mule deer, white-tailed deer, elk, and peccary are among the best-known mega (large) fauna historically found across El Norte. Hundreds of migratory birds spend autumn and winter in central or southern Mexico, migrating to El Norte for the spring and summer. Species from the interior of Mexico often overlap with species from the far north to create bewildering arrays of flora and fauna. In the lower Rio Grande Valley of south Texas, the ocelot, jaguarundi, chachalaca (a bird of the pheasant family), and wild turkey are examples of overlapping species.[14]

Colorado and New Mexico have more than 800 vertebrate species. More than 6,000 vascular and 2,000 nonvascular plant species in more than 450 recognized plant communities represent various terrestrial ecosystems. Arizona, California, and Texas have thousands of native plant and animal species, inhabiting close to a thousand recognized plant communities, and many are **endemic.** California currently lists 8,375 vascular plants as part of its natural heritage. The Texas natural heritage list includes more than 5,500 vascular plant species; 126 of 1,245 vertebrate species are listed as endemic (see table 9).

◼ Ancestral Civilizations and Environmental Change

Ancestral Anasazi, Mogollon, Hohokam, and Shoshone cultures played an important role in the environmental history of El Norte. Like Mesoamerican civilizations, the ancestral societies of El Norte developed agriculture, architecture, ethnobotany, artisan crafts, and trade. Some were city builders with trade networks; customary laws governing subsistence activities; and religious, kinship, and civic forms of social and political organization.[15] These parent civilizations are tied to the historic first nations. The Anasazi ancestors evolved into the Rio Grande Pueblo cultures, Hopi, and Zuñi; Hohokam ancestors became the Tohono O'odham and Pima; and ancestral Athapaskan- and Uto-Aztecan–speaking peoples became the Apache, Navajo, and Ute.

A critical issue in the study of ancestral civilizations is what William Denevan calls the "myth of a pristine wilderness."[16] This myth has racist and romantic aspects. The racist side is entangled with the imagination of a nation-building people invested in Manifest Destiny. Anglo-Americans needed to imagine an empty landscape to justify the "billion acres of public land" forcibly taken from Native American and Mexican-origin communities.[17] The "taming of the wilderness" was triumphantly declared a glorious victory in the march of civilization against "savagery" and "barbarism." The mirror image of this is the romantic myth of "noble savages" living in perfect harmony with nature. This romantic myth erases the history of the ancestral cultures: They are irrelevant to the environmental history of El Norte because they left everything undisturbed and unused. The romantic ideology excused whites for making use of something Indians (and Mexicans) were neglecting and wasting.

Charles Redman cautions against seeing the humanized landscapes of pre-contact America as resulting from conscious native conservation. Ancestral indigenous civilizations clearly modified the environment through activities like land clearance for settlement and farming, the setting of intentional brush fires, and the construction of irrigation networks and other communal structures for the control and use of water and land. Redman suggests that the ancestors of Native Americans caused deforestation, soil erosion, and increased salinity of groundwater and soil. The abandonment of Chaco Canyon around 1150 CE, evidently when it ceased to be agriculturally productive, is presented as the prime example of Anasazi-induced ecological degradation.[18]

A contrary view, drawing on data from tree-ring studies (dendrochronology), suggests the ecological collapse of Chaco was compounded by climate change. It was most likely drought that ended effective inhabitation of Chaco.[19] Indeed, not all Anasazi pueblos were abandoned at this time, and many in wetter upland areas like the San Juan, Las Animas, and La Plata watersheds persisted for another 250 years.

Ecological change occurred throughout the pre-contact history of El Norte. Ancestral civilizations developed complex bodies of place-based ecological knowledge. They saved seeds and planted domesticated crops. They used wild plants for medicine and food and managed the landscape with fire to encourage the **habitat** of species they hunted or collected. They altered rivercourses to divert water to crop fields and captured rainfall and moisture in pebble-mulch fields. They built towns, villages, seasonal hunting camps, and gathering stations. They built roads to support networks of trade and social exchange. These aboriginal cultures persisted in place for several thousand years without significantly impoverishing their environments, however. Between 1300 and 1450 CE, they left their ancestral homes to establish new communities and settlements as some of the first nations of El Norte.

■ First Nations and the Mexican-Origin People

At contact, Native American relations with Spanish and Mexican-origin people were hostile and violent. Conflict arose with the imposition of forced labor, the **encomienda** system that subjugated Indians to exploitation. Between the Pueblo Revolt of 1680 and Mexican independence in 1821, significant changes occurred in intergroup relations in New Mexico. During the short-lived Mexican Republic (1821–1848), relations between Pueblos and Mexicans moved toward peaceful coexistence, coinhabitation, and mutual aid. Mexican Americans lived and worked in native neighborhoods and communities. Norteña/o and native communities developed similar systems of customary law that nurtured civic institutions for local self-governance such as the acequia. On the eve of the military conflicts with the United States, the Mexican-origin people had established themselves within the borders of the traditional and ancestral homelands of the first nations. The Mexican-origin people had amalgamated as place-based cultures.

Native and Mexican-origin cultures exchanged numerous plants and animals, remedies, and local knowledge of the land, water, and wildlife habitat. Indigenous cultures made important contributions to the ethnobotany of the Mexican-origin people. They shared knowledge of hunting, foraging, and desert survival skills. In New Mexico the management of communal irrigation ditches (acequias) was a source of sustained contact and cooperative relations between Pueblo and Mexican-origin inhabitants. Cultural exchange flowed in both directions. The Mexican-origin people introduced sheep to the Navajo, who then developed a renowned wool-weaving tradition. The Pueblos adopted wheat as their own crop. Mexican-origin people introduced peaches, plums, apples, pears, and apricots, which the Pueblos and Navajo readily adopted for their family and communal orchards.

Anglo-Americans interceded in this process of cultural exchange by defining Mexicans as an inferior half-breed Indian race[20] and imposing strong taboos against the mixing of racial groups. Anglo-Americans generally recoiled from what they construed as miscegenation, a word implying the biologically wrongful mixing of races. They imposed a norm of racial segregation to keep whites from intermarrying with so-called Indian and Mexican races. This new racial hierarchy placed Mexicans in a position of inferiority relative to the purportedly more noble Indians. Indians were seen as fierce, courageous warriors, Mexicans as treacherous, cowardly thieves. This ideology defined Mexicans as an impure mixture of the Spanish and Mexican Indian races.

The Norteña/o Ecological Revolution, 1598–1848

Mexican-origin people established communities in most of the major watersheds of Texas, New Mexico, Colorado, Arizona, and California.[21] Four distinct bioregions were settled during the period of the Norteña/o ecological revolution, from 1598 to 1848 (see map 1):

1. Rio Arriba, or the upper Rio Grande watershed in northern New Mexico and southern Colorado (first settled in 1598);
2. south Texas including the lower Rio Grande Valley and the Nueces watershed (first settled in 1699);
3. Arizona, especially Tucson and the Santa Cruz River valley (first settled in 1752); and
4. Alta California, including the Los Angeles basin, the Central Valley, and the San Francisco Bay Area (first settled in 1769).

The distance from El Norte to Mexico City and other centers of Spanish colonial political and economic power was important. Even with the trade on the Camino Real (Royal Highway) and other wagon trails, El Norte was geographically isolated given limits of transportation and communication technologies. This isolation reduced regionwide pressures on ecosystems. Towns and villages based their subsistence strategies on local materials. External markets for products like timber, mutton, beef, and perishable crops simply did not exist.[22] Thus, geographic factors limited the scope and scale of ecological degradation during the Norteña/o ecological revolution.

At the time of the signing of the Treaty of Guadalupe Hidalgo in 1848, which ended the Mexican War and ceded El Norte to the United States, the Mexican-origin population in the region was about 82,000. New Mexico had a population of 60,000, Texas 14,000, California 7,500, and Arizona a scant 1,000 Mexican-origin inhabitants. Such small populations could not exert significant pressures on the environment.[23]

Norteñas/os were never a dominant force in Spanish colonial society and ascended to limited power only after Mexican independence in 1821. The colonial ecological revolution in Mexico was conceived and implemented by European or Mexican-born Spanish elites. The Mexican-origin people of El Norte were concentrated in the lower social classes of the empire, including the ranks of mine workers, farmworkers, day laborers, and small subsistence farmers.

The Norteña/o ecological revolution came quietly from below. Far from the centers of viceregal authority in Mexico, Norteñas/os followed unique patterns of ecological adaptation and developed their own ideologies of culture and nature, **modes of production,** customary laws, and forms of social organization. The Norteña/o communities represent a truly multicultural confluence of practices and technologies. Civilizations

| Map 1. Major settlement watersheds of El Norte (1598–1848) |

1. Lower Rio Grande Valley
2. El Paso, TX (Rio Grande) to Albuquerque, NM
3. Rio Arriba (San Luis Valley to Santa Fe, NM)
4. Tucson, Arizona (Santa Cruz Valley)
5. Los Angeles Basin
6. San Francisco Bay

■ Map 1. Major settlement watersheds of El Norte (1598–1848)

from Africa, the Middle East, Mediterranean Europe, and North America converged in the unique set of cultural practices embodied by the Norteña/o ecological revolution.

Land Grants and Cultural Landscapes

Mercedes (land grants) defined the early pattern of land use and settlement. Under Spanish and Mexican law, four principal types of grants were authorized. Pueblo grants confirmed aboriginal land rights for Eastern and Western Pueblo nations. Community grants, which were made to groups of five or more families to settle new watersheds, typically included

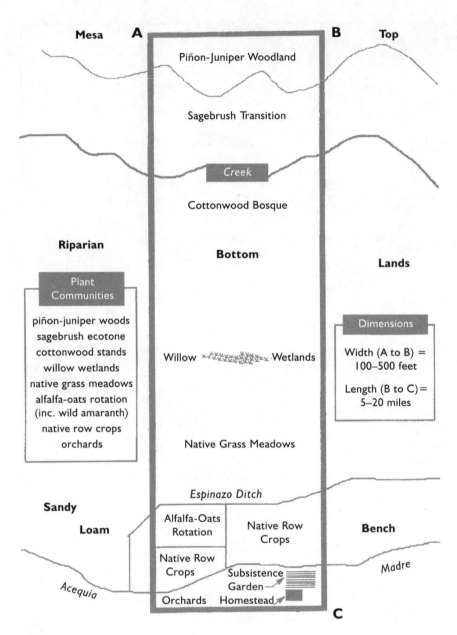

Mesa   A   B   Top

Piñon-Juniper Woodland

Sagebrush Transition

Creek

Cottonwood Bosque

Riparian   **Bottom**   **Lands**

Plant Communities

piñon-juniper woods
sagebrush ecotone
cottonwood stands
willow wetlands
native grass meadows
alfalfa-oats rotation
(inc. wild amaranth)
native row crops
orchards

Dimensions

Width (A to B) =
100–500 feet

Length (B to C) =
5–20 miles

Willow ~~~~~~~ Wetlands

Native Grass Meadows

Espinazo Ditch

Sandy   Alfalfa-Oats Rotation   Native Row Crops   **Bench**

Loam

Native Row Crops

Madre

Acequia   Subsistence Garden

Orchards   Homestead

C

9. Riparian long-lot.

large tracts of common lands. Individual grants were awarded to soldiers for service to the crown. A fourth type involved impresario grants to foreigners.

Many mercedes in northern New Mexico and southern Colorado were of the community type. These grants stipulated that each family would receive an individual parcel of land (*suerte*) for agriculture. The suertes were long, narrow, ribbonlike strips of land that gave settlers access to a river corridor, uplands, and fertile bottomlands. Cultural geographers refer to this land use pattern as the riparian long-lot (see figure 9). Each acequia farm thus maintained access to ecological zones across mesatops, foothills, and valley bottoms. The uplands were designated as common lands (ejidos), where settlers had rights to hunt and fish, graze livestock, and gather wood and wildcraft (medicinal plants). These rights were typically restricted under customary law to local subsistence uses.

Settlement of the Rio Grande corridor in south Texas followed a similar pattern. Common lands were important and local officials administered ejido use rights. Settlers in California and Arizona did not always follow this pattern of community land grants. In contrast, the secularization of the mission properties resulted in large cattle ranches controlled by elite families. By 1850, most of the lands of the former mission districts in California and Arizona were concentrated in 1,045 private landholdings of various sizes. About 800 of these ranchos were large, with 1,500 or more head of cattle. Ranchero elites had an estimated 2.2 million head of cattle at the start of the 1849 California gold rush.

Acequias

The acequia institution flourished in all four bioregions of El Norte. The acequia, which had roots in late antiquity, derived much of its customary law from Spanish, Arabic, and Pueblo Indian sources. Donald Worster notes that "authority over water distribution and management remains completely within the local community, with those who are the users. They have within themselves . . . all the skill and expertise required to build and maintain their water system."[24]

The eight hundred–year occupation of Spain by Muslim Moors influenced the development of the acequia institution. Much of the terminology in acequia law and irrigation derives from Arabic, as does customary law and practice. Customary water allocation practices can be seen as extensions

Topic Highlight 2. The Acequia: A Watershed Democracy

The acequia is a gravity-driven, earthenwork, communally managed irrigation institution with roots in late antiquity and strong Arabic influences. *Acequia* is derived from the Arabic term *as-Saquiya*, which translates as "the water bearer." Other examples of terminology for acequia irrigation derived from Arabic include *noria* (well), *atarque* or *presa* (dam), and *zanja* (irrigation ditch).

There are several different kinds of ditches in the acequia water web. The *acequia madre*, the "mother ditch," is the main-stem ditch off the water source. The *sangria*, or "bleeding ditch," is a lateral ditch running from the mother ditch to deliver water to fields. The *espinazo*, or "spinal ditch," typically delivers water to the center of irrigated fields.

The acequia is not just a sustainable irrigation technology but an important civic institution for local self-governance. The acequia is managed collectively by the *propietarios* (local landowners with water rights on the ditch), who elect a *mayordomo* (ditchrider or water master) on a one person, one vote basis. They also elect a *comisión* (a commission that oversees the work of the mayordomo). *Parciantes* (who are also propietarios) share water rights in the acequia association.

The customary law of the acequia derives from Roman, Spanish, and Arabic sources. Five basic principles underlie acequia customary law: (1) the communitarian value of water, (2) the non-transferability of water, (3) the right of thirst, (4) shared scarcity, and (5) cooperative labor and mutual aid.

The *communitarian value of water* holds that one cannot separate water from the landscape and its use in the community. Moreover, water rights are allocated on the basis of temporal priority as well as equity and fairness, and are dependent on ownership of farmland in the acequia corridor.

Water is an asset-in-place, meaning it cannot be transferred from an acequia to other users. Water is not a commodity to be owned or sold for money. It belongs to the community, and the irrigator has the right only to use the water, subject to rules that prohibit damaging other farmers or the land.

The *Islamic right of thirst* holds that all living things with thirst have a right to water, and human use of water cannot deny plants and animals their rightful share.

The right of thirst extends to parciantes on a ditch. The principle of *shared scarcity* holds that in times of drought, scarcity is shared and everyone uses less water, so that all may continue to farm.

The construction, maintenance, and operation of acequias are communal activities. Every spring, the acequia must be cleaned and repaired. All parciantes must contribute to ongoing maintenance by contributing their labor, assigning a *peon* (laborer) to perform the work, or paying a fine for failing to participate in the communal labor.

These principles have led many observers to describe the acequia system as a watershed democracy. The acequia is clearly one of the oldest institutions for local self-governance in the United States today. Yet acequia customary law conflicts with several contemporary U.S. water laws that treat water as a commodity, including the *doctrine of prior appropriation,* the concept that the first user of a water source has preferential rights to that water. The conflicts between acequia and Anglo concepts of water rights are discussed in chapter 7.

SUGGESTED READINGS

G. A. Hicks and D. G. Peña, "Community Acequias in Colorado's Rio Culebra Watershed: A Customary Commons in the Domain of Prior Appropriation," *University of Colorado Law Review* 74 (2003): 387–486.

D. G. Peña, "Cultural Landscapes and Biodiversity: The Ethnoecology of an Upper Rio Grande Watershed Commons," in *Ethnoecology: Situated Knowledge/Located Lives,* ed. V. Nazarea (Tucson: University of Arizona Press, 1999).

J. A. Rivera, *Acequia Culture: Water, Land, and Community in the Southwest* (Albuquerque: University of New Mexico Press, 1998). ■

of the Islamic right of thirst, the idea that all living things with thirst have a right to water. The *parciantes* (local irrigators) on each acequia elect a *mayordomo* (ditchrider) from among the farmers, who oversees the daily management of the acequia. The acequia is a vital civic institution for self-governance in the administration of watersheds and water rights (see topic highlight 2).[25]

Because rainfall is scarce during the growing season, acequia irrigation water comes from the snowpack that collects in the mountains over the

■ 10. Acequia riparian corridor along the Acequia del Cerro in the San Luis Valley of Colorado. The acequia is an irrigation ditch used by Chicana/o farmers in the Rio Arriba. Its water flow depends on snowmelt released from the mountains from May to October. This makes protection of the headwaters zone of critical importance to the irrigation community. Acequias are earthworks and their moist banks create dense corridors of native vegetation. The acequias are renowned for their sustainable use of renewable energy, recycling of water, maintenance of water quality, and protection of wildlife habitat.

course of the long winters. Each year, with the arrival of sunny spring days and later monsoonal rains, the snowpack melts and releases water into the watershed. The acequias divert some of the runoff water and capture the natural force of gravity to run their water webs without fossil fuels. The acequias are based on the renewable use of water and energy in a manner that does not deplete surface water or groundwater supplies or reduce in-stream flows in natural watercourses.[26]

Over generations, the dendritic networks of earthenwork, gravity-driven ditches created dense corridors of lush native vegetation (see figure 10). These acequia networks provide habitat and **biological corridors** for wildlife. This is an important example of the **ecological services** provided by the acequias (see table 10).[27] These beneficial ecological services are a significant aspect of the acequia as a sustainable institution for human inhabitation of El Norte.

Table 10 Economic and ecological services of the acequia landscape mosaic

SERVICE	EXAMPLE	BENEFITS
Agrobiodiversity	Seed-saving of heirloom varieties preserves crop genetic diversity in situ and continually improves productivity and pest resistance.	Agricultural sales
Food production	Riparian corridors and anthropogenic wetlands create habitat for medicinal and edible wild plants for home use or sale.	Artisan, subsistence, agricultural sales
Raw materials	Woodlots and orchards provide materials for food, firewood, tools, and handicrafts.	Artisan, subsistence, agricultural sales
Natural controls	Intercropping, **allelopathic** plants, and companion planting control weeds and insect pests without chemical inputs, preserving trophic webs in the agroecosystem.	Subsistence, agricultural sales, ecological value
Soil conservation	Riparian corridors act as a shield against wind erosion of soil.	Agricultural sales, ecological value
Soil formation	Acequia flood irrigation deposits fresh soil.	Agricultural sales, ecological value
Nutrient cycling	Perennial polycultures and companion planting add nutrients to the soil.	Agricultural sales, ecological value
Water supply	Ditch networks and anthropogenic wetlands store and retain water.	Ecological value
Water regulation	Riparian corridors and human-made wetlands control and buffer water flow through the local hydrological system.	Ecological value
Water treatment	Human-made wetlands absorb and filter pollutants and runoff and provide pH buffering.	Ecological value
Microclimatic regulation	Riparian corridors are populated by phreataphytes (plants with extensive root systems to tap groundwater) that contribute to local hydrological cycle through evapotranspiration.	Ecological value
Wildlife habitat	Riparian corridors and anthropogenic wetlands create habitat, food sources, and movement corridors for wildlife.	Ecological value, amenity
Recreation	**Cultural landscapes** and ecological landscapes provide opportunities for recreation and tourism.	Amenity
Cultural-ecological ethics	Local management of the acequia system by users encourages the reproduction of **land ethics** over the generations.	Ground work for future benefit flows

Self-Reliant Agro-Pastoral and Artisan Economy

The economic life of early communities revolved around self-sufficiency. Norteñas/os adopted numerous native crops, including maize, beans, squash, and chiles, and introduced new crops like wheat, barley, and other grains; olives; wine grapes; and numerous varieties of fruit and vegetables, many originally introduced to Spain by the Moors. They raised a diversity of domesticated animals and cultivated plants (see table 11). Maize, beans, and squash were typically planted together, a practice that fertilizes the soil, because legumes fix nitrogen in the soil. Planting squash inhibits weed growth because the sprawling crop smothers competing organisms. Norteña/o farmers were dedicated seed savers and adapted numerous cultivated varieties to the arid, high-altitude conditions found across El Norte.

Their livestock included milk cows, horses, sheep, and swine, and they sometimes bred sheep for wool, which local weavers used. The institution of the *mesta* (a type of grazing cooperative) played a role in livestock management.[28] With roots in medieval Spain and further social evolution in Mexico, the mesta supported cooperative stock-raising by helping younger sheepherders get started, and it regulated pastures to prevent overgrazing.

Production was oriented toward subsistence, but local and regional trade flourished. The most important trade route was the Camino Real, the 1,800-mile-long royal road between Santa Fe, New Mexico, and Mexico City. The California **ranchos** also maintained trade relations with the eastern seaboard. In the early 1800s rancheros shipped cattle hides to New England shoe manufacturers.

Artisans handcrafted a wide range of products from local materials obtained from the common lands. These included furniture, saddles, adobe ovens, and musical instruments. Many forest resources were used in handicraft production. Ponderosa pine was used to make furniture; piñon to make saddles and as firewood; cottonwood to make kitchen utensils; and juniper to make looms and roof beams (vigas). Douglas fir was the most important wood, used to make plows, corrals, and lumber for homes. Aspen was used to make musical instruments. The cutting of these species was limited to accessible lower-elevation forests, using hand axes and saws that did not cause massive deforestation.[29]

Subsistence hunting was important, and favored species included white-

Table 11 Principal domesticated animals and cultivated plants in historic acequia farms (Rio Arriba)

CROPS	ANIMALS	GRASSES
Beets (2)	Domestic cats	Alfalfa
Bolita beans[a]	Beef, milk cows (6)	Black grama[a]
Broccoli (3)	Chickens (8)	Blue fescue[a]
Cabbage (2)	Domestic dogs	Blue grama[a]
Calabacita (8)[a]	Ducks (5)	Brome[a]
Carrots (3)	Geese (3)	Luna crested wheat
Cauliflower (2)	Goats (5)	Redtop[a]
Chives	Guinea fowl	Timothy[b]
Cilantro	Hogs (6)	Western crested wheat
Cucumber (3)	Horses	
Decorative flowers (gladiolas, roses, etc.)	Rabbits	
English peas	Sheep (4)	
Fava beans[b]		
Garbanzos		
Garlic		
Lettuce (3)		
Maize (9)[a]		
Mint		
Onions (2)		
Oregano		
Parsley		
Pinto beans[a]		
Potatoes (5)		
Radishes (2)		
Sage (3)		
Scarlet runner beans		
String beans		
Sweet peas		
Turnips		
Vine tomatoes[a]		
Wheat (6)		
Crookneck squash[a]		
Zucchini		

Orchard crops
Apples (6)
Cherries (3)
Chokecherries[a]
Peaches (6)
Pears (2)
Plums (3) (1[a])

Source: Revised and updated from D. G. Peña, "Cultural Landscapes and Biodiversity: The Ethnoecology of an Upper Rio Grande Watershed Commons," in *Ethnoecology: Situated Knowledge/Located Lives,* ed. V. Nazarea (Tucson: University of Arizona Press, 1999).
Notes: Numbers in parentheses indicate horticultural varieties or breeds. Unmarked indicates exotic import (i.e., from European, Middle Eastern, Asian, or other stocks).
[a] Native **land race**.
[b] Naturalized exotic.

tailed and mule deer, antelope, and elk. Except for bison hunting on the high plains, hunting took place on the common grounds. Some commercial hunting occurred, with antelope skins and buffalo hides being exported on the Camino Real and to Spain via Mexican ports like Veracruz. The only species subjected to intense commercial hunting pressures was the beaver; throughout this period, a vigorous trade in furs developed, especially in California and New Mexico. However, most of the commercial hunters were itinerant French or Anglo fur trappers, not Norteñas/os.[30]

Self-Governance and Cooperative Labor

Institutions of self-governance were important in all the bioregions of El Norte. The Spanish laws for settlement and especially the *Recopilación de Leyes de los Reynos de las Indias* (1681) defined the framework for local governance through *ayuntamientos* (town councils). Although the town councils figured prominently in local self-rule, the acequia associations were just as important. Historian Andrés Tijerina notes the importance of local self-governance, which is evident in the water law of south Texas ranchero communities. These had

> a highly developed philosophy of water management . . . governed by basic principles of ancient law . . . Tejano water systems . . . included the dams, the irrigation canals or acequias, the aqueducts, and fields, many of which still carry water today. The influence of Hispanic water philosophy is fairly common in modern Texas, where vocabulary as well as law books include such words as suerte, porción, acequia, surco, agastodero, labor, arroyo, and canoa.[31]

Communities relied on cooperative labor, and the digging of acequias, often the first task, was done collectively. Families contributed to construction and maintenance of acequias. Constructing important buildings in the plazas (town squares) was also a collective endeavor. Cooperative labor extended to tilling, planting, cultivating, and harvesting, as well as the annual threshing of wheat.

Environmental Changes

Mexican-origin people introduced numerous new plants and animals. Agricultural activities, settlements, and the opening of trade routes modified local landscapes. Like Native Americans, the Mexican-origin people used fire to manage the mix of trees, brush, and other vegetative cover. The most significant ecological effects were in the areas closest to settlement. Overgrazing by sheep and cattle contributed to soil erosion and the formation of gullies (arroyos) in New Mexico, Arizona, and California. Some deforestation at lower elevations was a consequence of logging for fuel wood and lumber for construction of homes, corrals, and other structures.

In addition to the crops they introduced, Norteñas/os brought domesticated livestock, which many Native American communities adopted. The new livestock did not widely displace native species, but cattle brought new diseases like brucellosis, which spread to wild ungulates such as bison, pronghorn, and elk. The effect of livestock has occupied the attention of environmental historians. They describe a new "cowboy ecology" of cattle ranching as a biological invasion that led to the extinction of native plants and animals. Yet, during the early mission-rancho period, there simply were not enough sheep or cattle grazing on the land to cause much damage. For example, a 1774 report on the mission of San Gabriel, in California, listed a total of "thirty-eight head of cattle, thirty of sheep, twelve of goats, and twenty of swine, a filly, a stallion, five broken horses, two saddle mules, and fourteen pack mules," not exactly raging hoards of hoofed and cloven invaders.[32] After the missions were secularized, grazing increased but remained at sustainable levels. By 1827–1828, a French traveler reported that San Gabriel mission was secularized and controlled by a ranchero elite family. The landscape was described as "one continual pasture," with 150,000 cattle, 20,000 horses, and 40,000 sheep.[33] The heyday of the Mexican cattle ranching culture in California was the period between 1821 and 1849. Four hundred ranching families controlled the larger tracts of land, and each was running from two to ten thousand head of cattle. Yet as Donald Worster notes, the environmentally damaging growth of the cattle and sheep industries occurred during the period of Anglo-American expansionism, especially after the arrival of the railroads when markets for beef and wool expanded.[34]

Pastures and grasslands were not severely overgrazed, except for some localized pastures around the larger settlements of Albuquerque and Santa Fe during the eighteenth century.[35] Yet a shift in the composition of vegetation took place in settled areas as European and Asian species gradually replaced many native grasses. The seeds for these **invasive species** were probably in the hay brought by the Spanish on their voyage across the Atlantic. The upland mountain valleys and passes remained largely undisturbed, and on the whole native vegetation fared well across El Norte, especially in the upland headwater areas.[36] In south Texas, the brush country, or chaparral, fared well. The native grasses of the chaparral were two feet high, and early nineteenth-century reports exist of grass "breast high to a man on horseback."[37]

The largely subsistence hunting activities of Norteñas/os had little over-all effect on wildlife populations. Populations of ungulate species remained stable. In 1860, for example, antelope, mule deer, and elk herds in California numbered in the tens of thousands.[38] The Norteñas/os did not hunt large mammals such as the grizzly bear and Mexican gray wolf (*Canis lupus*) into extinction.

Summarizing the ecological changes prior to 1848, Norteñas/os used fire to manage the mix of grasslands and woodlands in their locales. They developed or introduced domesticated plants; collected wild plants for medicine and food; and introduced livestock to the environment. A signifi-cant change was the inadvertent importation of European and Asiatic weeds, particularly dandelions and sweet clovers. These activities altered the composition of the vegetation. Beneficial effects of human landscape change are also illustrated in the history of the Norteña/o ecological revo-lution, however. Over a period of four hundred years, the acequias created dense wildlife corridors of native vegetation including cottonwood, wil-low, and alder *bosques* (forests). This suggests that human landscape modi-fication is not inherently harmful and can sometimes provide habitat for native flora and fauna.

▮ The Industrial-Capitalist Ecological Revolution, 1848–1950

American military campaigns against Mexico between 1835 and 1848 re-sulted in Mexico losing close to two-thirds of its territory comprising all of El Norte including parts of Kansas, Nevada, and Utah. The industrial-capitalist ecological revolution unleashed forces that transformed the eco-systems, cultures, and economies of El Norte. Among these forces were the enclosure of the land grants and displacement of native peoples; the arrival of railroad mass markets; industrialization and urbanization; the rise of racially stratified labor markets; and the flow of Mexicans to the United States under a system of administered labor migration.

Enclosure and Displacement

Land loss was an important factor affecting Mexican-origin communities during the industrial-capitalist ecological revolution. After 1891, the Surveyor General and the Court of Private Land Claims adjudicated 35.4 million acres of Spanish and Mexican land grants, confirming only 2.05 million of these acres.[39] Many Mexican-origin communities lost land to the expansion of the railroads and the incursions of Anglo homesteaders. Unscrupulous lawyers took large portions of the land grants as payment for defending the claims of the Norteñas/os before the legal system. Large portions of the common lands were placed in the public domain, becoming part of the system of national forests, parks, and monuments.

The Office of the Surveyor General also played a role in land theft between 1869 and 1884. The Spanish and Mexican land grants had not been officially surveyed when the United States acquired Mexico's territory. The surveyor general was responsible for surveying these lands to establish their boundaries and fix legal descriptions. At least three of the surveyors general had ties to land speculators. Instead of protecting the land grants, they participated in the systematic theft of the common lands.[40]

The Treaty of Guadalupe Hidalgo contained provisions protecting the rights of Norteñas/os, but it was not enforced. Anglos used a variety of mechanisms to take land from Mexican Americans, including title fraud, taxation, condemnation by the government, and violence. In New Mexico, a group of land speculators and lawyers known as the Santa Fe Ring gained control of land grants through title fraud and lawsuits, then partitioned the common lands into private holdings. New tax and land registration laws were introduced, written in English and not intelligible to the majority of Spanish-speaking Norteñas/os. When they failed to comply with these laws, many lost their lands. Many land grant heirs, who did not have money to defend claims before the courts, turned over portions of their grants to lawyers in lieu of cash payments. In some cases, land grant documents were lost or destroyed.

The U.S. legal system was hostile to the confirmation of land grants. This pattern of hostility was cemented in 1897 when the U.S. Supreme Court issued its infamous *United States v. Sandoval* decision involving the San Miguel del Bado land grant in New Mexico. Malcolm Ebright summarizes this significant decision: "After the 1897 Sandoval decision, the land claims court rejected the common lands of every community grant that came up for adjudication. The vast acreage acquired by the United States now comprises most of the Carson and Santa Fe National Forests in Northern New Mexico."[41]

In Arizona, California, and Texas Mexican-origin people lost their land grants to Anglo American speculators and settlers. In California, the gold rush brought white squatters who overwhelmed the rancheros. New laws establishing land and poll taxes compounded the pressures exerted by squatters. Unable to respond to the new economic system, the rancheros mortgaged their land grant holdings to pay taxes and quickly lost their lands. In Texas, similar laws displaced the Mexican-origin people from the land. In addition, violence played a major role there, when groups such as the Texas Rangers forced Mexican Americans from the land to make way for new Anglo-owned cattle ranches. The Texas Rangers tolerated and even encouraged lynching to terrorize the Mexican Americans into sub-mission and to force families to sell their land grants to Anglo speculators for pennies an acre.[42] Displaced from their land, many Norteñas/os were forced into the ranks of the landless proletariat, moving to urban centers or finding work in mining camps, sugar beet fields, or railroad section gangs.

Railroad Mass Markets

The railroads arrived in the 1870s and benefited from government expro-priation of Spanish and Mexican land grants. Millions of acres were ap-propriated as rights of way for the alignment of rail routes. Railroads supported the growth of the livestock industry (see table 12). The most significant growth occurred in Texas, which dominated the cattle industry between 1870 and 1900. The growth of the Texas cattle industry led to overgrazing not only in Texas, but also in New Mexico. The New Mexico range was deluged with cattle from Texas, initiating the most severe de-struction of grasslands in the history of the state. Similar increases were evident in the number of sheep. In 1880, there were about twelve head of sheep per square mile in northern New Mexico. By 1900, the number had increased by 500 percent to 120 head per square mile. Frederick Gelbach argues that "rapid and extensive demise of grassland is the general out-come of American settlement. . . . Grass cover predominated in 1853, but began to disappear by the 1880s in concert with the postwar and railroad era of American ranching."[43]

Railroads facilitated settlement of El Norte by growing numbers of

Table 12   Growth of the cattle industry in selected states of El Norte, 1870–1900

	1870	1880	1890	1900
Arizona	30,000	142,000	502,000	320,000
California	1,001,000	916,000	1,258,000	878,000
New Mexico	57,500	347,900	1,631,500	803,000
Texas	4,600,000	4,932,000	8,587,000	6,700,000

Source: U.S. Senate, Committee on Agriculture and Forestry, The Western Range (Washington, DC: U.S. Government Printing Office, 1936).

Anglo-Americans, who quickly outnumbered the Mexican-origin population in every state except New Mexico. With the increased population came greater demands for goods, and the railroads provided the means for the expansion of mass markets for beef, wool, and other commodities. The Norteña/o loss of land accelerated. The Homestead Act of 1862 also contributed to this pressure as increasing numbers of white settlers squatted on the 640-acre square-grid parcels awarded by the federal government to encourage settlement and agricultural development.

Mexican and Mexican American workers played a major role in the construction of the railroads. By 1900, El Paso had become a major center for the recruitment of Mexican railroad section gangs. The Southern Pacific and Atchison-Topeka-Santa Fe Railroad companies were particularly aggressive in their search for Mexican workers. By 1908, at least sixteen thousand Mexicans were working on the rail lines.

Industrialization and Urbanization

Federal subsidies for agriculture, mining, timber, and other industries supported the growth of industry. In 1902, the federal government established the Bureau of Reclamation to promote the development of water resources in the arid lands of El Norte. Bureau-sponsored construction of large-scale dams and reservoirs radically transformed the **ecology** and economy of the region. Over the next seventy years, the bureau would construct 320 water storage reservoirs, 344 diversion dams, 14,000 miles of canals, 900 miles of pipelines, 205 miles of tunnels, nearly 35,000 miles of lateral ditches, 145 pumping plants, 50 power plants, and 16,420 circuit miles of electrical transmission lines.[44] This massive infrastructure

■ 11. Center-pivot irrigation sprinklers in a monoculture landscape rendered uniform to meet the needs of industrial economies of scale. These sprinklers irrigate "factories in the field" by mining the groundwater aquifers that lie below the surface. Only one type of crop is grown in these modern industrial monocultures, in this case potatoes. The system requires vast inputs of fossil fuels, pesticides, herbicides, and fertilizers. The use of tractors and other heavy equipment combined with the lack of natural cover vegetation accelerate the pace of soil erosion and compaction. The agrochemicals degrade water and soil quality as they leach into the environment. Pumping pivot sprinkler wells deplete the aquifers.

Farmworkers, most of them immigrants and people of color, are poisoned by pesticides and other agrochemicals. They experience poverty, lack of health services, and malnutrition. They are brutally repressed if they organize unions to demand their rights and a livable wage. They get deported without pay as "illegal aliens." Anthropologists may point to the polka-dot uniformity of these landscapes and note that there is little room for wildlife habitat or human dignity.

supported the rise of modern corporate agriculture in California and other western states. Deserts were converted to farmland under the power of federally subsidized water projects.

Industrialization transformed farming and ranching. The size of commercial farms increased, and the structure of agriculture changed dramatically. There was a shift away from the traditional **polycultures** favored by Norteñas/os to the modern **monocultures** favored by corporate agribusinesses (see figure 11). Instead of growing many different crops for subsistence and local trade, monoculture farmers produced large quantities of one crop for export to markets around the world. These modern monocultures were subsidized with cheap water and electricity produced by the Bureau of Reclamation dams and reservoirs.

Whereas Norteñas/os had strictly limited their use of timberlands to subsistence and domestic uses, the coming of the railroads led to massive exploitation of timber. The construction of the railroads required huge quantities of timber for railroad ties. The railroads also increased demand for timber and other forest products by linking a once-isolated geographic region to markets across the country. The enclosure of the Spanish and Mexican land grants, and their conversion to the public domain as part of the national forest system, was another significant factor in deforestation. In New Mexico, illegal logging took a major toll on the watershed forests of the historic acequia communities. The problem was so widespread that the courts were forced to intervene. Victor Westphall writes of "timber depredation" in New Mexico. By 1880, millions of board feet of timber had been cut illegally, and all but one of the sixty-five persons indicted were Anglos.[45]

Official data on timber cuts date to 1908 and demonstrate a steady increase in logging volumes. In Arizona and New Mexico, logging volumes increased from 40 million board feet (mbf) cut per year between 1908 and 1910 to 178 mbf cut per year during the decade from 1941 to 1950 (see table 13). Logging volumes in California increased more drastically. By 1850, there were dozens of sawmills in California. In 1940, forests in the Golden State yielded two billion board feet of timber per year.[46] The volume of logging in the national forests of El Norte was higher in that one year than the cumulative total over the previous three hundred years of Spanish-Mexican settlement.

Urbanization was another consequence of Anglo migration to the region. In 1848, the largest population centers were Albuquerque, Santa Fe, and Los Angeles, none of which had anywhere close to ten thousand residents. Population growth and concentration of people into cities accelerated after the arrival of the railroads and the construction of hydroelectric dams that provided cheap electricity to the emerging urban centers. In 1850, Los Angeles had 1,600 inhabitants; by 1910, it had 319,000. In a relatively brief period (1850–1950), the total population of El Norte increased from less than 100,000 to more than 19.7 million (see table 14). By 1920 most of the population (51.8 percent) was living in cities.[47] With the exception of those living in New Mexico, Mexican Americans became

Table 13   Logging levels in Arizona and New Mexico national forests

DECADE	AVERAGE ANNUAL CUT (million board feet)
1908–10	40
1911–20	76
1921–30	87
1931–40	98
1941–50	178
1951–60	275
1961–70	396
1971–80	375
1981–90	402

Source: C. W. Dahms, B. W. Geils, and D. Huebner, eds., *An Assessment of Forest Ecosystem Health in the Southwest,* General technical report RM-GTR-295 (Ft. Collins, CO: USDA, United States Forest Service, Rocky Mountain Forest and Range Experiment Station, 1997). This report is also available online at http://www.rms.nau.edu/publications/rm_gtr_295/.

increasingly urban-based. The Mexican-origin population in cities was segregated in **barrios** (inner-city neighborhoods) characterized by poor housing, crowding, and polluted conditions. The growth of the Mexican-origin population in the United States, especially after the Mexican Revolution (1910–1920), was increasingly shaped by the phenomenon of international labor migration from Mexico.

Administered Labor Migration and Racial Segregation in Labor Markets

Mexican migration to the United States began in earnest during the 1870s and became a major demographic force during the first two decades of the twentieth century. Following the railroads, Mexican workers found employment in a broad range of industries from sugar beets to mining. The industrialization of agriculture created an insatiable demand for Mexican workers. During the first three decades of the twentieth century, approximately one-tenth of Mexico's population shifted north of the border.[48] More than a million Mexicans migrated to the United States during this period.

Federal policies encouraged Mexicans to immigrate under conditions that increased their vulnerability and exploitation. U.S. immigration policy

Table 14 Population growth in El Norte (1850–1950)

	ARIZONA		CALIFORNIA		NEW MEXICO		TEXAS	
	TOTAL	MEXICAN-ORIGIN	TOTAL	MEXICAN-ORIGIN	TOTAL	MEXICAN-ORIGIN	TOTAL	MEXICAN-ORIGIN
1850	—	—	92,597	—	61,547	—	212,592	—
1860	—	—	379,994	—	93,516	—	604,215	—
1870	9,658	—	560,247	—	91,874	—	818,579	—
1880	40,440	19,562	864,694	54,831	119,565	106,710	1,591,749	81,895
1890	88,243	—	1,213,398	—	160,282	—	2,235,527	—
1900	122,931	39,466	1,485,053	48,576	195,310	93,356	3,048,710	198,841
1910	204,354	71,075	2,377,549	108,178	327,301	127,751	3,896,542	276,307
1920	334,162	108,377	3,426,861	159,560	360,350	145,696	4,663,228	475,736
1930	435,573	—	5,677,387	—	423,317	—	5,824,715	—
1940	499,261	100,098	6,907,387	459,920	531,818	198,372	6,414,824	639,431
1950	749,587	—	10,685,223	—	681,187	—	7,711,194	—

Source: The total population figures are from the United States Bureau of the Census, *Statistical Abstract of the United States*, table 16, p. 26. Available online at http://www.census.gov/population/cesnsudata/table-16.pdf. The Mexican-origin population figures are from M. P. Gutmann, R. McCaa, R. Gutierrez-Montes, and J. B. Gratton, *The Demographic Impact of the Mexican Revolution in the United States*, Paper 99-00-01 (Austin: Population Research Center, University of Texas, 2000), table 3, p. 6. The Mexican-origin population estimates include both native (U.S.-born) and foreign-born individuals.

reflected the dominant ideology that Mexicans were an inferior half-breed people, suitable as temporary labor but not as permanent settlers. This ideology led to a policy of administered labor migration under the Bracero Program (1942–1964) that sought to import Mexican workers on a temporary basis for specific occupational categories involving low-wage and hazardous jobs.[49]

Foreign- and native-born Mexican American workers were subject to occupational segregation in racially stratified labor markets. Mexican-origin workers were typecast as unskilled cheap labor and confined to blue-collar jobs. They were excluded from the ranks of organized unions, most notoriously from the American Federation of Labor (AFL). In response, Mexican-origin workers organized their own unions or joined organizations such as the Knights of Labor and the Industrial Workers of the World (IWW).[50] The occupational segregation of the Mexican-origin working class subsidized industries through cheap labor that could be deported at the first sign of resistance. The environmental injustices of this occupational segregation led to numerous conflicts and strikes over the course of the twentieth century.

Effects on Biodiversity

The California gold rush of 1849 led to overhunting of elk to supply meat to mining camps in the northern part of the state. By the late 1880s, antelope herds had been decimated as habitat was cleared for industrial agribusiness in the Central Valley. The massive landscape changes of modern corporate agriculture drove many individual species and entire plant and animal communities to extinction.[51]

Some species were harmed by predator eradication policies. These deliberate efforts to exterminate species deemed a threat to human safety or agriculture started as early as the 1860s. In California, the last native grizzly was shot by hired Anglo animal trappers in the Sierra Nevada of Tulare County in gold rush country. Aldo Leopold witnessed the killing of the last Mexican wolves in New Mexico, an experience that led to his famous phrase about the death of wildness in the extinguished "fierce green fire" in the eyes of a just-shot female wolf.[52] Similar predator control policies favored by the cattle and sheep industries led to extirpation of the Mexican wolf in Arizona and Texas as well.

Logging and mining caused serious damage to ecosystems. The volume of logging increased dramatically after 1848. Ecosystems were harmed not only by the massive volume of cuts but also by the construction of logging roads and skid trails (the paths created to drag timber out of the forests). In 1848, most of the forests in El Norte were roadless. The growth of industrial logging required the construction of vast networks of roads and skid trails. Between 1848 and the 1950s, roads were carved through the nation's public and private lands. By 1950, there were an estimated 380,000 miles of authorized roads on the national forest and grasslands, with an additional 60,000 miles of so-called ghost roads (unplanned or forgotten roads).[53]

Roads are among the most significant causes of the decline of biodiversity because they increase **habitat fragmentation.** Logging practices, especially clear-cutting (where all the trees in a given area are removed), caused widespread damage to watersheds by increasing sediment loads in creeks and rivers. Logging practices also removed streamside vegetation, eliminating shade and increasing water temperatures. Sedimentation and temperature changes damaged fish habitat and contributed to the extinction or endangerment of salmon and other aquatic species.[54]

Logging practices also harmed the acequia systems. Sediment choked acequias, often smothering the crops in flood-irrigated fields. Another serious effect was an acceleration in the rate at which snowpack turned into water flow. By removing or reducing the protective canopy of trees, logging exposed the snowpack to spring and summer rain-on-snow events. The resulting more rapid melting of the snowpack shortened the irrigation season for acequias downstream from logged areas.[55]

In mining, a destructive hydraulic power technology was developed in which powerful jets of water were used to dislodge gold from unconsolidated mineral deposits. The water and dislodged fragments of gold were channeled into sluices where the gold settled out and was collected while the lighter waste material was washed away. This practice produced enormous quantities of waste rock (tailings). Hydraulic mining destroyed landscapes, damaging habitat and water quality on an unprecedented scale. New mining technologies that emerged over the twentieth century produced new problems. Tailings and deep shafts have produced a phenomenon known as acid mine drainage, where heavy metals and toxic minerals are released into watercourses and groundwater. This produces severe contamination of rivers and creeks, resulting in the extermination of aquatic life and posing risks to human health.

Another factor damaging biodiversity was the introduction of exotic or invasive species. In 1769, Junípero Serra introduced three exotic plant species to California at his mission in San Diego Bay. During the entire Mexican period (1821–1848), Norteñas/os introduced a total of sixty-three non-native plant species. In the gold rush period (1849–1860), American pioneers introduced another sixty-three species. These numbers have steadily increased, from 292 (1922), to 437 (1951), 797 (1968), and 1,023 (1993).[56]

In summary, species extinctions in El Norte were largely associated with the industrial-capitalist ecological revolution. Modern monoculture farming destroyed habitat; increased soil erosion and compaction; and contaminated the water, soil, and farmworkers. The construction of dams and reservoirs destroyed habitat for terrestrial and aquatic species. Predator-control policies accelerated the decline of biodiversity, as did the increasingly rapid introduction of exotic plant and animal species.

■ A Century of Precursors

Conventional histories of the **environmental justice movement** (EJM) trace its roots to 1982 and African Americans' struggle against toxic waste dumps in Warren County, North Carolina. The roots of **environmental justice** run much deeper, however. In the case of the Mexican-origin people, the roots of the EJM can be traced to a century of struggles between 1877 and the 1970s.

The El Paso Salt War of 1877

The Salt War was an early precursor of Chicana/o struggles against the enclosure of commonly held resources. For a hundred years, Mexicans in El Paso made use of salt beds northeast of the town, curing meats and other perishables with the salt. The salt beds were common property and no one claimed exclusive ownership. In 1877, an Anglo-American entrepreneur built a fence around the salt beds and started charging local people for access.[57] Local mexicanos rebelled to restore community access to this important resource. The rebellion was crushed and numerous people killed when the governor of Texas imported hired gunmen from New Mexico.

Las Gorras Blancas, 1870–1899

From 1870 to 1899, New Mexico Chicanos organized the night riders known as Las Gorras Blancas (the white caps), who resisted encroachment on communal land grants. They cut barbed-wire fences; burned haystacks, barns, sawmills, and other buildings; and scattered livestock owned by Anglo land and cattle companies. These companies were based on the eastern seaboard or in foreign countries like Great Britain.[58] Mexican-origin people felt justified in these attacks on Anglos because they were being denied the land rights guaranteed under the Treaty of Guadalupe Hidalgo.

Cananea Strike of 1906

The Cananea mine in Sonora, across the border from Douglas, Arizona, was notorious as the site of record numbers of fatalities among workers, who died in explosions or from asphyxiation caused by the buildup of noxious gases. On November 19, 1906, Mexican workers went on strike against the owner, Anaconda Copper Company, a multinational corporation based in the United States. They were striking for three reasons: (1) to demand an end to the dual-wage system that imposed a Mexican wage of less than half what Anglo workers were paid for the same job; to protest the hated company store (*tienda de raya*), which maintained workers in a state of perpetual debt to the owners; and (3) to improve safety conditions in the mines. This strike was one of the first involving demands to improve workplace environmental conditions. The strikers were brutally repressed by the Arizona Rangers and the hated Rurales (rural mounted police) of the dictator Porfirio Díaz.[59]

Barrios, Freeways, and Baseball Parks

During the 1950s and 1960s, construction of the U.S. interstate highway system and the alignment of roads, bridges, and overpasses dissected numerous barrios. In Los Angeles, the construction of Dodger Stadium displaced the Mexican American community in Chávez Ravine.[60] Urban renewal projects displaced African American and Mexican American residents by the thousands across the United States. Gentrification, through which low-income areas are redeveloped to make way for higher-income residents and businesses, was another source of displacement wherever real estate developers evicted Mexican-origin residents to make way for supposedly higher and better land uses. The government took poor people's property to provide private property for developers.

In San Diego, the community responded by establishing Chicano Park underneath the Coronado Bay Bridge, which had bisected the barrio. Murals grace the concrete pillars that support the bridge.[61] The people of

Coronado barrio massed to reclaim the area as a community space before the city could construct a police substation there.

By 1953, the construction of the San Bernardino, Santa Ana, and Long Beach freeways in metropolitan Los Angeles had displaced thousands of Chicanas/os from their homes and businesses.[62] The construction of Interstate 10 through the heart of East Los Angeles and other communities of color was met with stiff resistance and protests. Barrio residents challenged the use of eminent domain to condemn property for the construction of freeways largely serving white suburban commuters.

Alianza Federal de Mercedes Libres, 1963–1968

The land grant movement was another important precursor of environmental justice.[63] The theft of land grants led to a century-long struggle to restore the rights of dispossessed heirs. In 1963, Reies López Tijerina established the Alianza Federal de Mercedes Libres (Federal Alliance of Autonomous Land Grants). The Alianza sought the return of land grants to the rightful heirs, focusing on common lands that had been converted to the public domain. The Aliancistas argued that the enclosure of land grants violated the Treaty of Guadalupe Hidalgo.

On October 15, 1960, Tijerina and 350 people who later formed the Aliancistas occupied the Echo Amphitheatre, a national forest campground north of Abiqui, New Mexico. They reasserted the use rights of heirs of the 1,400-acre Pueblo de San Joaquín de Chama land grant. This protest was followed by the famous Aliancista raid on the county courthouse in Tierra Amarilla. Tijerina and his colleagues sought to make a citizens' arrest of the district attorney for failure to uphold the rights of the grant heirs. In response, the U.S. government mounted the largest manhunt since the capture of Geronimo, using armored personnel carriers and federal troops to crush this protest. Tijerina surrendered when his relatives were imprisoned at an outdoor compound when nighttime temperatures were approaching freezing. His arrest and trial attracted national media attention and resulted in congressional hearings.

Early Anti-Pesticides Campaigns, 1965–1971

César Chávez, Dolores Huerta, and other activists established the United Farm Workers Organizing Committee (UFWOC) in the early 1960s. The UFWOC's goals were to organize farmworkers in seeking union recognition, collective bargaining rights, and union contracts to improve their wages and working and living conditions. Early UFWOC organizing efforts focused on unsafe uses of pesticides, a significant struggle that linked environmental and social justice concerns with labor rights. This campaign incorporated boycotts as a tool to force the growers to the negotiating table and to educate the public about the plight of farmworkers.[64]

Farmworkers understood that they were collectively affected by the unregulated use of pesticides in the fields. They organized a campaign to control and regulate the use of pesticides through litigation, legislation, public education, and collective bargaining contracts that would include provisions regarding the use of agroindustrial chemicals. They demanded public access to pesticide records and sought to ban the use of certain pesticides such as DDT. In 1970 the UFWOC won passage of a collective bargaining law in California, leading to the signing of the first labor contracts with grape growers. These contracts included health and safety clauses to address the pesticide problem at the point of production. The UFWOC also succeeded in banning some of the more acutely toxic pesticides.[65]

Fight against Indian Camp Dam, 1971–1976

Under Bureau of Reclamation programs, several dams were constructed in New Mexico, including Elephant Butte (completed in 1916), Caballo (1936), and Navajo (1963). These dams flooded thirty to forty thousand acres of irrigated farmlands, including some belonging to acequia farmers. The Navajo Dam inundated two Hispano communities—Rosa, New Mexico, and Arboles, Colorado—when it opened in 1963. The residents were forcibly relocated from lands they had lived on for generations.[66] The legacy of dam construction and displacement of Mexican American farmers flared into a major conflict with the proposal to construct the Indian Camp Dam outside Taos, New Mexico. Between 1971 and 1976, acequia farmers and other local Chicanas/os resisted the project. Their legal actions and protests succeeded when the conservancy district created to underwrite the project was annulled based on a technicality.[67]

■ Concluding Thoughts

The environmental history of México desconocido is much more than natural history. It is also the history of cultural, economic, legal, and social aspects of ecological change. This chapter has outlined transformations occurring under two ecological revolutions—Norteña/o and industrial-capitalist. Although Norteñas/os altered the environment in dramatic ways, these changes were largely sustainable and in some cases even beneficial for ecosystems. The example of the acequia as a beneficial form of anthropogenesis cannot be overlooked.

Large-scale environmental degradation of El Norte was principally a consequence of the industrial-capitalist ecological revolution. After 1848, the U.S. capitalist political economy displaced many Native Americans and Mexican Americans from their historic homelands and led to massive and largely harmful ecological changes. The processes that damaged the environment also harmed Mexican-origin communities. Ecological degradation and political economic domination led to a century of small-scale struggles in which Chicanas/os sought to address ecological damage and social injustice in a world torn apart by the ruthless commodification of nature and labor.

■ Discussion Questions

1. Compare and contrast the ecological worldviews of Native, Mexican, and Anglo-Americans. What are the differences between Spanish and **mestiza/o** ecological worldviews?

2. What is the significance for **cultural ecology** of regional historical differences in the encounter between Mexican peoples and Native Americans? With respect to Native American–Mexican-origin encounters, what do Texas, New Mexico, Colorado, Arizona, and California have in common? What differences are there? How did these similarities and differences affect the process of **cultural adaptation** to place?

3. What were the major environmental and cultural changes of the Norteña/o ecological revolution?

4. How did Native Americans contribute to the environmental knowledge of Mexican-origin communities?

5. Can anthropogenesis prove beneficial to **ecosystem integrity** and biodiversity? If so, under what conditions are **keystone communities** possible? What are the forces affecting the survival of cultures of habitat?

6. What were the major sources of environmental degradation in El Norte under the industrial-capitalist ecological revolution?

■ Suggested Readings

Briggs, Charles L., and John R. Van Ness, eds. 1987. *Land, Water, and Culture: New Perspectives on Hispanic Land Grants.* Albuquerque: University of New Mexico Press.

Ebright, Malcolm. 1994. *Land Grants and Lawsuits in Northern New Mexico.* Albuquerque: University of New Mexico Press.

Peña, Devon G., ed. 1998. *Chicano Culture, Ecology, Politics: Subversive Kin.* Tucson: University of Arizona Press.

Pulido, Laura. 1996. *Environmentalism and Economic Justice: Two Chicano Struggles in the Southwest.* Tucson: University of Arizona Press.

Rivera, José A. 1998. *Acequia Culture: Water, Land, and Community in the Southwest.* Albuquerque: University of New Mexico Press.

Scurlock, Dan. 1998. *From the Rio to the Sierra: An Environmental History of the Middle Rio Grande Basin.* General Technical Report RMRS-GTR-5. Ft. Collins, CO: USFS, Rocky Mountain Research Station.

■ Notes

1. Ernesto Galarza discerned eight major regions of settlement in El Norte by 1900: the San Francisco Bay basin, metropolitan Los Angeles, the Central Valley in California, the Salt River Valley in Arizona, all of Texas, the Denver metropolitan area, the "Border Belt," and the upper Rio Grande in northern New Mexico and south central Colorado. E. Galarza, "Mexicans in the Southwest: A Culture in Process," in *Plural Society in the Southwest,* ed. E. Spicer and R. H. Thompson (New York: Interbook, 1972), 266–67.

2. The term *first nations* emphasizes the idea that the first settled peoples in the Americas had institutions of political and normative self-governance.

3. D. Lavender, *The Southwest* (Albuquerque: University of New Mexico Press, 1980), 26–34.

4. See K. Basso, *Wisdom Sits in Places: Landscape and Language among the Western Apache* (Albuquerque: University of New Mexico Press, 1996).

5. A. Ortiz, *The Tewa World* (Chicago: University of Chicago Press, 1969).

6. Eugene Hunn, personal communication, January 18, 2002, Seattle.

7. T. Jaramillo, interview with the author, June 1998, El Poso, Sierra Culebra, Colorado (in the author's collection at the Rio Grande Bioregions Project, Department of Anthropology, University of Washington, Seattle). R. Garcia, "Notes on (Home)Land Ethics: Ideas, Values, and the Land," in *Chicano Culture, Ecology, Politics: Subversive Kin,* ed. D. G. Peña (Tucson: University of Arizona Press, 1998), 79–120. For cultural influences on Norteña/o culture, see G. Ochoa, *Atlas of Hispanic American History* (New York: Checkmark Books, 2001), 1–18. Ochoa outlines Roman, Visigoth, Spanish, Arabic, Native Mexican, and Native American cultures as the principal sources of an amalgamated Hispanic culture.

8. R. Nash, *Wilderness and the American Mind* (New Haven: Yale University Press, 1967); J. W. Powell, "Institutions for the Aridlands," *Century Magazine* 40 (1890): 112–20; D. Worster, *An Unsettled Country: Changing Landscapes of the American West* (Albuquerque: University of New Mexico Press, 1994), 1–28.

9. P. van Dresser, "The Bio-economic Community: Reflections on a Development Philosophy for a Semi-arid Environment," in *Indian and Spanish-American Adjustments to Arid and Semi-arid Environments,* ed. C. S. Knowlton (Lubbock: Texas Technical Press, 1964), 53–74; van Dresser, *A Landscape for Humans* (Albuquerque: Biotechnic Press, 1972); J. R. Van Ness, "Hispanic Land Grants: Ecology and Subsistence in the Uplands of Northern New Mexico and Southern Colorado," in *Land, Water, and Culture: New Perspectives on Hispanic Land Grants,* ed. C. L. Briggs and J. R. Van Ness (Albuquerque: University of New Mexico Press, 1987), 141–216; J. A. Rivera, *Acequia Culture: Water, Land, and Community in the Southwest* (Albuquerque: University of New Mexico Press, 1998); Peña, *Chicano Culture, Ecology, Politics;* J. K. Boyce, "From Natural Resources to Natural Assets," in *Natural Assets: Democratizing Environmental Ownership,* ed. J. K. Boyce and B. G. Shelley (Washington, DC: Island Press, 2003); D. G. Peña, "The Watershed Commonwealth of the Upper Rio Grande," in Boyce and Shelley, *Natural Assets,* 169–86; G. A. Hicks and D. G. Peña, "Community Acequias in Colorado's Rio Culebra Watershed: A Customary Commons in the Domain of Prior Appropriation," *University of Colorado Law Review* 74 (2003): 387–486.

10. *Black's Law Dictionary* (4th ed., 1968), 1712; P. Gómez, "The History and Adjudication of the Common Lands of Spanish and Mexican Land Grants," *Natural Resources Journal* 25 (1985): 1039; R. D. Garcia and T. Howland, "Spanish Land Grants in Colorado: Conflicting Values, Legal Pluralism, and Demystification of the Sangre de Cristo Land Grant," *Chicano-Latino Law Review* 16 (1995): 39–68.

11. E. Arellano, "Querencia: La Raza Bioregionalism" (unpublished report, Rio Grande Bioregions Project, Upper Rio Grande Hispano Farms Study, National Endowment for the Humanities Research Grant No. 22707-94); Peña, *Chicano Culture, Ecology, Politics,* 157–58; Hicks and Peña, "Community Acequias"; F. L. Brown and H. M. Ingram, *Water and Poverty in the Southwest* (Tucson: University of Arizona Press, 1987); M. Ebright, *Land Grants and Lawsuits in Northern New Mexico* (Albuquerque: University of New Mexico Press, 1994); Rivera, *Acequia Culture.*

12. A. de León, *They Called Them Greasers* (Austin: University of Texas Press, 1983).

13. F. R. Gelbach, *Mountain Islands and Desert Seas: A Natural History of the U.S.–Mexican Borderlands* (College Station: Texas A&M University Press, 1993).

14. D. G. Peña, *The Terror of the Machine: Technology, Work, Gender, and Ecology on the U.S.–Mexico Border* (Austin: CMAS Books, 1997), 286–90.

15. See the multivolume series *Handbook of North American Indians,* gen. ed. W. C. Sturtevant (Washington DC: Smithsonian Institution Press, 1978–2001); Lavender,

Southwest, 22–34; also see G. Ochoa, *Atlas of Hispanic-American History* (New York: Checkmark Books, 2001), 6–13.

16. W. M. Denevan, "The Pristine Myth: The Landscape of the Americas in 1492," in *The Americas before and after Columbus: Current Geographical Research,* ed. P. Godfrey Okoth and Patrick K. Kakwenzire (Kampala: USIS Kampala, 1993), 369–85; C. L. Redman, *Human Impact on Ancient Environments* (Tucson: University of Arizona Press, 1999), 195–99.

17. Quotation from G. M. Leonard, "The Importance of Resource Management," in *For the Conservation of Earth,* ed. V. Martin (Golden, CO: Fulcrum Books, 1988), 232.

18. Denevan, "Pristine Myth," 196.

19. Ibid., 118–22; also see T. A. Kohler, "Prehistoric Human Impact on the Environment in Upland North American Southwest," *Population and Environment: A Journal of Interdisciplinary Studies* 13 (1992): 255–68. Tree-ring studies at Chaco note critical climatic fluctuations that may have led to depopulation. See W. B. Gillespie, "Holocene Climate and Environment of Chaco Canyon," in *Environment and Subsistence of Chaco Canyon,* ed. F. J. Mathien (Albuquerque: National Park Service, Department of the Interior, 1985), 34–36.

20. See D. Montejano, *Anglos and Mexicans in the Making of Texas: 1836–1986* (Austin: University of Texas Press, 1987), 75–99; León, *They Called Them Greasers.*

21. Galarza, "Mexicans in the Southwest," 266–67. In 1833, the boundaries of the Mexican Republic included parts of Kansas, Nevada, and Utah but Norteñas/os did not settle in these areas until well after the Mexican War of 1846–1848.

22. The advent of the Santa Fe Trail and trade with Anglo-Americans in the early 1800s marked the start of relations with capitalist markets. Starting in the late 1700s, Spanish ports on the California coast initiated trade with Anglo ships bound to and from Boston and other centers of American capitalism on the eastern seaboard.

23. D. Scurlock, *From the Rio to the Sierra: An Environmental History of the Middle Rio Grande Basin* (Ft. Collins, CO: USFS, Rocky Mountain Research Station, 1998).

24. D. Worster, *Rivers of Empire: Water, Aridity, and the Growth of the American West* (New York: Pantheon, 1985), 31.

25. J. A. Westcoat Jr., "The 'Right of Thirst' for Animals in Islamic Law: A Comparative Study," in *Animal Geographies: Place, Politics, and Identity in the Nature-Culture Borderlands,* ed. J. Wolch and J. Emel (London: Verso, 1998), 259–79; I. G. Clark, *Water in New Mexico: A History of Its Management and Use* (Albuquerque: University of New Mexico Press, 1987); D. G. Peña, "Cultural Landscapes and Biodiversity: The Ethnoecology of an Upper Rio Grande Watershed Commons," in *Ethnoecology: Situated Knowledge/Located Lives,* ed. V. Nazarea (Tucson: University of Arizona Press, 1999); Rivera, *Acequia Culture;* Hicks and Peña, "Community Acequias."

26. Peña, *Chicano Culture, Ecology, Politics,* 260–65.

27. Peña, "Watershed Commonwealth."

28. W. Dusenberry, *The Mexican Mesta: The Administration of Ranching in Colonial Mexico* (Urbana: University of Illinois Press, 1963).

29. D. G. Peña and R. O. Martínez, "The Capitalist Tool, the Lawless, and the Violent: A Critique of Recent Southwestern Environmental History," in Peña, *Chicano Culture, Ecology, Politics,* 160.

30. D. J. Weber, *Taos Trappers: The Fur Trade in the Far Southwest, 1540–1846* (Norman: University of Oklahoma Press, 1981).

31. A. Tijerina, "Tejano Origins" (May 4, 1998), available online at http://www.tamu.edu/ccbn/dewitt/tejanoorigins.htm; also see A. Tijerina, *Tejano Empire: Life on the South Texas Ranchos* (College Station: Texas A&M Press, 1998).

32. Fr. F. Palóu, "A Spaniard Explores the Southern California Landscape, 1774," in *Green Versus Gold: Sources in California's Environmental History,* ed. C. Merchant (Washington, DC: Island Press, 1998), 68.

33. C. F. Carter, ed., "Duhaut-Cilly's Account of California in the Years 1827–28," *California Historical Society Quarterly* 8 (1929): 149; R. A. Billington, *The Far Western Frontier, 1830–1860* (New York: Harper Torchbooks, 1956), 7.

34. D. Worster, "Cowboy Ecology," in *Under Western Skies: Nature and History in the American West* (Oxford: Oxford University Press, 1998), 68.

35. R. MacCameron, "Environmental Change in Colonial New Mexico," *New Mexico History Review* 18 (1994): 17–39; Peña and Martínez, "Capitalist Tool," 141–77.

36. R. F. Dassman, "The Displacement of Wildlife," in *California's Changing Environment* (San Francisco: Boyd and Fraser, 1981), 9–19; Gelbach, *Mountain Islands and Desert Seas.*

37. Tijerina, *Tejano Empire,* 4.

38. Dassman, "Displacement of Wildlife."

39. S. Deutsch, *No Separate Refuge: Culture, Class, and Gender on an Anglo-Hispanic Frontier in the American Southwest, 1880–1940* (Oxford: Oxford University Press, 1987), 20.

40. Ebright, *Land Grants and Lawsuits,* 40–41.

41. Ibid., 48–49.

42. R. Acuña, *Occupied America: A History of Chicanos,* 3rd ed. (New York: Harper and Row, 1988), 27–31, 115–16.

43. Livestock figures are in Deutsch, *No Separate Refuge,* 21; Quotation from Gelbach, *Mountain Island and Desert Seas,* 111.

44. Worster, *Under Western Skies,* 53–78.

45. V. Westphall, *The Public Domain in New Mexico, 1854–1891* (Albuquerque: University of New Mexico Press, 1965), 113–14.

46. W. G. Robbins, "The Western Lumber Industry: A Twentieth Century Per-

spective," in *The Twentieth Century West: Historical Interpretations,* ed. G. D. Nash and R. W. Etulain (Albuquerque: University of New Mexico Press, 1989), table 8.1, 247.

47. W. Nugent, "The People of the West since 1890," in Nash and Etulain, *Twentieth Century West,* 52, table 1.1, 41.

48. Acuña, *Occupied America,* 188.

49. J. Samora, *Los Mojados: The Wetback Story* (South Bend: University of Notre Dame Press, 1971); E. Galarza, *Merchants of Labor* (Santa Barbara: McNally and Lottin, 1964).

50. On Chicana/o labor history, see *Aztlán: International Journal of Chicano Studies Research* 6, no. 2 (Summer 1975); Acuña, *Occupied America,* 141–97, 209–35, 278–79, 328–30.

51. Gelbach, *Mountain Islands and Desert Seas;* S. S. Pincetl, *Transforming California: A Political History of Land Use and Development* (Baltimore: Johns Hopkins University Press, 1999).

52. Dassman, "The Displacement of Wildlife," 23; A. Leopold, *Sketches Here and There* (Oxford: Oxford University Press, 1987), 129.

53. P. A. Michaels, "National Forests: Must All Roads Lead through the National Forests?" *Environmental Issues,* http://environment.about.com/library/weekly/aa020898.htm.

54. L. D. Harris, *The Fragmented Forest: Island Biogeography Theory and the Preservation of Biotic Diversity* (Chicago: University of Chicago Press, 1984); R. F. Noss and A. Y. Cooperrider, *Saving Nature's Legacy: Protecting and Restoring Biodiversity* (Washington, DC: Island Press, 1994).

55. R. Curry, "The State of the Culebra Watershed: The Impact of Logging on the Southern Tributaries," *La Sierra: National Edition* 1 (1995): 10–11; also see J. A. Jones and G. E. Grant, "Peak Flow Responses to Clear-Cutting and Roads in Small and Large Basins, Western Cascades," *Water Resources Research* 32 (1996): 959–74.

56. M. Barbour, B. Pavlik, F. Drysdale, and S. Linstrom, *California's Changing Environment: Diversity and Conservation of California Vegetation* (Sacramento: California Native Plant Society, 1993), 20.

57. Acuña, *Occupied America,* 47–48.

58. R. D. Ortiz, *Roots of Resistance: Land Tenure in New Mexico, 1680–1980* (Los Angeles: UCLA Chicano Studies Research Center Publications, 1980); R. J. Rosenbaum and R. W. Larson, "Mexicano Resistance to the Expropriation of Lands in New Mexico," in Briggs and Van Ness, *Land, Water, and Culture,* 269–310; R. J. Rosenbaum, *Mexicano Resistance in the Southwest: The Sacred Right of Self-Preservation* (Austin: University of Texas Press, 1981); Acuña, *Occupied America,* 70–74.

59. Acuña, *Occupied America,* 98–99, 148–49; J. W. Byrkitt, *Forging the Copper Collar: Arizona's Labor Management War, 1901–1921* (Tucson: University of Arizona Press, 1982); J. R. Kluger, *The Clifton-Morenci Strike: Labor Difficulties in Arizona,*

1915–1916 (Tucson: University of Arizona Press, 1970); J. Cockcroft, *Mexico: Class Formation, Capital Accumulation, and the State* (New York: Monthly Review Press, 1983).

60. A mural by Judith Baca, *The Great Wall of Los Angeles,* includes a panel, *The Division of the Barrios and Chávez Ravine,* which portrays the eviction of families and destruction of neighborhoods for freeways and the construction of Dodger Stadium. See L. Lippard, *Mixed Blessings: New Art in Multicultural America* (New York: Pantheon Books, 1990); S. E. Cockcroft and H. Barnet-Sánchez, eds., *Signs from the Heart: California Chicano Murals* (Venice, CA: SPARC; Albuquerque: University of New Mexico Press, 1993).

61. Office of Historical Preservation, *A History of Mexican Americans in California* (no date), available online at http://ohp.parks.ca.gov.

62. R. Romo, *East Los Angeles: History of a Barrio* (Austin: University of Texas Press, 1983), 169; Acuña, *Occupied America,* 295–98, and *A Community under Siege: A Chronicle of Chicanos East of the Los Angeles River, 1945–1975* (Los Angeles: UCLA Chicano Studies Research Center Publications, 1984).

63. P. Nabokov, *Tijerina and the Courthouse Raid* (Albuquerque: University of New Mexico Press, 1969); C. Knowlton, "Guerrillas of Rio Arriba: The New Mexico Land Wars," in *La Causa Politica: A Chicano Politics Reader,* ed. F. C. García (South Bend: University of Notre Dame Press, 1974).

64. L. Pulido, *Environmentalism and Economic Justice: Two Chicano Struggles in the Southwest* (Tucson: University of Arizona Press, 1996), 57–124; L. Pulido and D. G. Peña "Environmentalism and Positionality: The Early Pesticide Campaign of the United Farm Workers Organizing Committee, 1965–71," *Race, Gender, and Class* 6 (1998): 33–50.

65. Pulido and Peña, "Environmentalism and Positionality," 42–45.

66. F. L. Quintana, *Pobladores: Hispanic Americans of the Ute Frontier* (Aztec, NM: Frances Leon Quintana, 1991); S. Hawk, "A Study of Displaced Communities: Rosa, New Mexico, and Arboles, Colorado" (master's thesis, Southwest Studies Program, Colorado College, Colorado Springs, CO, 1994); C. Wilkinson, "Remembering Rosa," in *Arrested Rivers,* ed. C. Forsman, H. M. Harrison, and N. Harrison (Niwot, CO: University Press of Colorado, 1994).

67. S. Rodríguez, "Land, Water, and Ethnic Identity in Taos," in Briggs and Van Ness, *Land, Water, and Culture,* 352–54.

5

A Chicana/o Critique of Mainstream American Environmentalism

The first great fact about conservation is that it stands for development.
—Gifford Pinchot (1910)

These temple destroyers, devotees of raging commercialism, seem to have a perfect contempt for Nature, and, instead of lifting their eyes to the God of the mountains, lift them to the Almighty Dollar.
—John Muir (1910)

The impetus for federal environmental protection in the United States dates to the 1890s when the champions of **natural resource conservation** (Gifford Pinchot) and **wilderness preservation** (John Muir) staged a heated debate for the soul of **ecology** in America. At issue was whether nature was a natural resource to be exploited and managed for the benefit of humanity, or wilderness, a self-willing land to be preserved in a pristine and undisturbed state. By the end of the nineteenth century, these two philosophies had led the U.S. government to establish the first national parks, forests, and other protected areas. Environmentalists continued in one of these two camps until the 1960s. Environmentalism after the 1960s was influenced by activist-scientist Rachel Carson, who widely popularized the cause of ecology. Carson played a critical role in campaigns to protect wildlife and human health from the ill effects of pesticides.[1]

The late 1960s and the 1970s saw the rise of the so-called Group of Ten (G10). The G10 includes the National Audubon Society, Izaak Walton League, the Wilderness Society, Defenders of Wildlife, the Sierra Club, the National Parks and Conservation Association, the Environmental Defense Fund (EDF), the Natural Resources Defense Council (NRDC), the Friends of the Earth (FOE), and the Environmental Policy Institute (EPI). These large national environmental organizations benefited from the political opportunities presented when President Nixon signed legislation establishing

Table 15   Important federal environmental protection laws (since 1964)

YEAR	LAW	REGULATORY MANDATES
1964	Wilderness Act	Establishes a national system of wilderness areas where "man is only a visitor"
1970	National Environmental Policy Act (NEPA)	Establishes the Council on Environmental Quality to advise the president; establishes legal standards and procedures to complete EIS for all federally funded activities
1970	Clean Air Act	Establishes federal clean air standards and legal/scientific procedures for enforcement and compliance; the EPA is the designated enforcement agency
1972	Clean Water Act	Establishes federal clean water standards and legal/scientific procedures for enforcement and compliance; the EPA is designated enforcement agency
1973	Endangered Species Act	Establishes federal programs and procedures for the conservation of endangered wild plants and animals and the **habitat** in which they are found; the United States Fish and Wildlife Service (USFWS) is the designated enforcement agency
1980	Comprehensive Emergency Response, Compensation, and Litigation Act (Superfund)	Establishes federal programs to clean up uncontrolled or abandoned hazardous waste sites, as well as accidents, spills, and other emergency releases of pollutants and contaminants into the environment; the EPA is the designated enforcement agency

Source: For complete online text and links to each law, go to http://www.epa.gov/region5/defs/index.html.

the Environmental Protection Agency (EPA). Under pressure from the G10 and other environmentalists, the U.S. Congress enacted a series of laws designed to protect the environment (see table 15). Exemplary environmental laws include the Wilderness Act (1964), the **National Environmental Policy Act (NEPA)** (1970), the Clean Air Act (1970), the Clean Water Act (1972), and the Endangered Species Act (1973). Legal protection for wilderness areas, national parks, wildlife refuges, endangered species, and other environmental qualities like clean air and water were accomplishments of historic significance.

This chapter focuses on mainstream American environmentalism as expressed in the movements for natural resource conservation, wilderness preservation, and professional environmentalism (that is, the G10). I explain how each of these movements developed a specific definition of what the environment means, of the "nature of nature." Each has a different take on the causes of environmental degradation, and each proposes specific actions and strategies to resolve ecological problems. In a departure from conventional approaches to the history of environmentalism, I also offer critical comments on each movement from the perspectives of the **Mexican-origin people.**

▎ Natural Resource Conservation

Gifford Pinchot, a wealthy American forester trained in Europe, was the staunchest proponent of the philosophy of natural resource conservation. The second chief forester of the United States Forest Service (USFS), Pinchot used his position to promote federal policies for the management of hundreds of millions of acres in public timberlands and grasslands. Prior to the founding of the USFS in 1891, federal laws and policies allowed unregulated logging in a case of open-access plunder. Pinchot opposed unrestrained resource exploitation. He championed scientific conservation as a policy for the management of the public domain.

Pinchot viewed nature as a natural resource that should be scientifically managed and conserved for the benefit of present and future generations. Nature had utilitarian value as a resource of economic use to humans. Pinchot had studied the principles of German scientific forestry in Nancy, France, and later at Yale University. The science of silviculture, that is, of managing forests as units of production, was developed in Germany. There it transformed diverse, uneven-aged forests into **monoculture** tree plantations lacking diversity. The German system emphasized the production of the one or two most commercially valuable tree species and treated the rest as unwanted weeds to be controlled and eliminated. The natural regenerative cycle of fire was also eliminated. Under human control, the forests were simplified into a "one-commodity machine."[2]

Pinchot was committed to the idea that scientific experts should manage the forests, exerting human control over nature through science. Conservation was to be subordinated to development as dictated by principles of scientific efficiency. According to "the gospel of efficiency," the management of forests and other public lands was to be directed by scientists and engineers relying on presumed purely technical and nonpolitical criteria such as "maximum sustained yield" and efficiency. Technical experts would maintain neutrality and operate in the interests of the public without succumbing to political pressures or the undue influence of the timber barons and other private interests:

> The first principle of conservation is development, the use of the natural resources now existing . . . for the benefit of the people who live here now. . . . Conservation stands emphatically for . . . development . . . without delay. . . . [C]onservation stands for the prevention of waste . . . to understand that the prevention of waste in all other directions is a simple matter of good business. The first duty of the human race is to control the earth it lives on.[3]

Pinchot opposed the control of forests and timber resources by a few powerful corporations and individuals, asserting, "The natural resources must be developed and preserved for the benefit of the many, and not merely for the profit of a few."[4] Pinchot and his allies in the Progressive Reform Movement worked to drive monopoly interests out of the U.S. forests, but with limited success. Active in the establishment of several important organizations including the American Conservation League and the National Conservation Association, Pinchot worked to educate the public about scientific forestry and the importance of conserving natural resources for use by future generations. Despite this populist anti-corporate rhetoric, the philosophy of natural resource conservation was wed to an economic and utilitarian view of nature.

From the vantage point of Mexican American experiences, the natural resource conservation movement failed to address deep-rooted issues related to the **enclosure** of Spanish and Mexican community land grants. The first national forests (the Santa Fe and Kit Carson forests in New Mexico), established in the early 1890s, were composed at least in part of vast territories that had been managed as common lands during the Spanish and Mexican periods. Restrictive USFS management policies became enduring sources of **Chicana/o** grievances over the abrogation of land and water rights guaranteed by the Treaty of Guadalupe Hidalgo. In Colorado, New Mexico, Arizona, and California, the Mexican American people lost millions of acres of private and community-held lands after the Mexican War of 1846–1848.[5] Many of these lands were converted to the public domain and placed under the control of the USFS, the Bureau of Land Management (BLM), the National Park Service (NPS), and other federal and state land and wildlife management agencies.

Mexican-origin communities perceived the USFS as promoting commercial exploitation at the expense of traditional subsistence-level uses of the **commons.** Chicanas/os rejected arguments about the presumed industrial efficiency of scientific forestry. They were more concerned about restoring their traditional resource rights to community-owned lands they justifiably viewed as stolen. Chicanas/os did not see the benefits of scientific management. They understood the watersheds they had protected were severely damaged following decades of exploitation by large timber, mining, and cattle ranching industries. They blamed *la floresta* (the USFS) for allowing outsiders to exploit the stolen lands.

Mexican Americans had their own traditions and customs for management of community lands. For decades USFS officials and staff ignored and devalued this place-based ecological knowledge. Federal land management agencies took more than a century officially to acknowledge the injustices of lost land grants and the continued importance of national forests and grasslands to the survival of traditional land-based communities.[6] Mexican Americans experienced the scientific management of the national forests and other newly established public lands as part of the general orientation of policies that favored corporate exploitation of stolen lands.[7]

Some historians depict this conflict as a clash of **cultures** in which an inventive, technologically advanced Anglo-American culture overwhelmed the quaint but ecologically ignorant Mexican American culture.[8] In reality, this conflict was not a culture clash between an ecologically sophisticated culture and a backward one. It was more a clash between unequal powers—a regime that imposed federal control and one that fought to maintain local control over cherished ancestral common lands. As a New Mexican elder explains,

> [T]he trouble is with the Forest Service, they get the orders from Washington, D.C. . . . and to live over here is altogether different. Now they say, they look at the maps, they read the books, but between reading the book and doing what you're supposed to do here is two different things. And they want to follow the rules over there by the book. And we want to follow it over here by nature.[9]

Ideological differences between federal land managers and Mexican Americans resulted in conflicts for more than a century. Mexican Americans continue to emphasize local community rights and management of land, wildlife, and water. Mexican-origin people are connected to the land and forests through their work and cultural heritage. Federal land managers have failed to understand this and see the forests as publicly owned timberlands that should be scientifically managed to meet the objectives of maximum yield and taxpayer benefits. Scientific foresters have viewed land grant villages as a hindrance to the conservation goals of scientific management.[10]

▮ Wilderness Preservation

John Muir is the principal inspiration for the American philosophy of wilderness preservation. Critical of Pinchot and the conservation movement, Muir was among the founders of the Sierra Club in 1892. The Sierra Club became one of the largest and most influential environmental organizations in the United States. From the 1890s onward, Muir and the Sierra Club championed the cause of wilderness preservation by working to establish some of the first protected areas in the United States, including Yosemite National Park.[11] The preservationist movement defined nature as wilderness, as a place separate from the permanent presence or effects of humanity and civilization.

Muir objected to the utilitarian value that conservationists placed on nature. He believed that nature had its own intrinsic value independent of the value that humans placed on its use. The son of a preacher, Muir believed that the principal value of wilderness to humans was not material but spiritual and aesthetic. For example, he described Yosemite Valley as

"Nature's Cathedral." For Muir, wilderness preservation was essential to human spiritual welfare. In another example, Muir rallied against the building of the Hetch Hetchy Dam designed to provide San Francisco with water. The eventual construction of this dam inundated the Hetch Hetchy Valley in Yosemite National Park. In a widely quoted and eloquent critique of the project, Muir wrote with inspired religious allegory: "These temple destroyers, devotees of raging commercialism, seem to have a perfect contempt for Nature, and, instead of lifting their eyes to the God of the mountains, lift them to the Almighty Dollar."[12]

There was a clear fault line between the two classical approaches to environmental protection and land management in the United States. Pinchot and the conservationists viewed nature as a natural resource. They favored using science to manage natural resources to maximize benefits for the widest range of human uses, with the needs of future generations in mind. In contrast, Muir and the Sierra Club viewed nature as sacred wilderness, a place unsullied by human civilization. They favored preserving wildness for its own value, regardless of human needs for timber, minerals, and water.

The Mexican American people had a different experience with wilderness. In the land grant communities at the time of Pinchot and Muir, wilderness was inhabited, a wild but familiar place. It was home. It was not a mere natural resource, a **commodity**, or an empty and unknown space. Nature was inseparable from civilization, an intimate and intricately interconnected part of it. Land-based people, including Mexican Americans, use wilderness areas to hunt, fish, gather fuel wood and construction materials, harvest wild plants, and graze livestock. Their material culture is based on this direct relationship to wild spaces. Homes, roofs, fences, corrals, musical instruments, looms, carved saints, furniture, cooking utensils, and even food and medicines came from intimate knowledge of the forests.[13]

Over centuries Mexican Americans have developed a **sustainable** relationship with the landscape, maintaining the relatively wild (self-willing) state of the land by treading lightly with subsistence uses. The wilderness is also woven into local people's identities. As Teresa Jaramillo puts it, "I know La Sierra [The Mountain] because she is my home."[14] The place-based identities of the Mexican American people in the land grant villages are an important source of resistance to the outside forces of the state and the market.[15] This perspective has led Chicana/o communities into conflicts with corporate developers, federal scientists, and even elements of the wilderness preservation movement. The wilderness of the city-dwelling backpacking tourist is the Mexican American's familiar and beloved homeland.

■ Professional Environmentalism: The Group of Ten

By the first Earth Day in April 1970, American environmentalism was reaching the mainstream of American public life. It was developing into the financially well-endowed and highly professional G10. Membership in the G10 was predominantly urban, white, and middle class. The G10 embraced a corporate organizational culture and complete engagement with the federal environmental policy system. Committed to the "cult of expertise," the G10 relied on professional scientists, lawyers, and lobbyists.[16]

G10 groups have developed a strong base of local chapters and organizations. The Sierra Club and Audubon Society are known for having exceptionally strong and independent state-level organizations and local chapters. These local chapters are sometimes at odds with the national organizations in matters of philosophy and policy. It is important to recognize that not all environmentalists accept the ideologies or agendas espoused by the G10 national leadership.

Between 1970 and 1990, the G10 followed a corporate model in their national organizational structures and program activities. The executive directors and boards of the G10 agreed that a corporate model would greatly strengthen the hand of the environmental movement. As Gottlieb notes, "The groups needed to see themselves and their roles in new ways: as defenders of a system and the heads of multimillion dollar operations who by coordinating their common interests and goals could forge a mainstream identity."[17] Another major objective was the forging of a common national agenda. In 1985, the G10 published a book, *An Environmental Agenda for the Future,* that outlined a national environmental strategy.[18] The G10 agenda emphasized tougher regulation of agricultural and industrial air and water pollution, expanded protection for wilderness areas and endangered species, and a new focus on environmental hazards to human health.

The G10 sought dialogue with corporate leaders on environmental problems and policies, holding a series of meetings with the chief executive officers of six chemical companies: DuPont, Exxon Chemical, Union Carbide, Dow, American Cyanamid, and Monsanto. By the end of the decade, the G10 roundtable meetings had stalled, but the label stuck to refer to the mainstream or "shallow" environmental movement. Critics noted the large donations and grants to the G10 from the very corporations being targeted as responsible for ecological damage and pollution cleanup.[19]

The G10 focused on new opportunities to influence the enforcement and reform of federal environmental regulations by using the 1970 **National Environmental Policy Act (NEPA),** perhaps the single most important federal environmental protection law. The cornerstone of federal environmental law, NEPA establishes the general framework for the scientific analysis and mitigation of environmental impacts. NEPA defines the legal and scientific framework for **environmental impact studies (EIS),** the basic form of review extant at the federal, and increasingly, at the state levels. An important feature of the NEPA review process is that it encourages transparency and citizen participation, at least of those citizens with scientific, legal, or technical expertise.

This framework privileges scientific and legal expertise over other kinds of knowledge. By recruiting top scientists, lawyers, and other experts to the cause of environmentalism, the G10 redefined the traditional role of experts. Although the G10 had considerable success in using scientific and legal experts to advance a national environmental policy agenda, they inadvertently contributed to a technical assessment process that increasingly blocked most citizens from participating in decision making. As a result, the EIS became less democratic and accessible to the average person.[20]

Critics have noted that the EIS process has been appropriated by proponents of corporate and military values, who emphasize the logic and privilege the economic interests of larger market forces. Les Levidow states that "a profession of impact assessment has arisen to provide supposedly neutral expertise on proposed waste dumps, dams, mining, military exercises, and other projects." He continues by saying that the dominant form of expert-driven and top-down EIS is antidemocratic because "both human and environmental costs become reified as rationally calculable things, whose magnitude can be minimized or traded for other things." The dominant EIS model ultimately treats **ecosystems**—including air, land, water, and living organisms—as "non-priced natural resources." Advocates of this model define nature as "capital stock" in a system of "tradable development damage permits" that compensates affected communities for the various ills of ecological degradation.[21] The G10 was perhaps an unwitting accomplice in this market-based and antidemocratic bureaucratization of the EIS.

Mexican American communities also joined the widening **environmental justice movement (EJM).** The G10 and Mexican American activists had profound differences in their framing of environmental problems. The pesticides problem is illustrative of these differences. Like the Sierra Club, the Audubon Society, and other G10 organizations, Mexican American farmworkers battled against the unregulated use of pesticides as early as the 1960s. Farmworkers and environmentalists differed however in their definition of pesticides as a policy problem. Environmentalists viewed pesticides in terms of threats to wildlife, especially endangered birds. Farmworkers defined the problem primarily in terms of occupational health and work safety, even if they were sympathetic to the plight of wildlife.[22]

■ Rachel Carson and the Roots of Radical Environmentalism

Rachel Carson offered a brilliant and accessible critique of the dangers posed by human intervention in natural processes and ecosystems. Her book *Silent Spring* (1962) is a benchmark in the history of American environmentalism. Carson changed the way the public perceived environmental problems and forced environmentalists and policymakers to reexamine humans' role in the destruction of biological diversity. *Silent Spring* starts with a "fable for tomorrow" in which Carson describes the illusion of harmony spawned by prosperity and the false perception of progress occasioned by scientific advances in the "struggle of humans against nature":

> There was once a town in the heart of America where all life seemed to live in harmony with its surroundings. . . . Then a strange blight crept over the area and everything began to change. . . . There was a strange stillness. The birds, for example—where had they gone? . . . It was a spring without voices. On the mornings that had once throbbed with the dawn chorus of robins, catbirds, doves, jays, wrens, and scores of other bird voices there was no sound; only silence lay over the fields and woods and marsh.[23]

The silence of the birds in the springtime was the trope Carson used so effectively to convey her concern over the harmful effects of the use of DDT and other so-called economic poisons on wildlife and the environment.

Carson wrote of "the tide of chemicals born of the Industrial Age," and warned that "a different kind of hazard . . . lurks in our environment—a hazard we ourselves have introduced into our world as our modern way of life . . . evolved." She presented evidence that "new environmental health problems are . . . born of the never-ending stream of chemicals . . . pervading the world in which we live."[24] Carson understood that an increasing number of new maladies were threatening public health. The negative health effects of pesticides and other chemicals were not well understood in her time, but Carson outlined the then-existing empirical evidence to establish a clear causal link between chemicals in the environment and human health problems such as cancer and reproductive system disorders including birth defects.

Carson warned that the increasing dependency of agriculture on "economic poisons" was doomed to failure because insects and weeds would adapt, developing resistance to the chemical onslaught. She described a pesticide treadmill: The more poisons used, the greater the resistance of the targeted pests. This leads to a never-ending cycle of escalating use of pesticides and correspondingly greater resistance in pests.[25] This perspective on environmental problems was more radical than those of followers of Pinchot or Muir: It questioned the very logic of industrial capitalism. Carson understood that environmental problems would not be solved by conservation or wilderness preservation alone. Instead she urged scientists and the public to recognize and respect the complex interactions that tie all life together in a web of delicate interdependencies.

The chemical industry responded to *Silent Spring* with spiteful propaganda. Male scientists were paraded forth to criticize Carson's work. Chemical industry executives and their scientific apologists charged that *Silent Spring* was "dangerous for the United States because it was part of a Communist plot to ruin American agriculture, industry, and the economy, and to render this country defenseless before the East." The attacks focused as much on Carson's gender, personality, and character as on the scientific evidence she had amassed against pesticides. As M. Patricia Hynes notes, "*Silent Spring* altered the balance of power in the world."[26]

Carson's work undermined the dominant ideology that encouraged a misinformed and uneducated public to embrace blind faith in scientific progress and technological fixes. The publication of *Silent Spring,* and the scientific research that followed in its wake, led to changes in federal policies regarding pesticides and to the banning of several agroindustrial chemicals, including DDT. The EPA was created in part because of the influence of Carson's book.

Despite Carson's profound influence on environmentalism, there are some curious silences in *Silent Spring*. For one, Carson overlooked the plight of the largely Mexican-origin agricultural workforce. She did not recognize or acknowledge the emergent struggles among farmworkers against pesticide exposure and associated health problems. This oversight perhaps reflected Carson's white and privileged middle-class background. Her concern for the environmental correlates of public health focused on the general population, especially women and children, not on the heightened risks that minority populations face. Still, she inspired new waves of environmentalism by linking science to public policy **discourse.** She was among the first in a line of scientists who felt a responsibility to demystify science and make it accessible to the average citizen. This is one of the most significant and enduring implications of her work.

■ Concluding Thoughts

The conservationists, led by Gifford Pinchot, were **anthropocentric** (human-centered). They defined nature as a natural resource, a commodity to be managed scientifically for the benefit of humankind. In contrast, the wilderness preservationists, led by John Muir, were **biocentric** (life centered) or ecocentric (ecosystem centered). They defined nature as a place where wildlife and natural processes of evolution held sway. Muir's version equated nature with wilderness. The preservation of wilderness had intrinsic value independent of the human need for natural resources. Wilderness also had value for humans because it provided a context for spiritual renewal and a closer and more intimate relationship with creation.

These two conflicting schools influenced the evolution of American environmental law and public policy. Pinchot's agenda for scientific management of the forests became official federal policy with the establishment of a variety of laws governing "multiple and sustained uses" of public lands. Muir's agenda for wilderness preservation became public policy through the establishment of the National Park System and "primitive areas" that are the predecessors of modern-day wilderness reserves.

The emergence of the G10 signaled an important shift in American environmentalism toward increasing professionalization and bureaucratization. The G10 merged scientific and legal expertise to produce some of the most important public policies for environmental protection. The G10 shaped the national environmental agenda and contributed to the profession and politics of environmental impact studies. Rachel Carson championed a new approach to environmentalism that bridged the gap between scientists and the public. Her work led to major changes in the institutions charged with environmental protection and regulation. The work of the EPA was influenced by Carson's insights on the correlation between synthetic chemicals in the environment and human public health.

A failure to recognize the multicultural nature of American society was an underlying flaw of the first two waves of American environmentalism. The conservationists, on the rare occasions they acknowledged people of color, tended to view them as ignorant ecological thugs. This attitude was especially prevalent within the USFS and resulted in sharp, ever-escalating conflicts between government bureaucrats and land-based communities.[27] The wilderness preservation movement simply failed to recognize that for native local cultures the wilderness is a homeland. The G10 failed to recognize that the **built environment** is as important as national parks, forests, and wilderness areas. These differences led to conflicts between Mexican-origin people and both mainstream and radical environmental movements as Chicanas/os became active in the EJM in the 1980s and 1990s.

■ Discussion Questions

1. Compare the three strands of mainstream environmentalism in the United States (conservationism, wilderness preservation, and professional environmentalism). Account for differences in definitions of nature, explanations of the causes of environmental degradation, and recommended strategies to resolve ecological problems.

2. Discuss the effectiveness of legal strategies for environmental protection. Are laws such as the Endangered Species Act or the Wilderness Act effective? How are they circumvented? What are some current conflicts related to endangered species and wilderness protection?

3. What are the ethical and political implications of a professionalized and bureaucratic style of environmentalism as embodied by the G10? Conduct a research project in which you identify and discuss the shifting nature of corporate contributions to G10 budgets.

4. Why did the chemical industry attack Rachel Carson? Did her gender play a role in those attacks? What does this say about the nature of science and the politics of science in service to industry?

■ Suggested Readings

Carson, Rachel. 1962. *Silent Spring*. Greenwich, CT: Fawcett Publications.

Gottlieb, Robert. 1993. *Forcing the Spring: The Transformation of the American Environmental Movement*. Washington, DC: Island Press.

Hynes, M. Patricia. 1989. *The Recurring Silent Spring*. New York: Pergamon Press.

Nash, Roderick F. 1990. *American Environmentalism: Readings in Conservation History*. 3rd ed. New York: McGraw Hill.

■ Notes

1. R. Carson, *Silent Spring* (Greenwich, CT: Fawcett Crest Books, 1962).

2. See J. C. Scott, *Seeing Like a State* (New Haven: Yale University Press, 1998), 11–22.

3. G. Pinchot, "The Birth of Conservation," in *The Progressive Conservation Movement, 1890–1920* (Cambridge: Harvard University Press, 1959), 1–4, 265–66 passim.

4. Ibid., 78.

5. R. O. Acuña, *Occupied America: A History of Chicanos* (Boston: Addison-Wesley, 1999); C. L. Briggs and J. R. Van Ness, eds., *Land, Water, and Culture: New Perspectives on Hispanic Land Grants* (Albuquerque: University of New Mexico Press, 1987); W. deBuys, *Enchantment and Exploitation: The Life and Hard Times of a New Mexico Mountain Range* (Albuquerque: University of New Mexico Press, 1985); M. Ebright, *Land Grants and Lawsuits in Northern New Mexico* (Albuquerque: University of New Mexico Press, 1994); V. Westphall, *The Public Domain in New Mexico, 1854–1891* (Albuquerque: University of New Mexico Press, 1965).

6. The USFS issued its Hassell Report of 1968 only after Chicana/o activists led by Reies López Tijerina had exploded onto the scene during the infamous Tierra Amarilla courthouse raid. In this report the USFS for the first time officially acknowledged that federal policies were undermining the survival of the "Spanish American" land grant villages that had for centuries relied on the forests for subsistence.

7. D. G. Peña and R. O. Martínez, "Upper Rio Grande Hispano Farms: A Cultural and Environmental History of Land Ethics in Transition, 1598–1998" (final report, National Endowment for the Humanities, Grant RO22707-94. Rio Grande Bioregions Project, Department of Anthropology, University of Washington, Seattle, WA, January 2000).

8. deBuys, *Enchantment and Exploitation;* H. Rothman, "Cultural and Environmental Change on the Pajarito Plateau," *New Mexico Historical Quarterly* 64 (1989): 185–

212, and *On Rims and Ridges: The Los Alamos Area since 1880* (Lincoln: University of Nebraska Press, 1992). For a critique, see D. G. Peña and R. O. Martínez, "The Capitalist Tool, the Lawless, and the Violent: A Critique of Recent Southwestern Environmental History," in *Chicano Culture, Ecology, Politics: Subversive Kin,* ed. D. G. Peña (Tucson: University of Arizona Press, 1998), 146–57.

9. Fermín Arguello quoted in E. Rubine, "Then and Now: Habitus and the Power of Community in the Upper Rio Grande," in *Voces de la Tierra: Four Hundred Years of Acequia Farms in the Rio Arriba, 1598–1998,* ed. D. G. Peña and R. O. Martínez (Tucson: University of Arizona Press, forthcoming), 42–43.

10. deBuys, *Enchantment and Exploitation*; also see D. G. Peña, *Gaia en Aztlán: Endangered Landscapes and Disappearing People in the Politics of Place* (forthcoming).

11. D. Worster, "John Muir and the Roots of American Environmentalism," in *The Wealth of Nature: Environmental History and the Ecological Imagination* (Oxford: Oxford University Press, 1993), 184–202.

12. Ibid., 97.

13. Peña and Martínez, "Capitalist Tool," 160.

14. T. Jaramillo, interview by Devon G. Peña, June 1998, El Poso, Sierra Culebra, Colorado. In the author's collection at the Rio Grande Bioregions Project, University of Washington, Seattle.

15. D. G. Peña, "Identity, Place, and Communities of Resistance," in *Just Sustainabilities: Environmental Justice in an Unequal World,* ed. J. Agyeman, R. D. Bullard, and B. Evans (London: Earthscan; Cambridge: MIT Press, 2003).

16. R. Gottlieb, *Forcing the Spring: The Transformation of the American Environmental Movement.* (Washington, DC: Island Press, 1993), 117–48.

17. The corporate model was inspired by the corporate Business Roundtable, a group of chief executive officers from G10 organizations and Fortune 500 companies who met quarterly to discuss common political-economic interests in the wake of the growth of the environmental movement. See Gottlieb, *Forcing the Spring,* 120–21; quotation on p. 120.

18. J. H. Adams et al., eds. *An Environmental Agenda for the Future* (Washington DC: Island Press, 1985).

19. On the roundtables, see Gottlieb, *Forcing the Spring,* 123. For a critique of mainstream environmentalism, see C. Merchant, *Radical Ecology: The Search for a Livable World* (London: Routledge, 1992), 159–61, table 7.1.

20. F. Fischer, *Citizens, Experts, and the Environment: The Politics of Local Knowledge* (Durham: Duke University Press, 2000), 109–23; also see F. Fischer, "Participatory Expertise: Toward the Democratization of Policy Science," in *Advances in Policy Studies since 1950,* ed. W. Dunn and R. Kelley (New Brunswick: Transaction Press, 1992), 351–76.

21. Quotations in L. Levidow, "The Eleventh Annual Meeting of the International Association for Impact Assessment," *Capitalism, Nature, Socialism* 3 (1992): 117–18,

121–22, 122; also see D. G. Peña, *The Terror of the Machine: Technology, Work, Gender and Ecology on the U.S.–Mexico Border* (Austin: CMAS Books, 1997), 306–8.

22. L. Pulido and D. G. Peña, "Environmentalism and Positionality: The Early Pesticide Campaign of the United Farm Workers Organizing Committee, 1966–71," *Race, Gender, and Class* 6 (1998): 33–50.

23. R. Carson, *Silent Spring* (Greenwich, CT: Fawcett Publications, 1962), 13–14.

24. Ibid., 168.

25. Ibid., 217–43.

26. M. P. Hynes, *The Recurring Silent Spring* (New York: Pergamon Press, 1989); quotations on 17 and 3.

27. deBuys, *Enchantment and Exploitation;* for a critique, see Peña and Martínez, "The Capitalist Tool."

6

A Chicana/o Critique of Radical American Environmentalism

[T]he bleak, sometimes horrific, conditions that oppress us are created not only by the polluters, but also by the architects of policy, science, and health care who at best patch things up with distracting, ineffective, and sometimes dangerous "solutions."
—Lin Nelson (1990)

We don't have the complexion for protection.
—Southwest Network for Environmental and Economic Justice (1992)

A third wave of environmentalism, which emerged during the 1980s, encompassed different strands of radical **ecology.** These nonreformist social movements had a shared vision of fundamentally transforming political and economic institutions.[1] Radical American environmentalism includes schools of **deep ecology,** social ecology, **ecofeminism, ecosocialism,** bioregionalism, anti-toxics, and **environmental justice.** Each school has a distinct social movement, political organization, and history of activism. Each has defining values for environmental protection and specific beliefs about the nature of nature. Each has a different take on the history and causes of ecological degradation and proposes specific strategies to address ecological and social problems. Throughout this chapter I draw on the experiences and struggles of the **Mexican-origin people** to offer critical comments about radical environmentalism.

Deep Ecology

Norwegian philosopher Arne Naess first used the term **deep ecology** in a 1972 essay. Naess drew a sharp distinction between the "shallow" and "deep" ecology movements. He viewed the shallow ecology movement as reform oriented, narrowly focused on pollution and resource depletion, and concerned with the health and affluence of people in developed countries. In contrast, he defined deep ecology as a movement oriented toward long-range, revolutionary change. Naess rejected shallow ecology's **anthropocentrism,** the idea that humans are at the center of existence and have a right to dominate and exploit nature. He proposed a "relational, total-field image" based on **biocentrism** or ecocentrism (see table 16).[2]

In this philosophy existence is centered on all life forms, not just on humans. All life forms are intrinsically important independent of their utility to humans. Therefore, humans must learn to live in "mixed communities" with all species. Naess argues that social class hierarchies lead to domination of some humans by others. This domination is the fundamental problem of civilization and the primary source of ecological crisis. Naess opposes pollution and resource depletion but warns that a focus on these problems results in a failure to see the more fundamental connection between the domination of nature and the exploitation of humans.

Deep ecology influenced direct-action organizations, such as Earth First! and Greenpeace, and conservation biologists, including those affiliated with the Wildlands Project. Radical environmentalists share many of the objectives of classic **wilderness preservationists,** but they differ markedly in their strategies and tactics. Earth First! eschewed reformist legislative or bureaucratic regulatory approaches in favor of nonviolent direct-action campaigns involving activities such as lawsuits, protests, blockades, and even sabotage (that is, monkey wrenching).[3]

Activists in Earth First! and other like-minded organizations envision a system of wilderness areas "off-limits to industrial human civilization." These areas would allow "no human habitation (except, in some cases, indigenous peoples with traditional life-styles)." Protected areas would serve as "preserves for the free-flow of natural processes." These activists outline an ambitious national system of preserves comprising more than 700 million acres. They seek to ban logging, mining, water diversion, industrial activity, agriculture, and grazing to protect **ecosystem** functioning.[4]

Earth First! activists have had conflicts with communities of color. Activist Christopher Manes proclaimed that AIDS and starvation caused by drought were nature's responses to human overpopulation and damage to the environment. He proposed that the poor and hungry of the Third World should be allowed to starve. Further, he claimed humans should engage in voluntary extinction by committing mass suicide to rid the planet of the most harmful species in planetary history. Other activists, such as Ed Abbey and Dave Foreman, were staunchly anti-immigration.

Table 16 Comparison of dominant western industrial-scientific and deep ecology paradigms

DOMINANT WESTERN INDUSTRIAL-SCIENTIFIC PARADIGM	DEEP ECOLOGY PARADIGM
Anthropocentric (human-centered)	Biocentric (ecology-centered)
Dominant over nature	In harmony with nature
Natural environment viewed as resource for humans	All nature viewed as having intrinsic worth (biospherical equality)
Necessity of material/economic growth for growing human population	Elegant simplicity in material needs (material goals serve the larger goal of self-realization)
Belief in ample resource reserves	Belief in limited earth supplies
Use of highly technological progress and solutions	Use of appropriate technology; nondominating science
Consumerism	Doing with enough; recycling
National/centralized community focus	Minority tradition/bioregional focus

Source: Adapted from B. DeVall and G. Sessions, Deep Ecology: Living as if the Earth Mattered (Salt Lake City: Peregrine Smith, 1985), figure 5-1.

Abbey provoked severe criticism from Latinas/os after inflammatory attacks against Mexican immigrants whom he described as a "culturally-morally-genetically inferior people." Mexicans were one of the biggest threats to the environment: "They come to stay, and they stay to multiply," Abbey once wrote.[5] He recommended that the U.S. military seal off the Mexican border to keep the "wetbacks" (his term) out.

Social Ecology

Social ecology seeks to eliminate all forms of hierarchy. Philosopher Murray Bookchin argues that social ecology "offers no case whatsoever for hierarchy in nature and society; it . . . challenges the very function of hierarchy as a stabilizing or 'ordering' principle in *both* realms." Bookchin criticizes the "image of the natural world that sees nature . . . as blind, mute, cruel, competitive, and stingy." The idea of nature as a "seemingly demonic 'realm of necessity' " is a Western myth. The concept of progress, in which modern-thinking people seek "the extrication of humanity from the muck of a mindless, unthinking, and brutish domain," is another facet

Table 17 Organizational values of localism in social ecology

VALUE	OBJECTIVE	ORGANIZATIONAL FORM
Decentralization	Local authority	Libertarian municipalities
Democratization (political)	Citizen participation	Participatory democracy and consensus in decision making
Democratization (economic)	Worker and community participation	Worker self-management of cooperatives; community or worker ownership of means of production
Amalgamation	Regional coordination	Confederation of municipalities
Sustainability	Ecological and social integrity	"Moral economy" on a human scale

Source: Author's elaboration based on M. Bookchin, *The Modern Crisis* (Philadelphia: New Society Publishers, 1986); and J. Biehl, *The Politics of Social Ecology: Libertarian Municipalism* (Montreal: Black Rose Books, 1998).

of this myth. Bookchin proposes that we recognize a "deep-seated continuity between nature and society." Doing so requires redefining nature as "a participatory realm of interactive life-forms whose most outstanding attributes are fecundity, creativity, and directiveness, marked by complementarity that renders the natural world the grounding for an ethics of freedom rather than domination."[6]

For Bookchin, domination precedes exploitation. This is evident in the origin of one of the earliest forms of human domination: patriarchy, the subordination of women by men.[7] The underlying causes of environmental degradation derive from society's dysfunctional, hierarchically organized, and destructive relationship with nature. All subordinate Others—nature, woman, worker, farmer, colony—are affected by conditions of domination and ecological degradation.

Social ecologists seek a system of libertarian municipalism, a type of local participatory democracy inspired by colonial New England town meetings. Decisions are made at the town and county levels by direct consensus of the citizens. Libertarian municipalism requires the radical diffusion (instead of concentration) of political power and authority (see table 17). Localism is favored over centralism. Democratization involves the participation of local residents in decision making. On a larger scale, self-governing municipalities can form a network of associations or a confederation of municipalities consisting of delegates from all the local communities.[8]

Social ecologists are critical of capitalism, defined as a highly centralized "corporate market-based" system. They embrace **workplace democracy,** which is the elimination of management hierarchies, allowing workers to manage their own production. They further challenge the ownership of the means of production, supporting worker- or community-owned cooperatives over corporate ownership.[9] The Green Party–USA, founded in 1991, is an organization based at least partially on the theories and principles of social ecology. Green Party members call for the abolition of the corporate market-based system and for local self-governance through direct citizen democracy. By 1994, more than 142 local groups were affiliated with the Green Party–USA. By 2000, more than 130 Green Party candidates were holding elected office in thirty different states.[10]

For generations many Mexican American communities have embraced similar principles of decentralism, localism, participatory democracy, and communal ownership of the means of production. Traditions of **mutual aid** are based on local self-help and the marshalling of communal resources in the service of individuals needing assistance. Spanish and Mexican community land grants are enduring examples of community ownership of the means of production. In Los Angeles and other major urban areas, Mexicans and Mexican Americans are forming housing cooperatives and other communal organizations that seek local control over housing and public spaces in their communities. The **acequia** irrigation institutions of the Southwest are renowned as indigenous watershed democracies.[11] These examples illustrate the existence of grassroots localism in Mexican American communities. It seems ironic that Bookchin and Biehl limit their philosophical sources to values drawn from ancient Greek civilization and colonial New England civic **culture** (a bad time for Native Americans). The historical perspectives and political values of social ecology will be enriched by an understanding and respect for other cultural communities in expanding ideals of cultural citizenship (the concept that groups of people have collective rights to culture and cultural survival).

■ Ecofeminism

French social theorist Françoise d'Eaubonne proposed the concept of ecofeminism in 1974. This form of radical environmentalism, which has many different strands, is based on the idea that domination and exploitation of women and of the environment are interconnected. By the late 1970s, U.S. activists and writers were discussing ecofeminist concepts in the context of political and social struggles associated with the women's, antiwar, antinuclear, and reproductive rights movements.[12]

Carolyn Merchant and Ariel Salleh have outlined the various schools of liberal, cultural, social, and socialist ecofeminist thought. Significant theoretical debates exist among the various strands of ecofeminist philosophy.[13] Liberal ecofeminists seek equality: They want to make certain that pollution is not disproportionately targeting women, and they want women to participate equally with men in existing institutions dedicated to environmental protection and resource conservation. Cultural ecofeminists espouse more radical changes. They start with the idea that "the psychology of patriarchal masculinity is the root of the problem."[14] They want to abolish what they see as the violent, objectifying culture of masculinity, and many pursue separatist communities. Some cultural ecofeminists argue that women are closer to nature because of their reproductive biology.

Social ecofeminists reject the idea that patriarchy is the root problem;

instead, they focus on hierarchy as the underlying factor in all forms of domination. They do not agree that reforming the existing market and state system through gender equality is sufficient for meaningful political change. Rather, more radical changes in the organization of political and economic institutions are needed to overcome the tyranny of social hierarchy. They shun the idea that biological differences place women closer to nature.[15] Human alienation from nature and exploitation of the environment cut across gender, class, and race. Instead of a liberal reform of the existing structure of domination, or a cultural revolt against patriarchy and masculinist domination, social ecofeminists propose to transform the structure of social hierarchies through a movement based on local grassroots democracy, cooperative reorganization of the economy, and communities that respect ecological limits.

Socialist ecofeminists identify the capitalist system of economic exploitation and its control of science and technology as the underlying problem. Capitalist expansion and concentration of economic (and political) power require ever more costly destruction of the **natural conditions of production.** Socialist ecofeminists suggest that Marxist theory has overemphasized "the role of **commodity** production in determining how we use and conceive of nature."[16] They propose a broader focus that includes the sphere of social reproduction (that is, the production of labor, culture, and social life through the provision of nutrition, health care, education, childrearing, and so on). Ecological struggles related to the conditions of social reproduction are widening the confrontation between communities and the state, presumably becoming more important than the classical struggles of labor against capital.

Ecofeminists participate in a broad range of grassroots networks, organizations, conferences, and working groups. Their activism establishes connections among struggles against capitalist exploitation, militarism and war, the proliferation of nuclear and biological weapons, the nuclear power industry, and the cultures of violence against women and other marginalized groups. Socialist ecofeminists have undertaken political campaigns to demilitarize the global market economy and redirect social wealth toward the restoration of ecosystems and the rebuilding of sustainable farms, villages, towns, and cities.[17]

Women of color challenge the various strands of ecofeminism by recasting the critique of patriarchal capitalism in the context of what they view as a more fundamental critique of colonialism and racial domination.

Feminists of color propose that class, gender, race, nation, and sexual domination are all mutually interconnected. The inequalities of race and class are reproduced within ecofeminist theory and practice. According to Dorceta Taylor, "In the past, ecofeminism, like other sectors of the environmental movement, did not pay attention to the environmental struggles of women of color in the United States . . . and . . . women-of-color environmental justice activists still receive only marginal recognition from ecofeminists."[18]

Some **Chicanas** criticize ecofeminism for an elitist emphasis on theoretical **discourse** and inattention to the actual lived connections between race, class, and gender in women's experiences with oppression and domination.[19] **Environmental justice movement (EJM)** activists illustrate the significance of the direct lived experience of poverty, discrimination, and violence at the hands of the dominant white power structure. Direct experiences with violence and ecological degradation lie beyond the social spaces usually occupied by white middle-class women. Not all women live and work in polluted places. Not all women experience racial profiling and police brutality. Not all women are subject to the poverty of deprivation and hunger. Chicana theorists observe that white women enjoy the privilege of access to white male power,[20] and of being sheltered in a clean and safe middle-class environment. These differences in the material conditions of life that white women versus women of color experience are associated with divergent ideologies of nature, perceptions of **environmental risk,** ability to take action, and forms of plausible organization.

■ Ecosocialism

Marx identified two contradictions of capitalism. The first contradiction is the tendency, outlined in *Das Capital,* for the rate of profit to decline even as capital expands its global reach and becomes concentrated in fewer hands. This leads to an overproduction crisis as each individual capitalist seeks to lower costs to maintain profitability by out-producing his or her competitors, but "the unintended effect is to reduce the total market demand for commodities." The second contradiction is characterized as an underproduction crisis. Individual capitalists lower costs in part "by externalizing costs unto labor or nature," but "the unintended effect of this is to raise costs on other capitals . . . and lower profits."[21]

The second contradiction is a central concept in ecosocialist theory. Capital resists the tendency for the rate of profit to fall by seeking to expand the production base. The economic system destroys the natural conditions of production and provokes an ecological crisis, continually threatening to exceed the **carrying capacity** of the earth. James O'Connor states that the "basic cause of the second contradiction is capitalism's self-destructive appropriation and use of labor power, space, and external nature or environment." The global capitalist development of the past fifty years "would have been impossible without deforestation, air and water pollution, pollution of the atmosphere, global warming, and the other ecological disasters."[22]

The second contradiction is associated with a shift in **agency** (the actors involved in organizing for social change). Ecosocialists see a shift from working-class struggles in capitalist production to struggles by marginalized social groups in new ecological movements. The environmental justice and grassroots antitoxics movements are noted as two examples of this shift. These "social movements push capitalism to respond . . . by introducing more environmental and natural resources planning—sustained yield forests, environmental health policies, [and] toxic waste disposal practices."[23] Ecosocialists have been elected to city councils, water boards, and planning commissions, where they have pressed for public ownership of property; cooperative forms of production; and guaranteed housing, health, employment, and education.[24]

Ecosocialists and Mexican Americans have worked together in the Green Party–USA. Some activists consider the principles of ecosocialism to be compatible with the values expressed in many Mexican American communities in the context of struggles for social, economic, and environmental justice. EJM networks have integrated ecosocialist principles into their ideologies and strategies. Many EJM activists understand environmental problems in their communities by framing them in terms of conditions related to economic exploitation and socioeconomic (race-class) inequality.[25]

▉ Bioregionalism

The basic idea of bioregionalism is that any given local area of the **biosphere** is defined by the natural boundaries of watersheds and landforms. Bioregionalists propose that we should recognize how nature provides spatial principles for human **inhabitation** of places. The interaction of water and land defines the basic biophysical properties of the local ecosystem and the diversity of **habitats** in a given locality. Each **bioregion** is thus endowed with its own unique **biota,** its stock of native flora and fauna. Locally adapted human communities characterize each bioregion. They are shaped by adaptation to the ecosystem and a unique sense of place that includes local knowledge of ecology.[26]

Bioregionalism presents a sharp contrast to the modern industrial-scientific **paradigm.** Kirkpatrick Sale argues that the place-centered **environmental ethics** of bioregionalism challenge the scale, economy, polity, and social structure of the dominant paradigm.[27] Instead of nations, states and counties, bioregionalists envision polities at the watershed scale like the confederated municipalities that Bookchin and other social ecologists propose. Bioregionalists emphasize conservation, stability, self-sufficiency, and cooperation as underlying principles of place-based economics. This contrasts with the focus on exploitation, change and progress, global inter-dependency, and competition in the dominant economic paradigm. Bio-regionalists adopt political principles of decentralization, complementarity, and diversity as opposed to the centralization, hierarchy, and uniformity of the dominant paradigm (see table 18).

Bioregionalists celebrate the cultural distinctiveness of places and are keen to protect the place-based knowledge of endangered local cultures. The blending of biological and cultural diversity enables "dwellers in the land" to engage in the practical rediscovery of the nature-culture connec-tion. These ideas are associated with the concept of *reinhabitation,* which involves restoring the original livelihoods, **cultural landscapes,** and natural landscapes of places.[28]

Bioregionalists have established many independent activist organiza-tions. The largest and most significant of these is the North American Bioregional Congress (NABC), founded in 1984 and now known as the Turtle Island Bioregional Congress. An important precursor of the NABC was the Ozark Area Community Congress (OACC), cofounded by David Haenke, a self-described homesteader and appropriate technology activist. Originating in Kansas, the OACC has held an annual congress every year since 1980.[29]

Bioregional principles are similar to the land- and water-use ethics of some traditional rural Mexican American cultures in places like south Texas, northern New Mexico, southern Colorado, south central Arizona, California, and the Pacific Northwest. Many Chicana/o communities share strong traditions of watershed consciousness and local self-governance.

Table 18   Comparison of the bioregional and dominant industrial-scientific paradigms

	BIOREGIONAL PARADIGM	INDUSTRIAL-SCIENTIFIC PARADIGM
Scale	Region	State
	Community	Nation
Economy	Conservation	Exploitation
	Stability	Change and progress
	Self-sufficiency	World economy (interdependency)
	Cooperation	Competition
Polity	Decentralization	Centralization
	Complementarity	Hierarchy
	Diversity	Uniformity
Society	Symbiosis	Polarization
	Evolution	Growth/violence
	Division (unity in diversity)	Monoculture (compulsory acculturation)

Source: Adapted and revised from K. Sale, *Dwellers in the Land: The Bioregional Vision* (Philadelphia: New Society Publishers, 1991), 50.

Watershed scientist Robert Curry reminds us that the historical pattern of Mexican settlement in the Southwest followed a watershed-based or bioregional framework: "Remember that in California, General Vallejo drew the first county boundaries based on watersheds." Several grassroots organizations have explicitly embraced bioregional principles. The Colorado Acequia Association (CAA) calls itself a "bioregional" or "watershed-based" organization for environmental justice."[30]

The Antitoxics Movement

The grassroots antitoxics movement emerged in the aftermath of the August 1978 evacuation of the Love Canal neighborhood in upstate New York because of contamination from uncontrolled hazardous waste sites. The Love Canal evacuation led to the establishment of the Citizen's Clearinghouse for Hazardous Waste (CCHW). Lois Gibbs, a white middle-class mother, became the central figure in the founding of the antitoxics movement. This was a grassroots movement of volunteers, not a cadre of professional and highly paid lawyers, scientists, and lobbyists. The antitoxics movement concentrated on human health hazards in the **built environment** (neighborhoods, towns, and cities). The CCHW, and later the National Toxics Campaign (NTC), enlarged the scope of environmentalism by focusing on the risks to human health posed by toxicity.[31]

The underlying cause of environmental degradation according to the antitoxics movement is the collusion between government and industry that allows unregulated contamination and ill-advised siting and mismanagement of hazardous waste facilities in residential neighborhoods. The movement pushed for the adoption of new laws forcing governments and corporations to clean up contamination, punish polluters, and compensate victims. The movement worked for accountability through public disclosure and community right-to-know laws. This legislation, passed in the 1980s, established the right of individuals and communities to access government data on environmental risks and pollution sources. The movement also sponsored research on exposure to hazardous wastes and the correlation with incidence of cancers, reproductive and respiratory disorders, birth defects, and other medical conditions. Many antitoxics activists value the practice of kitchen table science, that is that those involved in the movement have been housekeepers or mothers who conducted and shared their own research with others. Their homes often double as meeting and organizing spaces.[32]

A basic principle of the antitoxics movement is that pollution should not just be cleaned up; in the immediate future, it should be prevented.[33] Prevention is more effective than cleanup because it eliminates the tendency of many communities to practice NIMBY ("not in my back yard") activism, which simply shifts the problem elsewhere. In 1984 the NTC drafted its "Citizens' Bill of Rights." The bill outlined seven rights: (1) the right to be safe from harmful exposure; (2) the right to know; (3) the right to cleanup; (4) the right to participation; (5) the right to compensation; (6) the right to prevention; and (7) the right to protection and enforcement. In 1980, the U.S. Congress passed the Comprehensive Environmental Response, Compensation, and Liability Act (CERCLA), commonly known as the Superfund Act. This law levied a tax on the chemical and petroleum industries to pay for toxic waste cleanup and provided broad federal authority to respond directly to releases or threatened releases of hazardous substances that may endanger public health or the environment. For six years, the NTC worked on a national legislative agenda to establish right-to-know laws and reauthorize the Superfund Act. The movement succeeded with the passage in 1986 of the Superfund reauthorization, which designated $9 billion for cleanup of the worst toxic waste sites in the country.[34]

The issues raised by the antitoxics movement resonated with Mexican American and other communities of color, many of which have their own histories of struggles over toxic waste sites in residential neighborhoods, pesticides in the workplace, lead paint in homes, lack of clean drinking water, and similar health risks in the built environment. The antitoxics movement remained narrowly focused in white communities, however. EJM activists criticized it for benefiting from white privilege because activists accepted the concentration of federal Superfund resources in white communities at the expense of cleanup in communities of color.

■ The Environmental Justice Movement (EJM)

The EJM represents a major shift in the direction of American environmentalism.[35] It precipitated radical changes in environmental activism by redefining the political values of environmentalism; expanding the concept of the environment; and challenging racism in the G10, radical environmental movements, and government agencies such as the EPA. A principal accomplishment of the EJM is the linking of environmental, economic, and social justice issues in a new paradigm that offers a critique of and alternative to mainstream environmentalism.

The EJM has deep roots but effectively began in the early 1980s with protests against **environmental racism.** Environmental racism refers to "racial discrimination in environmental policymaking." It encompasses "discrimination in the enforcement of regulations and laws . . . the deliberate targeting of communities of color for toxic waste disposal and the siting of polluting industries . . . the official sanctioning of the life-threatening presence of poisons and pollutants in communities of color . . . [and a] history of excluding people of color from . . . environmental groups, decision-making bodies, commissions, and regulatory bodies."[36]

Environmental racism is a form of institutionalized discrimination— an interrelated set of political practices, power structures, and relations of domination that intentionally or unintentionally target individuals or groups for disparate treatment on the basis of their race, ethnicity, national origin, class, gender, or sexual orientation. Environmental racism operates through geographic, social-organizational, and procedural inequities (see

Table 19 Principal forms of environmental racism

GEOGRAPHIC INEQUITIES	←	SOCIAL-ORGANIZATIONAL INEQUITIES	←	PROCEDURAL INEQUITIES
1. Disproportionate siting of hazardous and toxic waste sites 2. Disproportionate siting of infrastructure such as power plants and transmission towers, dams and reservoirs, roads, highways, railroads, urban renewal projects, etc. 3. Disproportionate siting of polluting industry and manufacturing facilities, and industrial zones 4. Disproportionate siting of extractive industries, including mining and logging 5. Differential access to recreational facilities, parks, and open space 6. Disproportionate impact of gentrification in both rural and urban communities 7. Disproportionate exposure to toxics in work, home, and neighborhood		1. Disproportionate access to data on toxins in work, home, and neighborhood 2. Disproportionate access to health care and medical services and facilities 3. Greater incidence of multiple hazard exposures compounded by effects of low income and limited resources (shelter, food, clothing, medical care) 4. Discrimination in the hiring and staffing patterns of the EPA and G10 5. Institutional inequity in environmental protection apparatus: Superfund monies directed to white communities 6. Environmental protection apparatus legitimates high-risk technologies such as waste incinerators		1. Objectivist semantics and cult of expertise, which limit and create bias in the science of environmental impact studies and risk assessment, thwarting equitable cleanup of toxic waste sites 2. Lack of access to regulatory agencies, scientists, and other decision makers during EIS review process 3. Attacks on the authority of local knowledge and privileging of scientific and legal experts 4. Undue burden of proof imposed on the victims instead of the perpetrators of environmental risk and harm

Note: The left-to-right arrows between the column heads indicate a presumed pattern of causality in the literature. That is, procedural inequities are seen as determining social-organizational inequities, which then result in disproportionate adverse effects expressed in patterns of geographic inequity. For example, the procedural inequity of undue burden of proof can result in the social-organizational inequity that legitimates projects involving high-risk technologies, which then results in a geographic inequity involving disproportionate exposure to toxics in work, home, and neighborhood.

table 19). This powerful concept led to an extraordinary variety of empirical and theoretical research that has informed the strategies and tactics of the EJM. The contributions of the EJM have always moved beyond a critique of environmental racism toward a diverse social movement for grassroots participatory democracy, economic and social justice, and ecological sustainability.[37]

In 1987, the United Church of Christ Commission for Racial Justice published its landmark study, *Toxic Wastes and Race*. This study documented the disproportionate siting of unregulated toxic waste dumps in low-income communities of color. It cited 1983 government data showing that three of every four toxic waste sites in the United States were located in low-income communities of color. In addition, it documented that 75 percent of Latinas/os in southwestern states were drinking pesticide-tainted water.[38] Early environmental justice research focused on problems related to disproportionate impacts, the fact that communities of color were more likely to be harmed by environmental risks. Another major approach focused on the politics of the **environmental impact statement (EIS)** and the definition, quantification, and distribution of environmental risks.

A key event in the history of the EJM was the First National People of Color Environmental Leadership Summit held in Washington, DC. The delegates at the summit adopted the Principles of Environmental Justice on October 27, 1991.[39] These principles offered a radical new vision of environmental issues and called for a mass social movement for grassroots **ecological democracy** (see topic highlight 3).

The delegates at the first Environmental Leadership Summit rejected the idea of establishing one all-encompassing national organization, instead opting for a network model. Richard Moore of the Southwest Network for Environmental and Economic Justice (SNEEJ) coined the phrase "building a net that works" to explain this strategic choice. At the time of the first Environmental Leadership Summit, the structure of the EJM consisted of six regional networks of grassroots organizations that either participated in the organization of the 1991 summit or were founded shortly thereafter: the Asian Pacific Environmental Network (APEN), the Farm Worker Network for Economic and Environmental Justice (FNEEJ), the Indigenous Environmental Network (IEN), the Northeast Environmental Justice Network (NEJN), the Southern Organizing Committee for Social Justice (SOC), and SNEEJ.

PREAMBLE

We the people of color, gathered together at this multinational People of Color Environmental Leadership Summit, to begin to build a national and international movement of all peoples of color to fight the destruction and taking of our lands and communities, do hereby re-establish our spiritual interdependence to the sacredness of our Mother Earth; to respect and celebrate each of our cultures, languages and beliefs about the natural world and our roles in healing ourselves; to insure environmental justice; to promote economic alternatives which would contribute to environmentally safe livelihoods; and to secure our political, economic, and cultural liberation that has been denied for over 500 years of colonization and oppression, resulting in the poisoning of our communities and land and the genocide of our peoples, do affirm and adopt these Principles of Environmental Justice:

1. **Environmental justice** affirms the sacredness of Mother Earth, ecological unity and the interdependence of all species, and the right to be free from ecological destruction.
2. **Environmental justice** demands that public policy be based on mutual respect and justice for all peoples, free from any form of discrimination or bias.
3. **Environmental justice** mandates the right to ethical, balanced, and responsible uses of land and renewable resources in the interest of a sustainable planet for humans and other living things.
4. **Environmental justice** calls for universal protection from nuclear testing, extraction, production, and disposal of toxic/hazardous wastes and poisons and nuclear testing that threaten the fundamental right to clean air, land, water, and food.
5. **Environmental justice** affirms the fundamental right to political, economic, and cultural and environmental self-determination of all peoples.

6. **Environmental justice** demands the cessation of the production of all toxins, hazardous wastes, and radioactive materials, and that all past and current producers be held strictly accountable to the people for detoxification and containment at the point of production.

7. **Environmental justice** demands the right to participate as equal partners at every level of decision-making including needs assessment, planning, implementation, enforcement, and evaluation.

8. **Environmental justice** affirms the right of all workers to a safe and healthy work environment, without being forced to choose between an unsafe livelihood and unemployment. It also affirms the right of those who work at home to be free from environmental hazards.

9. **Environmental justice** protects the rights of victims of environmental injustice to receive full compensation and reparations for damages as well as quality health care.

10. **Environmental justice** considers governmental acts of environmental injustice a violation of international law, the Universal Declaration on Human Rights, and the United Nations Convention on Genocide.

11. **Environmental justice** must recognize a special legal and natural relationship of Native Peoples to the U.S. government through treaties, agreements, compacts, and covenants affirming sovereignty and self-determination.

12. **Environmental justice** affirms the need for urban and rural ecological policies to clean up and rebuild our cities and rural areas in balance with nature, honoring the cultural integrity of all our communities, and providing fair access to all to the full range of resources.

13. **Environmental justice** calls for strict enforcement of principles of informed consent, and a halt to the testing of experimental reproductive and medical procedures and vaccinations on people of color.

14. **Environmental justice** opposes the destructive operations of multinational corporations.

15. **Environmental justice** opposes military occupation, repression and exploitation of lands, peoples and cultures, and other life forms.

16. **Environmental justice** calls for the education of present and future generations which emphasizes social and environmental issues, based on our experience and an appreciation of our diverse cultural perspectives.

17. **Environmental justice** requires that we, as individuals, make personal and consumer choices to consume as little of Mother Earth's resources and to produce as little waste as possible; and make the conscious decision to challenge and reprioritize our lifestyles to insure the health of the natural world for present and future generations.

Adopted today, October 27, 1991, in Washington, DC ■

The EJM generated intense political pressure that resulted in **Executive Order 12898,** signed by President Bill Clinton on February 11, 1994. Clinton's historic order established the guidelines for implementation of a federal environmental justice policy. The executive order mandated that "each Federal agency shall make achieving environmental justice part of its mission by identifying and addressing, as appropriate, disproportionately high and adverse human health or environmental effects of its programs, policies, and activities on minority populations and low-income populations in the United States and its territories and possessions."[40] By August 1994, the Clinton administration had appointed the National Environmental Justice Advisory Committee (NEJAC), a signal of the influence of the EJM in national politics.

If the underlying cause of ecological and social problems was environmental racism, as EJM activists assert, presumably the solution lay in achieving **environmental equity,** meaning that environmental protection would be extended equally to all social groups without race or class discrimination. The implementation of 12898 and the establishment of NEJAC were capstone achievements of the struggle for environmental equity. Many EJM theorists and activists rejected the environmental equity model, however, because it fell short of fully embracing the Principles of

Environmental Justice, especially the sixth principle, which calls for "the cessation of the production of all toxins, hazardous wastes, and radioactive materials, and . . . detoxification and containment at the point of production." The EPA has embraced the equitable distribution of environmental risks under a liberal reformist model that does not reduce the use of high-risk and destructive technologies or challenge the regulatory power structure embedded in a corporate-dominated system.[41]

The equity-based model accords primacy to scientific experts. It reinforces a cult of expertise dominated by quantitative analysis and promotes adherence to market-dominated values.[42] The bottom line of this model is the rationale that contamination and degradation are inescapable consequences of the capitalist system. The best one can do is to mitigate their effects and minimize the risks they pose. To paraphrase Ynestra King, We all get the same toxins in our piece of the same rotten carcinogenic pie.[43]

The Principles of Environmental Justice propose a distinctly more radical ethic of containment and prevention; namely, cessation of toxicant production and detoxification at the point of production. Any amount of risk, no matter how minimal, is unacceptable. The Principles of Environmental Justice call for the radical transformation of capitalist technology and support the autonomy of local communities against the tyranny of the global market system.[44]

Some scholar-activists are critical of the EJM's overemphasis on the literature and politics of toxicity. Environmental racism often involves disparate exposure to toxic and hazardous wastes. However, the deterioration of home, work, and neighborhood environments encompasses a broader range of economic and political threats to ecological and community integrity. Some have cautioned against the focus on toxicity, urging environmental justice scholars and activists to acknowledge that forces such as gentrification, tourism, second home and resort development, deforestation, and the loss of communal lands and water rights are additional factors in the ravaging of many communities of color.[45]

Environmental justice research has not focused sufficient attention on the intersections of race, class, gender, and other differences in ecological politics. This is especially true for the study of the EJM itself: the history and politics of ideologies and identities, approaches to resource mobilization, organizational forms, and terrains of struggle. Laura Pulido provides clues to this complexity in a study of the "people of color identity" in the EJM. She found that "[d]espite scholars' recent emphasis on the fragmentary nature of identity, few have documented the process of identity formation among successful broad-based contemporary social movements."[46] Radical critics have tended to disparage politics based on identity because they view it as the source of political fragmentation of the left in the period since the 1960s.[47] Pulido demonstrates how the EJM used the ostensibly unitary identity of people of color to build one of the most successful, broad-based social movements in recent American history.[48]

■ Concluding Thoughts

The EJM challenged the traditional Anglo-American dichotomy between nature and culture, wilderness and civilization.[49] The movement called for equity across generations, among different human groups and cultures, and in human relations with other species. It shifted the discourse on ecological protection beyond the limits of the dominant models of **natural resource conservation** and wilderness preservation. Under the EJM model, the environment became the place where humans live, work, play, and worship. This simple definition allowed the EJM to provoke changes in the politics of environmental regulation and **ecosystem management.** It challenged discriminatory administrative laws and procedures in federal agencies. EJM activists confronted the G10 with evidence of racism and exclusionary politics. While environmental racism persists, communities of color continue robust struggles for grassroots ecological democracy; that is, a society in which environmental protection is extended to everyone and local communities control their own ecological and economic destinies.[50]

■ Discussion Questions

1. Compare the ten major strands of environmentalism in the United States, accounting for the differences in how they define nature and the environment, how they explain the principal causes of environmental degradation, and how they propose to resolve the ecological crisis.

2. Conduct bioregional research and answer the following questions: What are the major rivers in your home place, and where do they originate? Where does your drinking water come from? What are five native plants in your area? Are any of them used for food or medicine? What are the major landforms that define the topography of your locale? What are the native cultures of your area?

What has happened to them? What is the origin of important place-names in your locale? Name a native species (flora or fauna) that is now extinct. What caused its extinction?

3. What is environmental racism? Is race the principal factor determining the experience of environmental problems?

■ Suggested Readings

Bullard, Robert D. 1993. *Confronting Environmental Racism: Voices from the Grassroots.* Boston: South End Press.

———. 1994. *Unequal Protection: Environmental Justice and Communities of Color.* San Francisco: Sierra Club Books.

DeVall, Bill. 1988. *Simple in Means, Rich in Ends: Practicing Deep Ecology.* Salt Lake City: Peregrine Smith.

Gottlieb, Robert. 1993. *Forcing the Spring: The Transformation of the American Environmental Movement.* Washington, DC: Island Press.

Merchant, Carolyn. 1992. *Radical Ecology.* London: Routledge.

■ Notes

1. C. Merchant, *Radical Ecology: The Search for a Livable World* (London: Routledge, 1992); R. Gottlieb, *Forcing the Spring: The Transformation of the American Environmental Movement* (San Francisco: Sierra Club Books, 1993).

2. A. Naess, "The Shallow and the Deep, Long-Range Ecology Movement: A Summary," *Inquiry* 16: 95–100. Bill DeVall and George Sessions popularized Naess's ideas in the United States. See B. DeVall and G. Sessions, *Deep Ecology: Living as if Nature Mattered* (Salt Lake City: Peregrine Smith Books, 1985); B. DeVall, *Simple in Means, Rich in Ends: Practicing Deep Ecology* (Salt Lake City: Peregrine Smith Books, 1988). For a critique, see G. Bradford, *How Deep Is Deep Ecology?* (Ojai, CA: Times Change Press, 1989) and P. F. Cramer, *Deep Environmental Politics: The Role of Radical Environmentalism in Crafting American Environmental Policy* (New York: Praeger, 1998). On biocentrism, see Naess, "Shallow and the Deep," 95–96; also see Merchant, *Radical Ecology,* 86–93.

3. See E. Abbey, *The Monkey Wrench Gang* (New York: Avon Books, 1975); D. Bevington, "Earth First! in Northern California: An Interview with Jodi Bari," in *The Struggle for Ecological Democracy: Environmental Justice Movements in the United States,* ed. D. Faber (New York: Guilford Press, 1998), 248–71; S. Chase, ed., *Defending the Earth: A Dialogue between Murray Bookchin and Dave Foreman* (Boston: South End Press, 1991); J. Davis, ed., *The Earth First! Reader: Ten Years of Radical Environmentalism* (Salt Lake City: Peregrine Smith Books, 1991).

4. Quotations from R. Scarce, *Eco-Warriors: Understanding the Radical Environmen-*

tal Movement (Chicago: Noble Press, 1990), 66; also see C. Manes, *Green Rage: Radical Environmentalism and the Unmaking of Civilization* (Boston: Little, Brown and Co., 1990), 74; D. Foreman and H. Wolke, *The Big Outside: A Descriptive Inventory of the Big Wilderness Areas of the United States* (Nevada City, CA: Harmony Books, 1992).

5. D. G. Peña, ed., *Chicano Culture, Ecology, Politics: Subversive Kin* (Tucson: University of Arizona Press, 1998), 30–31. The Foreman-Abbey group was judged too anti-labor, anti-left, and macho by Jodi Bari, who envisioned a progressive mix of radical environmentalism and new left (pro-labor, pro–civil rights) philosophies. See U. Heider, *Anarchism: Left, Right, and Green* (San Francisco: City Lights Books, 1994), 48–53. Abbey quotations from E. Abbey, "Immigration and Liberal Taboos," in *One Life at a Time, Please* (New York: Henry Holt, 1988).

6. M. Bookchin, "The Concept of Social Ecology," in *Ecology: Key Concepts in Critical Theory,* ed. C. Merchant (Atlantic Highlands, NJ: Humanities Press, 1994), 160; M. Bookchin, *The Modern Crisis* (Philadelphia: New Society Publishers, 1986), 50, 59, 55; see also pp. 66–67.

7. Bookchin, *Modern Crisis,* 23, 67.

8. See J. Biehl, *The Politics of Social Ecology: Libertarian Municipalism* (Montreal: Black Rose Books, 1998), 53–62, 101–10.

9. Ibid., 114–18.

10. Heider, *Anarchism,* 65; M. Feinstein, *Green Party Members Holding Elected Office in the United States, 2000,* available online from http://www.feinstein.org/greenparty/electeds.html.

11. J. A. Hernández, *Mutual Aid for Survival: The Case of the Mexican American* (Melbourne, FL: Krieger Publishing, 1983); G. A. Hicks and D. G. Peña, "Community Acequias in Colorado's Rio Culebra Watershed: A Customary Commons in the Domain of Prior Appropriation," *University of Colorado Law Review* 74: 387–486.

12. F. d'Eaubonne, *La Féminisme ou la Mort* (Paris: Horay, 1974); for English excerpts, see F. d'Eaubonne, "The Time for Ecofeminism," in Merchant, *Ecology,* 174–97. For U.S. ecofeminism, see I. Diamond and G. Orenstein, eds., *Reweaving the World: The Emergence of Ecofeminism* (San Francisco: Sierra Club Books, 1990); J. Plant, ed., *Healing the Wounds: The Promise of Ecofeminism* (Philadelphia: New Society Publishers, 1989); G. Kirk, "Ecofeminism and Chicano Environmental Struggles: Bridges across Gender and Race," in *Chicano Culture, Ecology, Politics,* 177–200.

13. Merchant, *Radical Ecology,* 183–210, 193–96; A. Salleh, *Ecofeminism as Politics: Nature, Marx, and the Postmodern* (London: Zed Books, 1997). J. Biehl, *Rethinking Ecofeminist Politics* (Boston: South End Press, 1991); K. J. Warren, ed., *Ecofeminism: Women, Culture, Nature* (Bloomington: Indiana University Press, 1997); M. E. Zimmerman, *Contesting Earth's Future: Radical Ecology and Postmodernism* (Berkeley: University of California Press, 1994).

14. Salleh, *Ecofeminism as Politics,* 103.

15. While social ecofeminists agree that women are cultural and biological beings, they reject the notion that this somehow places them closer to nature. Men are also sensuous, embodied, and socially located beings. Women and men are thus equally capable of nurturing relationships with the earth. See E. Carlassare, "Essentialism in Ecofeminist Discourse," in Merchant, *Ecology,* 220–34; and T. Doyle and D. McEachern, *Environment and Politics* (London: Routledge, 1998), 51–54.

16. Salleh, *Ecofeminism as Politics,* 155; quotation from D. Pepper, *Eco-socialism: From Deep Ecology to Social Justice* (London: Routledge, 1993), 61.

17. Salleh, *Ecofeminism as Politics,* 17–32; Kirk, "Ecofeminism and Chicano Environmental Struggles."

18. See D. E. Taylor, "Women of Color, Environmental Justice, and Ecofeminism," in *Ecofeminism: Women, Nature, Culture,* ed. K. J. Warren, 38–81; quotation on p. 69.

19. M. Davis, "Philosophy Meets Practice: A Critique of Ecofeminism through the Voices of Three Chicana Activists," in Peña, *Chicano Culture, Ecology, Politics,* 201–31.

20. A. Hurtado, "Relating to Privilege: Seduction and Rejection in the Subordination of White Women and Women of Color, *Signs* 14 (1989): 833–55; also see Davis, "Philosophy Meets Practice," 216–17.

21. K. Marx, *Das Capital,* vol. 1 (New York: Vintage Books, 1977). The quotations are from p. 4 of J. O'Connor, "The Second Contradiction of Capitalism: Causes and Consequences," *Center for Ecological Socialism Pamphlet* 1 (1991): 1–10. For an edited collection of works by Marx and Engels, see R. C. Tucker, ed., *The Marx-Engels Reader* (New York: W. W. Norton, 1978). Also see H. Cleaver, *Reading Capital Politically* (Austin: University of Texas Press, 1979).

22. O'Connor, "Second Contradiction of Capitalism," 4–5.

23. J. O'Connor, "Socialism and Ecology," in Merchant, *Ecology,* 152–72; quotation from Merchant, *Radical Ecology,* 149.

24. W. Contreras Sheasby, "Growing the Red/Green Paradigm: Ecological Socialism in Root and Branch," *Synthesis/Regeneration* 22 (Spring 2000), available online at http://www.greens.org/s-r/22/22-14. Merchant, *Radical Ecology,* 167–68, 235–40.

25. A. Szasz, *Ecopopulism: Toxic Waste and the Movement for Environmental Justice* (Minneapolis: University of Minnesota Press, 1994); L. Pulido, *Environmentalism and Economic Justice: Two Chicano Struggles in the Southwest* (Tucson: University of Arizona Press, 1996).

26. See R. F. Dassman, *The Conservation Alternative* (New York: Wiley, 1975), and *Environmental Conservation* (Somerset: Wiley, 1984); G. Snyder, *Turtle Island* (New York: New Directions Books, 1974), and *A Place in Space: Ethics, Aesthetics, and Watersheds* (Washington, DC: Counterpoint Press, 1995); DeVall, *Simple in Means, Rich in Ends,* 58–64; K. Sale, *Dwellers in the Land: The Bioregional Vision* (San Francisco: Sierra Club Books, 1987). For commentary, see Peña, *Chicano Culture, Ecology, Politics,* 28–37.

27. Sale, *Dwellers in the Land.*

28. R. Dassmann and P. Berg, "Reinhabiting California," *The Ecologist* 7 (1977): 399–401; V. Andruss, C. Plant, J. Plant, and E. Wright, eds., *Home! A Bioregional Reader* (Philadelphia: New Society Publishers, 1990); P. Berg, ed., *Reinhabiting a Separate Country: A Bioregional Anthology of Northern California* (San Francisco: Planet Drum Foundation, 1978).

29. D. Aberley, "Interpreting Bioregionalism," in *Bioregionalism,* ed. M. V. McGinnis (London: Routledge, 1999), 26–27.

30. Quotation from ibid., 2. Colorado Acequia Association, *Statement of Principles* (San Luis, Colorado, 1999). Copy of organizational brochure in the author's collection; also see D. G. Peña, "Identity, Place, and Communities of Resistance" in *Just Sustainabilities: Environmental Justice in an Unequal World,* ed. J. Agyeman, R. D. Bullard, and B. Evans (London: Earthscan; Cambridge: MIT Press, 2003).

31. Penny Newman and Cora Tucker also played major roles in the early antitoxics movement; see Gottlieb, *Forcing the Spring,* 207–34. L. Gibbs, "Action from Tragedy," in "Feminism and Ecology," special issue, *Heresies* 13 (1981); also see Merchant, *Radical Ecology,* 162–63.

32. G. Cohen and J. O'Connor, eds., *Fighting Toxics: A Manual for Protecting Your Family, Community, and Workplace* (Washington, DC: Island Press, 1990). On kitchen table science, see J. Seager, *Earth Follies: Coming to Feminist Terms with the Global Environmental Crisis* (London: Routledge, 1993), 194–98; also see Kirk, "Ecofeminism and Chicano Environmental Activism," 182, 190–91; L. Nelson, "The Place of Women in Polluted Places," in Diamond and Orenstein, *Reweaving the World,* 172–87.

33. Kirk, "Ecofeminism and Chicano Environmental Activism," 162.

34. For the "Citizens' Bill of Rights," see Merchant, *Radical Ecology,* 163; on the Superfund Act, see G. Cohen, introduction to *Fighting Toxics,* 7.

35. D. E. Taylor, "The Rise of the Environmental Justice Paradigm: Injustice Framing and the Social Construction of Environmental Discourses," *American Behavioral Scientist* 43, no. 4 (2000): 508–80.

36. B. F. Chavis Jr., foreword to *Confronting Environmental Racism: Voices from the Grassroots,* ed. R. D. Bullard (Boston: South End Press, 1993), 3.

37. For EJM perspectives on sustainable development, see D. G. Peña, "The Scope of Latino/a Environmental Studies," *Latino Studies* 1 (March 2003): 47–78; and Agyeman, Bullard, and Evans, *Just Sustainabilities.*

38. Lee, *Toxic Wastes and Race* (New York: United Church of Christ, Commission for Racial Justice, 1987); GAO, *Siting of Hazardous Waste Facilities and Their Correlation with the Racial and Economic Status of Surrounding Communities* (Washington, DC: GPO, 1983); Lee, "Beyond Toxic Wastes and Race," in Bullard, *Confronting Environmental Racism,* 41–52.

39. C. Lee, ed., *Proceedings: The First National People of Color Environmental Leader-*

ship Summit (New York: United Church of Christ, Commission for Racial Justice, 1992); also see the documentary film *Documentary Highlights of the First People of Color Environmental Leadership Summit* (New York: United Church of Christ, Commission for Racial Justice, 1991).

40. See the EPA's Web site at http://www.epa.gov/swerosps/ej/html-doc/execordr .htm for the original text of Executive Order 12898; the quotation is on p. 1. For the EPA's programmatic response to Executive Order 12898, see Office of Environmental Justice, Environmental Protection Agency, *Environmental Justice Strategy: Executive Order 12898* (Washington, DC: GPO, 1995); available online at the URL cited above.

41. The EPA defines environmental equity as "the [equitable] distribution of environmental risks across population groups." See EPA, *Environmental Equity: Reducing Risk for All Communities,* vol. 1, *Workgroup Report to the Administrator* (Washington, DC: GPO, 1992), 1.

42. P. Almeida, "The Network for Environmental and Economic Justice in the Southwest: An Interview with Richard Moore," in Faber, *Struggle for Ecological Democracy,* 159–87.

43. D. G. Peña and J. C. Gallegos, "Local Knowledge and Collaborative Environmental Action Research," in *Building Community: Social Science in Action,* ed. P. Nyden, A. Figert, M. Shibley, and D. Burrows (Thousand Oaks, CA: Pine Forge Press, 1997), 85–91. Ynestra King's comments in Kirk, "Ecofeminism and Chicano Environmental Struggles," 191.

44. This critique of the EPA policy was evident at a meeting of EJM activists sponsored by the Ford Foundation in February 1998 in Santa Fe, New Mexico as part of the Natural Assets Project. Also see D. Faber, "The Struggle for Ecological Democracy and Environmental Justice," and "The Political Ecology of American Capitalism: New Challenges for the Environmental Justice Movement," in Faber, *Struggle for Ecological Democracy,* 1–59; D. G. Peña, "Autonomy, Equity, and Environmental Justice" (paper prepared for the Provost's Lecture Series on Race, Poverty, and the Environment, Brown University, Providence, RI, April 2003).

45. D. G. Peña as quoted in J. Adamson and R. Stein, "Environmental Justice: A Roundtable Discussion," *Interdisciplinary Studies in Literature and Environment* 7: 155–70;. D. G. Peña, "Chicanos and Environmental Justice" (paper presented at the National Association for Chicano Studies, Albuquerque, New Mexico, April 1990).

46. Taylor, "Women of Color;" L. Pulido, "Development of the People of Color Identity in the Environmental Justice Movement of the Southwestern United States," *Socialist Review* 26, no. 3–4 (1996): 145–80; quotation on p. 146.

47. A. Ross, *Universal Abandon? The Politics of Postmodernism* (Minneapolis: University of Minnesota Press, 1988); J. Handler, "Postmodernism, Protest, and the New Social Movements," *Law and Society Review* 26 (1992): 697–731; for a critique of this

view, see Pulido, *Environmentalism and Economic Justice,* 207–11, and "People of Color Identity," 145–50.

48. Peña, "Identity, Place, and Communities of Resistance," and "Scope of Latino/a Environmental Studies."

49. D. G. Peña, "The 'Brown' and the 'Green': Chicanos and Environmental Politics in the Upper Rio Grande," *Capitalism, Nature, Socialism* 3 (1992): 79–103.

50. See Faber, *Struggle for Ecological Democracy.*

Ecological Politics and the Mexican-Origin People, 1980-2002

The environment is the place where we live, work, play, and worship.
—Teresa Leal (2001)

Is the Earth local?
—Joseph C. Gallegos (2001)

Environmental justice has been described as the environmentalism of everyday life.[1] This concept of the environment is a compelling alternative to mainstream concepts of nature as natural resource, wilderness, or functioning **ecosystem.** In this chapter I focus on the period since the early 1980s, a time of vital participation by **Mexican-origin people** in the **environmental justice movement (EJM).** A widely spun web of interconnected neighborhood associations, labor groups, civil rights organizations, and local communities is linked through regional and multinational networks. For example, the multiracial SNEEJ includes local grassroots affiliates from more than a hundred different communities in Arizona, California, New Mexico, Colorado, Texas, and Mexico.

Environmental justice struggles are part of the history of Mexican American **social movements.** I present keystone cases to illustrate the variety of ideologies, organizational forms, and terrains of struggle within the EJM. Farmworkers, factory workers, land grant heirs, **acequia** farmers, urban **barrio** residents, and rural **colonia** residents are the social forces underlying this movement. In addition, a significant Mexican American middle class has emerged, bringing to the movement professionals in fields such as law, science and engineering, business, and education.[2] Mexican-origin communities have participated in protests against the **North American Free Trade Agreement (NAFTA,)** the **World Trade Organization (WTO),** and **globalization** since the 1990s. Table 20 outlines the principal **Chicana/o** environmental justice clusters and terrains of struggle.[3]

Table 20 Social groups and terrains of struggle in the Chicana/o environmental justice movement

SOCIAL GROUP OR SECTOR	TERRAINS OF STRUGGLE

Farmworkers	1. Workplace health and safety hazards
	  ■ Pesticides and other toxic substances
	  ■ Short hoe use
	  ■ Lack of potable water
	2. Worker control of production to manage environmental risks
	3. Worker-owned cooperatives
	4. Revival of collective bargaining contracts
	5. Emergent biotechnologies and environmental risk (e.g., genetically engineered crops, genetically engineered organisms (GEOs), and increased exposure to herbicides)
	6. Farmworker housing, education, and medical care
	7. Malnutrition

Factory workers	1. Workplace health and safety hazards
	  ■ Exposure to toxic chemicals and fumes
	  ■ Assembly line speed-up
	  ■ Inadequate ventilation
	  ■ Poor ergonomic design of work environments and hazardous machines
	  ■ Sexual/sexist harassment
	2. Violence against labor organizers
	3. Violence against maquila workers (serial/mass murders)
	4. Worker control of production to manage environmental risks
	5. Worker-owned cooperatives
	6. Access to medical care

Land grant communities	1. Restoration of common lands of Spanish and Mexican mercedes 2. Restoration of historic use rights of land grant heirs 3. Citizen participation and co-management of lands with USFS, BLM 4. Displacement by gentrification and subdivisions 5. Environmental and social effects of military installations (Los Alamos National Lab) on land grants
Acequia farmers	1. Protection of water rights (establishment of water trusts) 2. Legitimation of acequia customary law 3. Watershed protection and restoration (from damage by logging, mining, subdividing) 4. Gentrification and the preservation of farmland, **cultural landscapes**, and open space (establishment of land trusts)

	5. Cooperative economic development
	6. Sustainable agriculture (organic certification, agroecology)
	7. Community-supported agriculture for local food security
Urban barrio residents	1. Cleanup of hazardous waste sites, solid waste dumps, incinerators
	2. Elimination of lead and other toxic substances in homes
	3. Cleanup of toxic plumes in groundwater sources of drinking water
	4. Displacement of homes and businesses by freeway alignments and other urban infrastructure
	5. Community-based public health
	6. Community-owned economic development alternatives
	7. Reclamation of urban common space
	8. Social and environmental effects of industrial parks
	9. Housing & urban habitat projects
	10. Gentrification and affordable housing
	11. Transit racism
	12. Recycling
	13. Urban horticulture
Rural colonia residents	1. Access to housing
	2. Lack of potable water
	3. Productive recycling
	4. Sanitation systems
	5. Contaminated soils in residential lots
	6. Lack of access to health care
Overlapping groups	1. Politics and science of EIS
	2. Environmental racism and EPA accountability
	3. Environmental racism in the Group of Ten
	4. Military installations in rural and urban communities
	■ Pollution of groundwater sources of drinking water
	■ Soil contamination in residential areas
	■ Threats to local quality of life
	■ Loss of historic settlement areas
	■ Economic development impacts
	5. Urban horticulture and local food security
	6. GEOs; No Patents on Life campaign
	7. WTO, globalization
	8. Transborder and binational environmental degradation and management (maquilas, NAFTA, transboundary pollution)
	9. Violence against workers and community activists
	10. Zapatistas and indigenous autonomy
	11. Just sustainability and just transition campaigns

Nos Matan en Cosechas Tóxicas: Farmworkers and the Environment

There are more than four million farmworkers in the United States today, of which a hundred thousand are minor children. At least two-thirds of these workers are immigrants, and 80 percent of the immigrants are from Mexico.[4] "They are killing us in toxic harvests" is a statement heard among farmworker organizers in reference to the environmental hazards these four million people face.

Farmworkers launched the first anti-pesticide campaign in the mid-1960s, envisioning democratic change through the power of collective bargaining. They fought for worker control of production as the basis for attaining environmental and economic justice. Their vision of environmental and economic justice endures in contemporary struggles. Baldemar Velasquez of the Farm Labor Organizing Committee (FLOC) emphasizes the link between labor rights and environmental protection: "We are always using labor agreements to challenge problems, violations of the law, environmental issues like pesticides, and conditions in labor camps." The struggles of farmworkers extend beyond resisting **environmental racism** in working and living conditions to embrace the struggle for **sustainable** and equitable agriculture.[5]

Latina/o immigrants account for a disproportionate number of workplace fatalities and injuries. The workplace risks they face are compounded by federal laws that exempt small businesses from pesticide regulations and the provision of basic needs like safe drinking water and sanitary latrines.[6] California data on the incidence of pesticide-related illnesses and fatalities show a steady increase during the 1990s over previous decades. The death rate among farmworkers in 1996 was 20.9 per 100,000 workers compared to an average for all industries of 3.9 per 100,000 workers. State laws are inadequate to protect farmworkers from pesticide exposure. For example, California has legal penalties for violation of exposure rules or failure to provide workers with training and safety equipment. Yet in more than half of reported incidents, growers are not fined, instead being served with meaningless notices of violation.[7] Enforcement is further limited by budget cuts that have reduced the number of pesticide safety inspectors.

Pesticide residues in vegetables and fruits have been a major concern for environmentalists, who sought to ban the more dangerous substances. As a result, by the late 1970s and early 1980s, agribusiness was shifting from hydrocarbon to organophosphate pesticides, which have a shorter half-life. By the time produce reaches the consumer, residues are well below levels considered unsafe under federal laws. Compared to the older hydrocarbon pesticides, however, organophosphates are hundreds or even thousands of times more acutely toxic at the point of production. What may be safer for consumers is more dangerous to farmworkers and wildlife who face immediate exposure in the fields.[8]

 ### ¿Donde Están?
Farmworker Health Care and Housing

Farmworkers have an average life expectancy of forty-nine years. Rates for infectious and chronic diseases, malnutrition, and infant and maternal mortality by far exceed U.S. averages and are closer to patterns in Third World nations. The EPA receives at least 300,000 reports of pesticide poisoning each year, far less than the actual number. A number of chronic illnesses correlated with pesticide exposure are common in farmworker populations. Pesticide-related health problems are compounded by the conditions of rural poverty, including lack of access to medical care, substandard housing, and malnutrition.[9] Child labor is persistent, and conditions in labor camp housing are evidence of grower and regulatory agency mistreatment of farmworkers. Crowded and unsanitary conditions in labor camps across the country pose a health hazard. Farmworkers and their families are forced to live in one-room shacks without heating, running water, or toilet facilities. In California's Imperial Valley, farmworkers are living in caves or holes dug out of cliffs. For roofing they use tattered plastic tarps and scrap tin held in place with rocks, dirt, or discarded tires.[10]

Farmworkers and Biotechnology

Genetically altered foods pose concerns regarding consumer food safety and farmworker health and safety. Commercial agricultural biotechnology is of concern to farmworkers because of the potential for sustained exposure to toxicants. One type of agricultural biotechnology involves genetically engineered organisms (GEOs), also known as transgenic crops. These crops are genetically altered to survive higher chemical treatment

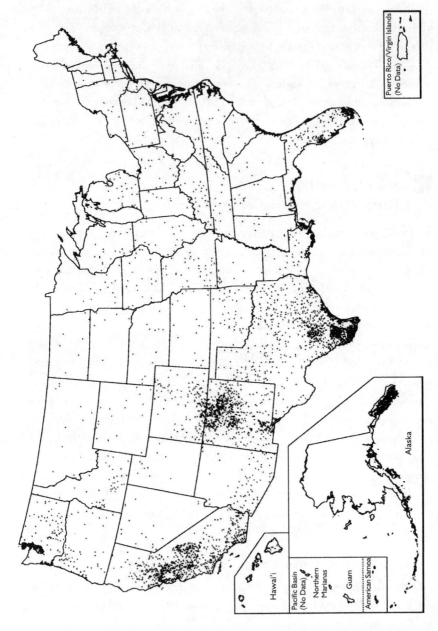

■ Map 2. Distribution of U.S. Latina/o farms, 1992; one dot = five Spanish-origin farms

Puerto Rico/Virgin Islands
(No Data)

protocols (especially herbicide resistance). Farmworkers will bear the burden of toxic exposure in fields planted with herbicide-resistant GEOs.[11]

Farmworker Environmental Justice Organizations

The Farm Worker Network integrates environmental issues under the rubric of a demand for **workplace democracy** and worker control of production.[12] FLOC has made quality-of-life issues such as adequate housing, nutrition, and health care an integral part of a strategy based on fair trade collective bargaining agreements that promote equitable and nonexploitative relations between consumers in the First World and producers in the Third World.[13] Thus, the environmentalism of farmworkers does not divide the environment into disembodied parts like nature, workplace, and home. Environmental problems are inseparable from working and living conditions.

Organizing campaigns for sustainable agriculture have existed since the 1970s. Worker-owned cooperatives have been established in California, Texas, New Mexico, Colorado, and other states. During the 1970s and 1980s, the UFW promoted strawberry cooperatives in California. These early efforts proved largely unsuccessful, but new cooperatives are being established every year. As the number of white-owned family farms continues to decrease, the number of Latina/o farms is increasing at a dramatic pace. Between 1987 and 1997, the number of Latina/o-owned and -operated farms increased by more than 40 percent.[14] Latina/o farmers are located in every state but 72 percent are in five states: California, Colorado, Florida, New Mexico, and Texas (see map 2). Together they control more than ten million acres of land. About 80 percent are of Mexican origin, and many are former migratory farmworkers.

▪ Nos Matan en Malditas Fábricas: Factory Workers and the Environment

I once heard a **maquiladora** worker in Juárez explain that the managers "kill us in wretched factories." She was referring to the hundreds of workers killed every year in factories on both sides of the border. Occupational segregation by race and gender affects workers' experiences with workplace **environmental risks.** Research shows that Mexican American and other workers of color are "disproportionately concentrated in occupations and industries that pose greater risks of work-related injuries, unsafe working conditions, and environmental hazards."[15]

Dying on the Job: Workplace Health and Safety

Studies have documented violation of health and safety standards in unregulated industries. Work-related injuries, mutilations, and deaths are higher in manufacturing operations with large concentrations of workers of color. Injuries and deaths are correlated with environmental racism in the internal organization of such workplaces. Inside factories, the division of labor relegates Mexican-origin workers to low-paying, high-risk jobs. Health and safety hazards include exposure to toxic chemicals and fumes, assembly line speedup, inadequate ventilation, bad lighting, poor ergonomic design of tools and workstations, and hazardous machinery. Workers face persistent racial and sexual harassment, domestic violence, rape, and—in Juárez—hundreds of unsolved serial murders. Microelectronics assembly workers are exposed to chemicals associated with a wide variety of diseases including cancer, cardiovascular illness, and respiratory or reproductive system disorders.[16]

Resisting Environmental Racism in the Workplace

Environmental justice groups like SNEEJ have joined with labor unions and independent worker groups to organize against workplace environmental racism. Worker struggles against environmental racism in the microelectronics and semiconductor industries are widespread on both sides of the border. The case of GTE Lenkurt in Albuquerque illustrates the problems facing workers. In 1987, this company reached a $2.5 million settlement with workers as compensation for a long history of workplace toxics contamination. Assembly operations were subsequently relocated to Juárez, Mexico. At least twenty-five former workers have died from work-related illnesses since the plant relocation.[17]

Workers have organized campaigns to address the international dimensions of environmental racism in the workplace. One such case is the Echlin Corporation, a manufacturer of brake pads with plants in Irvine, California, and Mexico City. Chicana/o workers with the United Electrical Workers local union launched a binational campaign to help Mexican workers improve working conditions. They supported rank-and-file struggles for an independent union. The corporation fired pro-union workers on both sides of the border, closed the U.S. plant, and entirely relocated to Mexico. The struggle in Mexico continues despite the firing and blacklisting of workers.[18]

Fuerza Unida illustrates the importance of the fight against the geopolitical mobility of corporate capital. Fuerza Unida was established in 1990 when workers at Levi Strauss in San Antonio organized an independent union to fight plant closings and layoffs. More than ten thousand workers and fifty-eight plants were affected by the relocation of production to Costa Rica and Mexico. Workers were pressured to make wage concessions or face the risk of further plant relocations. Fuerza Unida was a precursor of the protests against NAFTA, the **World Trade Organization (WTO),** and globalization—all of which increase corporate mobility in the global flows of production and undermine local worker unions and organizations.[19]

■ Se Robaron Nuestra Tierra Madre: Land Grants and the Environment

"They stole our Mother Earth" is a saying among land grant activists. In the late nineteenth century, Las Gorras Blancas cut barbed-wire fences and dreamed of undivided landscapes. These precursors of the EJM fought for the day when the rightful heirs would reclaim their ancestral **commons.** The resurgence of land grant struggles since the 1980s proves the persistence of this militant memory of place. A strong sense of place and a fierce cultural attachment to the land and water define identities and ecological politics in many land grant communities in the Rio Arriba.[20]

Struggles to Restore Lost Lands

Mexican land grants were lost to unjust **enclosures** driven by the U.S. government's push to establish the national forests after 1891. Additional common and family lands were lost to theft and unethical partitioning by unscrupulous lawyers, land barons, and federal bureaucrats. Of an estimated 35 million acres, only 2.05 million were patented or confirmed. A 2001 General Accounting Office (GAO) report estimates that New Mexico has a total of 152 community land grants, referring to "land grants that set aside common lands for the use of the entire community."[21]

The land grant movement has historically revolved around direct action and legal struggles to restore lost community lands. These grants include areas that are part of the national forest timber and range lands administered by the USFS. Other lost common lands are managed by the BLM and other federal and state land management agencies. Legal restoration of community land grants remains a priority of the movement.

La Compañía Ocho: Co-management of National Forests

Efforts to increase local control (or co-management) of national forest lands have led to bitter clashes with government foresters and environmentalists. An example is the Vallecitos Federal Sustained Yield Unit northwest of Taos, New Mexico. In 1948, the Vallecitos Unit was carved out of a section of the Kit Carson National Forest that was originally part of the common lands of the Vallecitos de Lovato land grant, erroneously rejected by the surveyor general in 1886.[22]

Shortly after the 1967 Tierra Amarilla courthouse raid, the U.S. Congress held hearings on the so-called land grant question. In 1968, the USFS released its Hassell Report on Hispanics and the national forests in northern New Mexico. The report called for modifying policy to support the goals of rural poverty reduction and economic stability of forest-dependent communities. Yet Vallecitos Unit administrators did not pursue these reforms until 1975, when the community established a local advisory committee.[23]

Local forest workers constantly protested the volume of timber cuts as excessive and unsustainable. They also opposed a succession of timber harvest agents for failing to hire local people. In 1985, environmentalists joined local loggers to lobby for restrictions on the volume of proposed timber cuts. The community called on la floresta (the Forest Service) to follow policies favoring small contracts for "thinning and for harvesting of forest products for traditional uses such as firewood and construction materials."[24] Local forest workers established La Compañía Ocho in 1990. In 1997, they received their first timber contract, La Manga timber sale. Forest Guardians initiated an ill-advised conflict with La Compañía Ocho over La Manga. They alleged that the cut would destroy one of the "last old growth" ponderosa stands in northern New Mexico within the historic **habitat** range of the Mexican spotted owl (*Strix occidentalis*). La Compañía Ocho finally won the timber contract, but the conflict deepened divisions between land grant communities and white environmentalists.

Ganados del Valle: Traditional Grazing Rights

Ganados del Valle (livestock of the valley) is a community-owned livestock and artisan weavers cooperative based in Los Ojos, New Mexico. In 1987, Chicana/o sheepherders launched a civil disobedience campaign to protest the lack of access to their traditional grazing range on the enclosed Tierra Amarilla land grant.[25] This grant is enclosed in a checkerboard pattern that includes national forest mixed with state wildlife management areas, private ranches and forests, and tribal reservations.

Ganados is the latest in a long line of grassroots organizations to emerge in the more than one hundred–year struggle over common lands.[26] As is true of other areas of northern New Mexico, poverty is highly racialized in Tierra Amarilla. Laura Pulido has written that the conflict between Ganados and environmentalists over grazing rights on public lands revolved around the struggle to reestablish the "ecological legitimacy" of traditional land-based local **cultures.** The **legitimation** of traditional livestock producers as sustainable stewards of the land was stymied by the arrogance of state wildlife managers and the political influence of environmentalists. These groups viewed the sheepherders through the racialized lens of white middle-class and managerial positions. The "Hispanic" sheepherders were "quaint" but "ignorant" ecological thugs.[27] Ganados responded by romanticizing their relationship to the land and presenting themselves as an endangered local culture.

Restoring the Commons: Land Rights and the Taylor Ranch

Land rights struggles may involve private enclosures of community mercedes. An important example is the Sangre de Cristo Land Grant in the San Luis Valley of south central Colorado. The Taylor family of New Bern, North Carolina, enclosed the 80,000-acre commons in 1960, ending more than one hundred years of local use and access under **customary law.** The heirs filed suit in 1981 to restore their historic use rights to the commons in *Rael v. Taylor*.[28]

Between 1991 and 1998 the courts repeatedly ruled against plaintiffs' claims of usufruct (that is, use) rights to the common lands possessed by the Taylor family. In a dramatic turn of events, the Colorado Supreme Court on June 24, 2002, issued its third opinion on the case, restoring some of the plaintiffs' historic use rights. Settlement is complicated by the recent sale of the Taylor Ranch to Lou Pai, a billionaire and former chief executive officer of Enron Energy Services Corporation.[29]

Between 1995 and 2000, massive industrial-scale logging devastated the subalpine and montane forests of the Taylor Ranch. The logging harvested an estimated 210 million board feet on the 34,000 acres of land stocked with merchantable timber. Timber operations were met by an intense anti-

■ 12. Anti-logging protestors, La Sierra, San Luis Valley, Colorado. These protestors are on a road leading into the Taylor Ranch, the enclosed common lands of the Sangre de Cristo Land Grant in the San Luis Valley of south central Colorado. Local protests against logging started in June 1995 and continued for five years. The unique coalition of protestors included acequia farmers and ranchers, land-rights activists, environmental justice organizers, and radical environmentalists from Earth First!, Greenpeace–Boulder, Ancient Forest Rescue, and other groups. Notice the young woman (bottom right) holding a sign that reads, Sin agua no hay vida, "Without water there is no life."

logging campaign, which the *New York Times* characterized as the "hottest environmental dispute in the southern Rockies." This anti-logging campaign is significant in the history of American environmentalism because it marks the first multiethnic coalition of traditional farmers and ranchers, land grant activists, environmental justice organizers, and radical environmentalists. More than a hundred protestors were arrested, including local women and children participating in logging road blockades and lockdowns (see figure 12).[30]

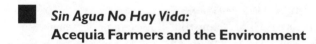

Sin Agua No Hay Vida:
Acequia Farmers and the Environment

"Without water, there is no life" is a traditional saying from the Rio Arriba. For decades, acequia farmers have confronted a daunting range of issues, including damage to watersheds and the complicated legal standing of traditional water rights. They have defended the authority of the customary law of the acequia and have sought equal standing under modern water law regimes. They have organized campaigns for watershed protection and ecological restoration projects to repair damage caused by industrial logging, mining, overgrazing, subdividing, and other harmful and exploitative activities. Land and water trusts are emerging to protect historic acequia farmlands from development and encroachment by real estate speculators and other outsiders. Acequia farmers are active in the sustainable agriculture movement and support local food security.[31] They have developed programs to certify organic local growers, provide cooperative economic development opportunities to "limited resource" farmers, and offer training in land and water management practices.

Acequias and Environmental Racism

Acequia farmers have struggled against the contamination of their water supplies from acid mine drainage and leaks and spills from mined waste tailings. The Molycorp molybdenum strip mine in Questa, New Mexico, has extensively damaged the watershed and enclosed land grant. Battle Mountain Gold, Inc. (BMG), in San Luis, Colorado, is another target of acequia-led EJM struggles. The Culebra acequia members opposed the proposed BMG strip mine and cyanide leach vat gold processing mill. The acequias hired a team of lawyers, hydrologists, and ecologists to argue their case in the state district water court. Local acequia farmers testified knowledgeably about problems with the reclamation and monitoring plans.[32] Their assessment proved more accurate than that of BMG's scientific experts when the corporation failed to reclaim the lands and contain pollution from the site.

The Culebra acequia members have opposed other development proposals, including a hog farm (really a confined animal feeding operation), a state prison, a municipal solid waste dump for Front Range cities including Denver and Colorado Springs, and plans for assembly-line sweatshops. All these proposals were defeated through acequia members' participation in the county's land use planning commission, itself a result of the struggles of the local acequia association to protect the watershed.[33]

The Colorado Acequia Association (CAA), founded in 1998, has roots in the 1990s anti-logging campaign against the Taylor Ranch and efforts by La Sierra Foundation to acquire and co-manage the land grant. Deeply rooted in the traditions of customary law that have governed the local watershed democracy for generations, the CAA led efforts to establish a county land-use planning commission and participated in developing a land use code and watershed protection ordinance based on the principles of conservation biology and environmental justice.[34]

New Mexico Acequias: Authority in Land and Water Use Planning

New Mexico acequia associations have fought to protect their water rights, customary laws, watersheds, and ancestral farmlands. The New Mexico Acequia Association, founded in 1988, and the Congreso de Acequias (Acequia Congress), established in 1999, are important actors in regional ecological politics. The Taos Valley Acequia Association was established in 1988 to address threats to the water rights of the sixty-six acequias in that watershed. Over the past twenty years, Taos acequia farmers have had to contend with threats posed by the expansion of Taos Ski Valley and the construction of condominiums and second homes in the foothills of the Sangre de Cristo Mountains. Illegal culverts and poorly designed roads cause erosion, dumping sediment into the acequias. In 1995, the Acequia de San Antonio in Valdez, New Mexico began posting public signs on crossings over the acequia madre declaring its authority to regulate land use practices that damage or threaten the traditional acequia system.[35]

Restoring Acequia Customary Law

New Mexico and Colorado acequia associations face legal challenges to their traditional water rights. Conflicts endure between customary acequia water law and the U.S. legal doctrine of prior appropriation (first in use, first in right). Preserving and protecting their water rights has been a difficult process, but most acequia associations have succeeded in doing so. The acequia institution developed in the context of relatively isolated and autonomous local communities during the lengthy Spanish and Mexican periods. The administrators of modern water law tend to view acequia practices as wasteful and inefficient. **Customary law** allows for communal sharing of scarce water resources in times of drought, whereas the appropriative rights regime demands that the most senior rights have priority in times of drought. Acequia law establishes that its officers are elected on a one-farmer, one-vote basis. The modern doctrine of prior appropriation apportions voting rights on the basis of the size of irrigated acreage (bigger irrigators get more votes).[36] These conflicts have led to successful efforts by New Mexico acequia associations to gain passage of legislation and favorable court decisions protecting traditional values of local governance.

From Toxic to Exotic Racism: Acequias and the Tourism Industry

Local struggles for watershed protection run deep and involve multiple issues from the legal standing of acequia water rights to resistance against toxic racism caused by mining and other industries. In addition, many communities face displacement and ecological devastation from the new amenity industries, driven by tourism.[37] The new and allegedly more sustainable economy of tourism, and especially the nature and culture appreciation industry, layers exotic racism on top of the existing toxic racism.

Exotic racism markets the landscapes and cultures of Chicana/o rural communities as **commodities** to be sold for the amusement and enjoyment of tourists. Bucolic scenery, the "quaint" adobe village architecture, and artisan handicrafts are featured attractions. Because tourism increases the demand for land, acequia farms are being blacktopped to make way for resorts, condominium clusters, shopping centers, roads, and other facilities that serve tourists. Acequia-irrigated fields, orchards, and pastures are overvalued by a globalized real estate market that ruthlessly offers ancestral landscapes at $80 to $100,000 an acre. The pressure to sell increases with the property taxes.[38]

■ Hacen Ruinas de Nuestras Vecindades: Political Ecology of the Barrio

"They make ruins of our neighborhoods" complained barrio residents during the construction of the interstate highways in the 1960s and 1970s. Mexican-origin people are at the heart of a demographic transition called Latinization, a dramatic rise in the Latina/o population that is remaking the major urban centers of the United States. The new Latina/o urban core consists of more than twenty-two million people in the five most populous urban states and is "reinventing the U.S. big city" (see table 21).[39] Environmental racism is part of Chicana/o urban life. The largest concentration of hazardous waste landfills in the United States is on the south side of Chicago, composed of predominantly African American and Latina/o neighborhoods.

Table 21   Largest Latina/o populations by state, county, and city (in rank order)

STATES WITH LARGEST LATINA/O POPULATIONS (1997)		COUNTIES WITH LARGEST LATINA/O POPULATIONS (1997)		CITIES WITH LARGEST LATINA/O POPULATIONS (1992)	
California	9,941,014	Los Angeles (CA)	4,000,642	New York	1,783,511
Texas	5,722,535	Dade (FL)	1,139,004	Los Angeles	1,391,411
New York	2,570,382	Cook (IL)	867,520	Chicago	545,852
Florida	2,105,689	Harris (TX)	852,177	San Antonio	520,282
Illinois	1,182,964	Orange (CA)	761,228	Houston	450,483

Source: M. Davis, *Magical Urbanism: Latinos Reinvent the U.S. Big City* (London: Verso Books, 2000), table I.

Southwest Organizing Project: Defying the Urban Grid

SWOP was a collective response by Chicanas/os in Albuquerque to an urban environment characterized by pervasive patterns of discrimination and police brutality. Communities of color experience the urban environment as the site of domination, power, and resistance. They often lack access to ecological amenities such as uncrowded housing, open space and parks, and recreational facilities. Often surrounded by toxic **brownfields,** polluting industries, and deteriorating housing, degraded urban neighborhoods are treated as sacrifice zones (areas defined as environmentally expendable).[40]

SWOP activists perceive the barrio as encapsulated by the fortress of police power. For them, the **built environment** is a place that dehumanizes and punishes residents under a regime of constant surveillance and spatial control of the "grid" through racial segregation and profiling. This concept of the built environment is important to Chicana/o environmental justice activists because it emphasizes the spatial dimensions of power in the urban environment. Activists developed a critique of discrimination in employment, housing, the police, and justice system.[41]

Urban Habitat: Creating Livable and Just Cities

SWOP encouraged communities to shift from reactive struggles against environmental racism to proactive campaigns for healthy and livable cities. Mexican-origin urban residents are participating in movements for better housing, community-based health care, alternative economic development, brownfield reclamation, urban horticulture, and local food security. Environmental justice activists have campaigned for "urban habitat" as championed by the Earth Island Institute in the San Francisco Bay Area. People are demanding and reclaiming urban community space, the common places that promote conviviality. The reclamation of urban space involves self-help housing projects, urban gardens, and cleanup of contaminated soils and brownfields.

Kettleman City: Confronting Racism in the EPA

El Pueblo para el Aire y Agua Limpio in Kettleman City is an important example of the Chicana/o grassroots movement against toxic racism.[42] This especially poignant and iconic struggle implicates the EPA and a large corporation in the deliberate exclusion of the community from lawful participation in the process of environmental review. For decades residents of this community in California's San Joaquin Valley were denied equitable access to the scoping, research, and public commentary processes that are required under the **National Environmental Policy Act (NEPA)** for all federal **environmental impact studies.** By 1990, the Kettleman City struggles had revealed a legacy of environmental racism inside the EPA. This struggle catalyzed multiracial and multistate coalitions and led to the EPA accountability project in 1991, eventually resulting in **Executive Order 12898** and the establishment of NEJAC and the EPA Office of Environmental Justice.

Toxics and the Military: Tucsonans for a Clean Environment

On the south side of Tucson, Mexican-origin and Tohono O'odham communities waged a struggle against pollution from the Hughes (now Raytheon) Air Force Missile Plant No. 44. Local grassroots mobilization began in the mid-1980s and eventually resulted in a multimillion-dollar settlement for affected families and Superfund designation for the site.[43]

Between 1955 and 1977, Hughes Aircraft Corporation dumped large amounts of trichloroethylene (TCE) and other untreated chemicals into arroyos surrounding the plant next to Tucson International Airport. This resulted in a plume of toxic groundwater contamination. In 1981, Pima County officials closed domestic drinking water wells in the area of Tucson affected by the TCE plume. Local residents reported high rates of chronic illnesses. A local journalist published a series of articles on the TCE plume and the poisoning of the community's drinking water. By 1987, Native and Mexican American activists had organized Tucsonans for a Clean Environment (also TCE). They mobilized 1,600 affected families to file suit against Hughes Aircraft and the U.S. Air Force. In 1991, they agreed to a settlement of $85 million, at the time the largest award for a water pollution case in U.S. history.[44]

Madres del Este de Los Angeles: Engendering Organized Communities

Established in 1985, MELA is one of the oldest and most prominent grassroots organizations in the Chicana/o EJM. Most MELA activists are Mexican American women who have used their role as mothers to engender ecological struggles. Aurora Castillo and Juana Gutiérrez, in concert with a local Catholic parish priest, were among the early organizers of this grassroots environmental justice organization.

Mexican-origin communities in the Los Angeles basin face the intrusion of locally unwanted land uses. High-income white communities do not want toxic waste incinerators in their neighborhoods, and they have the political power to make sure public officials locate such unwanted facilities in politically powerless localities like East and South Central Los Angeles. By leading opposition to proposals to locate a toxic waste incinerator, a state prison, and a fuel pipeline in East Los Angeles, MELA redefined ecological politics and challenged the imposition of locally unwanted land uses on communities of color. MELA epitomizes the central role of women in the EJM. MELA members recognized that as Mexican Americans they would be marginalized and ignored by politicians and decision makers. By presenting a public face as mothers, MELA activists sought respect within the political system and the media.[45]

SNEEJ and Intel Inside New Mexico

SNEEJ launched a campaign against Intel because industrial subsidies, site development, and manufacturing operations all pose significant threats to workers, communities, and the environment. The Intel chip-making plant in New Mexico is located on a mesatop overlooking the Rio Grande in the Rio Rancho suburb northwest of Albuquerque. Environmental justice activists were opposed to the granting of subsidies and tax breaks to lure the company to the area; they felt this policy rewarded a corporation that was already responsible for three Superfund sites in the Silicon Valley.[46]

SWOP, SNEEJ, and Native American tribes expressed concern over the adverse environmental effects of Intel's FAB 11 plant. The wafer (computer chip) fabrication plant uses two to three million gallons of water a day in a desert city where water resources are already stretched beyond **carrying capacity.** Intel is mining the groundwater aquifer at the rate of 1.5 billion gallons or 4,500 acre-feet per year.[47] Over time this pumping will lower the water table because the rate of withdrawal exceeds the recharge capacity of the aquifer. Neighboring well users will have to pay to follow the water when Intel's consumption depletes the aquifer.

A Think/Act Tank:
The Los Angeles Labor and Community Strategy Center

The Labor and Community Strategy Center in Los Angeles has been at the heart of the EJM in southern California since the mid-1980s. The center is a multiracial and anti-corporate "think tank/act tank" whose work "spans all aspects of urban life." It emphasizes rebuilding the labor movement; fighting for environmental justice, true mass transit for the masses, and immigrant rights; and actively opposing the growing criminalization, racialization, and feminization of poverty.

Among the grassroots environmental justice campaigns of the Strategy Center is the Bus Riders Union (BRU), a multiracial organization that has waged a decade-long struggle for equitable and sustainable mass transit. The BRU is involved in civil rights litigation against the Los Angeles Metropolitan Transit Authority. Ricardo Zelada, a Salvadoran and plaintiff in the BRU Title VI lawsuit, explains the struggle as one against transit racism: "The same people who use the bus are both poor workers and racial and ethnic minorities—that's where racism and the proletarian character of our 'class' of bus riders comes together. . . . [T]he government removes funds from areas in which ethnic minorities and the poor are concentrated—the bus system—and concentrates and transfers funds to a place where the majority is white and they are not so poor and there are few riders altogether—the trains."[48]

Inner-City Milpas: Local Food Security and Urban Horticulture

Raquel Pinderhughes has studied the connection between urban food self-sufficiency and environmental justice. Urban agriculture "has the potential to transform blighted, vacant lots into vibrant green community spaces" that "bring people together to create safe open spaces that facilitate community social networks and interactions." Agriculture in urban areas also "supplements household food security and reduces stress on household food budgets." **Traditional environmental knowledge** is transferred across generations wherever urban agriculture provides opportunities for elders and youth to work together.[49]

Urban agriculture contributes to local food security among low-income families "marginalized by the mainstream food system." The urban agriculture movement builds the capacity of local people to be more self-sufficient in terms of food.[50] The movement draws on the tendency among many Mexican-origin immigrants and Mexican Americans to engage in home gardening. Zapoteca and Mixteca immigrants from Oaxaca maintain horticultural spaces in thousands of back and front yards, vacant lots, and even alleys and street medians across the Los Angeles basin.[51] This grassroots subsistence horticulture is evident in other U.S. rural and metropolitan areas wherever native mexicanos have settled. This ethnobotanical and agroecological knowledge is being tapped by the environmental justice urban agriculture movement.

 ### *Somos Humanos y No Lo Olvidan:* Rural Colonias and the Environment

Colonia residents are portrayed by racist media and government officials as filthy, poor, uneducated, and unmotivated victims of their own sloth. They are depicted as living in subhuman conditions. Colonia residents reply, "We are humans and don't forget it."[52]

Colonias and Subdivision Regulations

Colonias are low-income subdivisions built without legal protections for residents and homeowners. In Texas, colonias were exempt from laws regulating subdivisions until community members and environmental justice activists pressed for more regulation.[53] A 1990 GAO survey identified 872 colonias in Texas, 14 in New Mexico, and none in Arizona or California. This estimate was based on erroneous assumptions about colonia settlements in California and other southwestern states; in fact, hundreds of colonias exist in these other states. A more recent survey by the Texas Water Development Board found far more colonias than did the GAO study; the official estimate for Texas alone now stands at 1,471.[54]

Drinking Water and Wastewater

Colonias lack water and sanitation systems, conditions that contribute to high rates of water-borne diseases including dysentery and chronic diarrhea. Potable water is often delivered by *piperos,* fly-by-night operators who sell water from tanker trucks. "Residents wait as the piperos pump a week's supply of water into fifty-five gallon metal drums that once held industrial chemicals. . . . [I]n Nogales, Sonora . . . the water the piperos deliver . . . is itself badly contaminated by toxic chemicals. . . . [T]he city permits the piperos to continue to draw their water from a municipal well that was recently found to be polluted with industrial solvents [used in the maquiladora industry]."[55]

Colonia residents lack access to public health-care facilities and have serious problems associated with toxic contamination of soils on home lots and surrounding lands. These communities are captive to the larger forces surrounding water development politics in the Southwest. Real estate and subdivision developers continuously lobby state legislators to avoid "overregulating" private property and to protect developers' rights. Colonias contribute to border environmental problems wherever untreated human wastes (*aguas negras*) flow into surface streams and leach into groundwater aquifers.[56]

Colonias and Environmental Justice

Texas border colonia residents are organizing to demand access to potable water, sanitation systems, and health-care facilities. Some colonias are organizing housing construction cooperatives that draw on the strong self-help and **mutual aid** traditions followed by urban squatters in Mexico. In Juárez, SOCOSEMA, the municipal dump workers' cooperative, offers an inspiring model of the possibilities of autonomous economic and political self-organization among colonia residents.[57] Members used their cooperative resources to support self-help housing, access to clean water, and literacy education, as well as a shortened workday (from fifteen hours to about six) to allow for these community activities. In El Paso County, Texas, a Catholic community-based group, the El Paso Interreligious Sponsoring Organization (EPISO), supported colonia residents' struggles during the late 1970s and 1980s. EPISO successfully pressed for water and sanitation facilities in the colonias, while attracting the support of public figures and the attention of the mass media and elected officials.[58]

Concluding Thoughts: Is the Earth Local?

When the Culebra Coalition launched its anti-logging campaign in June 1995, Zachary Taylor Jr., the manager of the enclosed common lands, denounced the protests as the actions of "a bunch of radical outsiders" and "just a handful of misled and misinformed locals."[59] Joe Gallegos, a local acequia farmer and mayordomo replied with a rhetorical question: "Is the Earth local?" He was referring to the idea that local people have developed a sense of place that defines their commitment to La Sierra. Locals were the heart and soul of the anti-logging struggle.

A commitment to protecting local or home places is a defining quality of the EJM. Farmworkers and acequia farmers, factory workers and barrio residents, land grant villagers and colonia residents all share a commitment to protect the environment because it is the place where they live, work, play, and worship. The EJM calls on people to "think and act locally," to defend the earth in the places we inhabit—all the earth, not just majestic mountains and emerald forests.

Discussion Questions

1. What are some of the health problems among farmworkers caused by long-term exposure to pesticides? What compounding socioeconomic factors affect rates of chronic illness, infectious diseases, and morbidity among this group?

2. How could the use of GEOs or transgenic crops affect farmworkers' health and safety?

3. Can Spanish and Mexican land grants be restored to community ownership and management? If not, what are the prospects for and potential problems of a policy that encourages local co-management of public lands?

4. Discuss the differences between equity and autonomy in the EJM.

5. What is the significance of Latina/o struggles for local food security? What are the social, cultural, and economic implications of the community garden movement in inner-city communities?

6. MELA activists used their identity as mothers to gain political clout. Is such use of identities effective as a strategy to gain legitimation of a movement's claims and grievances? If so, what identities are and are not effective?

■ Suggested Readings

Barry, Tom, and Beth Sims. 1994. *The Challenge of Cross-Border Environmentalism: The U.S.–Mexico Case.* Albuquerque: Resource Center Press; Bisbee: Border Ecology Project.

Cole, Luke W., and Sheila R. Foster. 2001. *From the Ground Up: Environmental Racism and the Rise of the Environmental Justice Movement.* New York: New York University Press.

Pardo, Mary. 1999. *Mexican American Women Activists: Identity and Resistance in Two Los Angeles Communities.* Philadelphia: Temple University Press.

Peña, Devon G. 2003. The Scope of Latino/a Environmental Studies. *Latino Studies* 1: 47–78.

Pulido, Laura. 1996. *Environmentalism and Economic Justice: Two Chicano Struggles in the Southwest.* Tucson: University of Arizona Press.

■ Notes

1. L. Pulido, personal communication, July 1994.

2. D. Montejano, "On the Future of Anglo-Mexican Relations in the United States," in *Chicano Politics and Society in the Late Twentieth Century,* ed. D. Montejano (Austin: University of Texas Press, 1999), 234–58.

3. SNEEJ, SWOP, the Farm Worker Network for Economic and Environmental Justice (FNEEJ), and the Indigenous Environmental Network (IEN) participated in the Seattle anti–WTO demonstrations in November 1999. For summaries of environmental justice struggles, see C. Rechtschaffen and E. Gauna, *Environmental Justice: Law, Policy, and Regulation* (Durham, NC: Carolina Academic Press, 2002); D. G. Peña, "The Scope of Latino/a Environmental Studies, *Latino Studies* 1 (2003): 47–78.

4. C. Marentes, "Food Production under Globalization and Neoliberalism: The Plight of the Workers of the Land" (paper presented at the 1997 Agricultural Missions Annual Meeting, Study Session on Economic Globalization, El Paso, TX, May 2, 1997).

5. B. Velasquez, telephone interview recorded by Rebeca Rivera, March 2001 (in the audio collection of the Rio Grande Bioregions Project, Department of Anthropology, University of Washington, Seattle). On the scope of farmworker protests, see D. G. Peña, "Environmental Justice and Sustainable Agriculture: Linking Social and Ecological Sides of Sustainability" (commissioned policy paper prepared for the Second National People of Color Environmental Leadership Summit, Washington, DC, October 2002), available online at http://www.ejrc.cau.edu/summit2/SustainableAg.pdf.

6. F. J. Frommer, "Immigrant and Hispanic Workers Describe Unsafe Working Conditions," *San Francisco Chronicle,* February 27, 2002.

7. M. Reeves, et al., *Fields of Poison: California Farmworkers and Pesticides* (San Francisco: Californians for Pesticide Reform, Pesticide Action Network; Sacramento:

California Rural Legal Assistance Foundation; Watsonville: UFW, 1997), 30, available online at http://www.igc.org/panna/resources/documents/fields.pdf.

8. A. Wright, *The Death of Ramón González: A Modern Agricultural Dilemma* (Austin: University of Texas Press, 1990); R. Gottlieb, *Forcing the Spring: The Transformation of the American Environmental Movement* (Washington, DC: Island Press, 1993), 240–44.

9. FLOC, *Farm Workers and Farm Labor Conditions,* available online at http://www.iupui.edu/~floc/fws.htm. Also see J. Kay, "California's Endangered Communities of Color," in *Unequal Protection: Environmental Justice and Communities of Color,* ed. R. D. Bullard (San Francisco: Sierra Club, 1994), 155–88; Y. Perfecto, "Farm Workers, Pesticides, and the International Connection," in *Race and the Incidence of Environmental Hazards,* ed. B. Bryant and P. Mohai (Boulder: Westview Press, 1992); E. Leon, *The Health Condition of Migrant Farmworkers,* Occasional Paper 71 (East Lansing: Julian Samora Research Institute, Michigan State University, August 2000).

10. FLOC, *Farm Workers and Farm Labor Conditions;* S. Greenhouse, "As U.S. Economy Booms, Housing for Migrant Workers Worsens," *New York Times,* March 31, 1998.

11. Peña, "Environmental Justice and Sustainable Agriculture," 3, 6; M. Teitel and K. A. Wilson, *Genetically Engineered Food: Changing the Nature of Nature* (Rochester, VT: Park Street Press, 1999); D. G. Peña, "Latinos and Biotechnology: Environmental and Health Risks of Emergent Technologies," *Aztlán: International Journal of Chicano Studies Research* (forthcoming).

12. The Farm Worker Network has nine affiliates: Comité de Apoyo a los Trabajadores Agrícolas (CATA, based in New Jersey), Centro Independiente de Trabajadores Agrícolas (CITA, New York), Confederación Nacional Campesina (CONFENACA, the Dominican Republic), Farm Labor Organizing Committee (FLOC–AFL–CIO, Ohio), Farm Worker Association of Florida (FWAF, Florida), Organización de Trabajadores Agrícolas de California (OTAC, California), Unión Sin Fronteras (USF, California), Unión de Trabajadores Agrícolas Fronterizos (UTAF, Texas), and Washington Farmworkers Union (WFU, Washington state).

13. The "fair trade" label is usually applied to coffee. Baldemar Velasquez explains the concept of fair trade in the context of farmworker union contracts: "We are working on a fair trade component to our collective bargaining contracts by asking that workers in offshore operations of American companies be paid wages and provided benefits comparable to those of workers in U.S. operations." (Personal communication to the author at the Second EJ Summit, Washington, DC, October 25, 2002).

14. R. Rochin, "The Conversion of Chicano Farm Workers into Owner-Operators of Cooperative Farms, 1970–1985," *Rural Sociology* 51 (1988): 97–115; D. G. Peña, "The Browning of the American Farm," *High Country News,* April 4, 2000; R. Rochin, "Hispanic Americans in the Rural Economy: Conditions, Issues, and Probable Future

Adjustments," in *National Rural Studies Committee: A Proceedings,* ed. E. Castle (Corvalis, OR: Western Rural Development Center, 1992).

15. A. de la Torre and A. Estrada, *Mexican Americans and Health: ¡Sana! ¡Sana!* (Tucson: University of Arizona Press, 2001), 18–19.

16. D. Faber, "The Political Ecology of American Capitalism: New Challenges for the Environmental Justice Movement," in *The Struggle for Ecological Democracy: Environmental Justice Movements in the United States,* ed. D. Faber (New York: Guilford Press, 1998), 39; Gottlieb, *Forcing the Spring,* 235–44, 270–306. On the concentration of Latinas/os in high-risk, low-wage jobs, see R. Morales and P. M. Ong, "The Illusion of Progress: Latinos in Los Angeles," in *Latinos in a Changing U.S. Economy,* ed. R. Morales and F. Bonilla (Newbury Park: Sage, 1993), 28–54; D. G. Peña, *The Terror of the Machine: Technology, Work, Gender, and Ecology on the U.S.–Mexico Border* (Austin: CMAS Books, 1997). On the health risks of chemical exposure, see R. Kazis and R. Grossman, *Fear at Work: Job Blackmail, Labor, and the Environment* (Philadelphia: New Society Publishers, 1991); D. Rosner and G. Markowitz, eds., *Dying for Work* (Bloomington: University of Indiana Press, 1987); C. Levenstein and J. Wooding, "Dying for a Living: Workers, Production, and the Environment," in Faber, *Struggle for Ecological Democracy,* 60–80; P. M. Ong and E. Blumenberg, "An Unnatural Trade-Off: Latinos and Environmental Justice," in Morales and Bonilla, *Latinos in a Changing U.S. Economy,* 207–25.

17. P. Almeida, "The Southwest Network for Environmental and Economic Justice: An Interview with Richard Moore," in Faber, *Struggle for Ecological Democracy,* 171–72; Peña, *Terror of the Machine,* 34; S. Fox, *Toxic Work: Women Workers at GTE Lenkurt* (Philadelphia: Temple University Press, 1991); SWOP, *Intel Inside New Mexico: A Case Study of Environmental and Economic Injustice* (Albuquerque: SWOP, 1995).

18. D. Bacon, "A Plant Closes in Revenge for Cross-Border Organizing" (November 30, 1998), available online at http://www.igc.org/dbacon/Mexico/01Pclose.htm.

19. E. Martínez, *De Colores Means All of Us* (Boston: South End Press, 1998), 82.

20. Peña, *Chicano Culture, Ecology, Politics;* D. G. Peña, "Identity, Place, and Communities of Resistance" in *Just Sustainabilities: Development in an Unequal World,* ed. J. Agyeman, R. D. Bullard, and B. Evans (London: Earthscan; Cambridge: MIT Press, 2003), 146–67.

21. GAO, *Treaty of Guadalupe Hidalgo: Definition and List of Community Land Grants in New Mexico,* Exposure Draft GAO-01-330 (January 2001), available online at http://www.gao.gov/new.items/d01330.pdf.

22. C. Wilmsen, "The Vallecitos Federal Sustained Yield Unit: A Case Study of Forest Management and Rural Poverty in Northern New Mexico" (paper presented at the annual meeting of the Association of American Geographers, San Francisco, CA, March 29, 1994), 5.

23. M. J. Hassell, *The People of Northern New Mexico and the National Forests*

(Albuquerque: U.S. Department of Agriculture, USFS, Southwestern Region, 1968). The Hassell Report was prepared in response to the Tierra Amarilla courthouse raid and the tense aftermath of Tijerina's arrest. The USFS interpreted the courthouse raid as a management crisis, not a justifiable human rights conflict. See D. G. Peña and R. O. Martínez, *Upper Rio Grande Hispano Farms: A Cultural and Environmental History of Land Ethics in Transition, 1598–1998* (final report, National Endowment for the Humanities Grant #RO227078-94. Rio Grande Bioregions Project, Department of Anthropology, University of Washington).

For policy recommendations, see S. Forrest, "The Vallecitos Federal Sustained Yield Unit: The (All Too) Human Dimension of Forest Management in Northern New Mexico," in *Forests under Fire: A Century of Ecosystem Management in the Southwest,* ed. C. J. Huggard and A. R. Gómez (Tucson: University of Arizona Press, 2001); Wilmsen, "Vallecitos Federal Sustained Yield Unit," 13, 45.

24. C. Wilmsen, "Fighting for the Forest" (Ph.D. diss., University of Wisconsin, 1997), 57, 67–69. Vallecitos Sustained Yield Unit Association as quoted in Wilmsen, "Vallecitos Sustained Yield Unit," 14.

25. See D. G. Peña, "The 'Brown' and the 'Green': Chicanos and Environmental Politics in the Upper Rio Grande," *Capitalism, Nature, Socialism* 3 (1992): 79–103; Pulido, *Environmentalism and Economic Justice* and "Ecological Legitimacy and Cultural Essentialism: Hispano Grazing in the Southwest," in *Struggle for Ecological Democracy,* 293–311; D. G. Peña and M. M. Mondragon-Valdéz, "The 'Brown' and the 'Green' Revisited: Chicanos and Environmental Politics in the Upper Rio Grande," in *Struggle for Ecological Democracy,* 312–48.

26. Peña and Mondragon-Valdéz, " 'Brown' and the 'Green' Revisited," 323.

27. Pulido, "Ecological Legitimacy," 296; Peña and Valdéz, " 'Brown' and the 'Green.' "

28. R. D. García and T. Howland, "Determining the Legitimacy of Spanish Land Grants in Colorado: Conflicting Values, Legal Pluralism, and Demystification of the Sangre de Cristo/Rael Case," *Chicano-Latino Law Review* 16 (1995): 39–68.

29. The case was renamed *Eugene Lobato et al. v. Zachary Taylor et al.* The justices agreed that the heirs of the Sangre de Cristo Land Grant have prior rights of usufruct to graze livestock, cut timber, and gather firewood. Despite the dissent of two justices, the court failed to include hunting and fishing in the set of usufructuary rights. See T. Noel, "Old Is New Again in Valley: High Court Returns Use of the Taylor Ranch to Costilla Residents," *Rocky Mountain News,* July 13, 2002; A. Bernstein, "Luck of the Draw: Divorce Forced Quiet ex-Enron Executive Lou Pai to Dump Stocks, Making Him a Very Rich Man, and a Target of Many Lawsuits," *Houston Chronicle,* March 3, 2002.

30. Quotation from J. Brooke, "In a Colorado Valley: Hispanic Farmers Battle a Timber Baron," *New York Times,* March 24, 1997; also see Peña, "Identity and Place in Communities of Resistance," in Agyeman, Bullard, and Evans, *Just Sustainabilities.*

31. G. A. Hicks and D. G. Peña, "Community Acequias in Colorado's Rio Culebra Watershed: A Customary Commons in the Domain of Prior Appropriation," *University of Colorado Law Review* 74 (2003): 387–486; Peña, "Environmental Justice and Sustainable Agriculture."

32. D. G. Peña and J. Gallegos, "Nature and Chicanos in Southern Colorado," in *Confronting Environmental Racism: Voices from the Grassroots,* ed. R. D. Bullard (Boston: South End Press, 1993), 141–60; Peña, "An Orchard, a Gold Mine, and an Eleventh Commandment," in *Chicano Culture, Ecology, Politics,* 249–78; D. G. Peña, R. Martínez, and L. McFarland, "Rural Chicana/o Communities and the Environment: An Attitudinal Survey of Residents of Costilla County," *Perspectives in Mexican American Studies* 4 (1993): 45–74; D. G. Peña and J. Gallegos, "Local Knowledge and Collaborative Environmental Action Research," in *Building Community: Social Science in Action,"* ed. P. Nyden et al. (Thousand Oaks: Pine Forge Press, 1997), 85–91.

33. Peña, "Identity, Place, and Communities of Resistance," 43.

34. Hicks and Peña, "Community Acequias"; R. Curry, M. Soulé, D. G. Peña, and M. McGowan, *Montana Best Management Practices: A Critique and Sustainable Alternatives* (report submitted to the Costilla County Land Use Planning Commission, San Luis, CO, on behalf of La Sierra Foundation and Costilla County Conservancy District, October 1997); D. G. Peña, "The Watershed Commonwealth of the Upper Rio Grande," in *Natural Assets: Democratizing Environmental Ownership,* ed. J. K. Boyce and B. G. Shelley (Washington, DC: Island Press, 2003), 169–86.

35. J. A. Rivera, *Acequia Culture: Water, Land, and Community in the Southwest* (Albuquerque: University of New Mexico Press, 1998), 189.

36. Peña, "Gold Mine," 249–65; Rivera, *Acequia Culture;* Hicks and Peña, "Community Acequias."

37. S. Rodríguez, "Land, Water, and Ethnic Identity in Taos," in *Land, Water, and Culture: New Perspectives on Hispanic Land Grants,* ed. C. L. Briggs and J. R. Van Ness (Albuquerque: University of New Mexico Press, 1987) 314–403, and "Art, Tourism, and Race Relations in Taos," in *Discovered Country: Tourism and Survival in the American West,* ed. S. Norris (Albuquerque: Stone Ladder Press, 1994), 143–60.

38. Peña and Martínez, *Upper Rio Grande Hispano Farms;* J. Gallegos, "Sangre de Tierra: Six Generations in the Life of an Acequia Farming Family" (unpublished manuscript in author's collection).

39. M. Davis, *Magical Urbanism: Latinos Reinvent the U.S. Big City* (London: Verso, 2000), 3–6.

40. J. Gauna, telephone interview recorded by Rebeca Rivera, March 2001 (in the audio collection of the Rio Grande Bioregions Project, Department of Anthropology, University of Washington, Seattle). The term *sacrifice zones* originated with Ward Churchill and Winona LaDuke; see W. Churchill and W. LaDuke, "Radioactive Colonization: Hidden Holocaust in Native North America," in *Struggle for the Land: Indigenous Resistance to Genocide, Ecocide, and Expropriation in Contemporary North*

America,* ed. W. Churchill (San Francisco: City Lights, 2002), 261–328; A. Gedicks, *The New Resource Wars: Native American Environmental Struggles against Multinational Corporations* (Boston: South End Press, 1993).

41. Interview with J. Gauna.

42. L. W. Cole and S. R. Foster, *From the Ground Up: Environmental Racism and the Rise of the Environmental Justice Movement* (New York: New York University Press, 2001); R. Austin and M. Schill, "Black, Brown, Red, and Poisoned," and J. Kay, "California's Endangered Communities of Color," in *Unequal Protection.*

43. R. Augustine, "Tucsonans Fight for a Clean Environment," in *People of Color Environmental Groups: 2000 Directory,* ed. R. D. Bullard (Flint, MI: Charles Stewart Mott Foundation, 2000), 32–33; J. N. Clarke and A. K. Gerlak, "Environmental Racism in Southern Arizona: The Reality beneath the Rhetoric," in *Environmental Injustices, Political Struggles,* ed. D. E. Camacho (Durham: Duke University Press, 1998), 82–100.

44. Clarke and Gerlak, "Environmental Racism in Southern Arizona," 84, 87–88. Jane Kay is the journalist who wrote the series for a Tucson newspaper, the *Arizona Daily Star*, between 1981 and 1985.

45. M. Pardo, *Mexican American Women Activists: Identity and Resistance in Two Los Angeles Communities* (Philadelphia: Temple University Press, 1999), and "Gendered Citizenship: Mexican American Women and Grassroots Activism in East Los Angeles, 1986–1992," in *Chicano Politics and Society,* 58–81, see especially 74–75; G. Gutiérrez, "Mothers of East Los Angeles Strike Back," in *Unequal Protection,* 220–33.

46. SWOP, *Intel Inside New Mexico,* 38.

47. Ibid., 56.

48. E. Mann, "A Race Struggle, a Class Struggle, a Women's Struggle All at Once: Organizing on the Buses of L.A.," in *Socialist Register 2001: Working Classes, Global Realities,* ed. L. Panitch, et al. (New York: Monthly Review Press, 2001).

49. R. Pinderhughes and K. Perry, "Poverty Reduction, Environmental Protection, Environmental Justice: The Urban Agriculture Connection," in *Natural Assets: Democratizing Environmental Ownership,* ed. J. K. Boyce and B. Shelley (New York: Russell Sage Foundation, 2002); Peña, "Environmental Justice and Sustainable Agriculture."

50. Pinderhughes and Perry, "Poverty Reduction," 12.

51. Author's observations during recent visits to Los Angeles. One Zapotec family maintains three separate milpas in a south central Los Angeles neighborhood. They are planted with land race varieties of maize, beans, squash, avocados, limes, chiles, and numerous aromatic or medicinal herbs. Many heirloom seeds are brought to the United States from Oaxaca in the immigrants' baggage.

52. Peña, *Terror of the Machine,* 215–17.

53. M. Pepin, *Texas Colonias: An Environmental Justice Case Study,* available online at http://itc.ollusa.edu/faculty/pepim/philosophy/cur/colonias.htm#OLE_what.

54. GAO, *Rural Development: Problems and Progress of Colonia Subdivisions near Mexico's.Border* (Washington, DC: Government Printing Office, 1990); Texas Water Development Board, *Water and Wastewater Needs of Texas Colonias* (Austin: TWDB, 1992); Pepin, *Texas Colonias.*

55. T. Barry and B. Sims, *The Challenge of Cross-Border Environmentalism: The U.S.–Mexico Case* (Albuquerque: Resource Center Press; Bisbee: Border Ecology Project, 1994), 35–36.

56. Ibid, 31; Pepin, *Texas Colonias.* Also see C. R. Bath, J. M. Tanski, and R. E. Villarreal, "The Failure to Provide Basic Services to the Colonias of El Paso County: A Case of Environmental Racism?" in *Environmental Injustices, Political Struggles,* 125–37.

57. Peña, *Terror of the Machine,* 213–43.

58. Bath, Tanski, and Villarreal, "Failure to Provide Basic Services," 132.

59. Peña, "Identity, Place, and Communities of Resistance," 43.

Conclusion

Mexican-Origin People and
the Future of Environmentalism

When Zachary Taylor Jr. logged La Sierra above San Luis, Colorado, he did more than cut four hundred-year-old Ponderosa pines and Douglas firs. He also transformed how local people experienced this place. "Taylor . . . is clear-cutting my soul," Joe Gallegos once told me at an anti-logging protest.[1] Each tree that was logged felt like a piece of Joe's memory being ripped away from the landscape for export on a seemingly endless convoy of logging trucks. Gallegos could not stand by and let the lifeblood of the **acequias** become dust on the floor of distant sawmills. He and other protestors resisted the logging because it violated their sense of place and identity. La Sierra is one place; it occupies one small spot on the map. But the timber baron's vision of that space as salable timber to be scientifically harvested and the acequia farmer's view of the place as a beloved homeland and precious watershed are disparate and irreconcilable. These two views of the land encapsulate the contradictions I explored in mapping the environmental history of México desconocido.

Arguably, all societies organize and use human labor to transform nature. We convert the natural conditions of life—the land, water, plants, and animals—into energy we consume to survive and reproduce. All societies transform the environment in this manner, but they differ in more than the size of their ecological footprints. Human groups do not necessarily share the same values to guide their transformation of nature. Nature is many things—the capitalist developer's exploitable natural resource, the environmentalist's pristine wilderness, the scientist's delicately balanced (or **chaotic**) **ecosystem,** the farmer's beloved homeland and precious watershed— and it is shaped by people's perceptions of time and place, extant forms of cultural organization and knowledge, specific histories and patterns of human inhabitation, and ever-changing power dynamics. This book was organized to reflect these interconnected themes of **ecology,** history and **culture,** and politics.

■ Future Trends and Emerging Issues

What is the future of the **environmental justice movement (EJM)** in Mexican-origin communities? It seems increasingly clear that the fate of the **Mexican-origin people** is tied to that of other Latina/o communities and of other communities of color. This is reflected in the multiracial and multinational membership of grassroots EJM organizations and their networks. The international dimensions of the movement are becoming more complex and important as the EJM converges with the anti-globalization movement. On the near horizon, the more salient issues for **environmental justice** theory and practice are legal, scientific, theoretical, and organizational. I close with a discussion of these challenges.

Assaults on Title VI

For nearly two decades, Title VI of the 1964 Civil Rights Act provided a firm basis for grassroots lawsuits to combat the disproportionate effects of **environmental racism.** Title VI is not an environmental law, but it precludes recipients of federal funds from engaging in activities that have discriminatory effects. Many environmental justice community groups and activists have effectively used this statute to oppose a wide variety of policies and programs deemed discriminatory to the environmental well-being of people of color. The U.S. Supreme Court ruled in the case of *Alexander v. Sandoval*, 532 U.S. 275 (2001), that individuals and community-based organizations do not have private rights of action under Title VI.[2] This decision has undermined the use of civil rights statutes in environmental justice litigation and organizing. How will the EJM respond to a legal environment that disqualifies citizen knowledge and is hostile to grassroots **agency** and democratic participation? Will activists seek new civil rights laws to restore the pivotal right of individuals and affected communities to directly challenge discrimination in environmental protection? What other legal approaches are available for the pursuit of environmental justice litigation? These questions are of utmost significance as communities of color work to sustain the EJM over the coming decades.

Genomics and Environmental Risk Assessment

The advent of the Human Genome Project, which is working to map the human genetic code, is a profound scientific development. Genomics, the comprehensive study of sets of genes and their interactions, is not a well-known or easily understood scientific field. The first step is for EJM activists and communities to educate themselves to address the legal, social, environmental, and ethical implications of human genetic technologies. The emerging areas of toxicogenomics (the study of how an organism's genetic material responds to environmental stressors or toxicants) and mass genotyping (the genetic profiling of the diversity of human subpopulations) are particularly worrisome because they involve theories, methods, and data that could be used to limit meaningful citizen participation in **environmental risk** assessment. There are indications that these new fields will converge in a major restructuring of the bureaucratic regulations and scientific standards governing environmental risk assessment. Mass genotyping could be used to estimate the susceptibility of particular subpopulations to given types of toxicants. The results presumably would define the exposure and risk thresholds of different toxicants for different subpopulations. In one application, databases could be used to require members of identified high-risk subpopulations to sign liability waivers as a precondition of employment in jobs involving exposure to particular toxicants. Such an approach to risk assessment would allow corporations to avoid responsibility for the regulation, containment, and elimination of toxic risks. They would be armed with a new scientific tool to pre-screen the workforce based on genetic profiling. The labor and civil rights implications of such a development are quite chilling and need to be addressed by environmental justice theorists and activists.

From Environmental Racism to Just Sustainabilities

A subtle shift has occurred in environmental justice theory over the past ten years. It involves a move away from a focus on environmental racism and engagement with the politics of risk assessment toward a focus on **sustainable development** in light of new movements for social and economic justice. This shift was already evident at the 1994 annual gathering of SNEEJ, where participants focused on the theme of building **sustainable** communities. The Second National People of Color Environmental Leadership Summit, in October 2002, also addressed the theme of sustainability. Discussions of local empowerment and sustainability have become central in EJM **discourse.**[3] What is sustainable development? Is it a "Trojan horse" of neoliberal design inside which lurk programs to weaken local communities through top-down **environmental managerialism**? Is a sustainable society possible without social justice? What will Mexican Americans do to help an increasingly transnational society move toward sustainability with social justice?[4]

Globalization, Neoliberalism, and Autonomy

The theory and practice of sustainable development must confront the neoliberal project that seeks to reverse the changes brought about by two decades of environmental justice struggles. Neoliberalism is based on the privatization of the social and **natural conditions of production;** elimination of non-tariff barriers to free trade, such as environmental and labor regulations; severe cuts in social spending (on housing, health, education, poverty reduction, and so on); and the imposition of a bureaucratic regime that is antidemocratic (it deliberately excludes average citizens and workers from participating in decision-making processes).[5]

Since January 1994, when the Maya rebel army of Zapatistas staged an insurrection in the southeastern Mexican state of Chiapas, struggles against neoliberalism have been a focus of **social movements** north and south of the U.S.–Mexico border.[6] The Zapatistas declared neoliberalism and the **North American Free Trade Agreement (NAFTA)** to be a death sentence for Mexico's indigenous masses.

Zapatistas represent a fight for autonomy. Zapatista concepts of local autonomy were first outlined in the "First Declaration from the Lacandón Jungle," wherein the indigenous rebels renounced the nation-state without falling into the myth of **globalization:** "By rooting themselves in their local spaces . . . [t]heir claims are no longer concentrated in demanding that the state meet their needs. Instead, their quests for liberation are defined by exercising their freedoms."[7] What is autonomy, and how is it different from equity? Equity strategies require the cooperation of the state as the ultimate administrator of justice. Autonomy strategies focus on a group creating its own liberties through local self-determination; recourse to **customary law** and practice; and the building of cultural, social, economic, and natural assets for self-reliance and independent livelihoods. The political and philosophical issues related to the theory and practice of autonomy must be thoroughly addressed. Autonomy theory may assist the EJM to become more effective as a force of fundamental social transformation.

Urban Ecology

A renewed focus is needed on the study of urban ecosystems as something more than the geographic grid for plotting the disparate effects of environmental racism. This is important to the future of the **Chicana/o** EJM because most Chicanas/os live and work in cities. Issues related to the politics of urban planning; gentrification; **brownfields** reclamation; access to affordable and safe housing, public health, and equitable mass transit; police brutality and racial profiling; and urban agriculture and local food security must continue to demand action in the EJM. Struggles for sustainable cities in the future will have to confront the misfit between the current regime, which emphasizes market-based planning, and demands for **ecological democracy** from citizens and communities asserting their rights to determine the environmental conditions of their life and work. What lessons can be drawn from our own diverse place-based knowledge? What strategies have urban communities used successfully to control their land use planning and development practices?

Place-Based Knowledge and Participatory Ecosystem Management

The ethic of local knowledge challenges the top-down and expert-driven politics of environmental risk assessment and **ecosystem management.** The EJM values local knowledge as the basis for elaboration of sustainable alternatives to global capitalism and neoliberalism.[8] Research on **traditional environmental knowledge (TEK)** usually focuses on rural land-based communities. What can we learn from local cultures about inhabiting both rural and urban places without impoverishing ecosystems? Scholars are only now studying the submerged history of Mexican-origin land and water use management traditions. They are rediscovering democratic principles that have guided indigenous organizations like the acequia associations in their roles as watershed managers. Can other local civic institutions of self-governance be identified and mobilized more widely so that communities elsewhere can become more active in self-management of the environment? How might the study of TEK support campaigns for participatory ecosystem management in different cities and regions?

Grassroots Transnationalism

Mike Davis notes how the Zapotec Indians of Oaxaca have created veritable transnational suburbs in the Los Angeles basin. They "have transplanted traditional village governments *en bloc* to specific inner city Catholic parishes." They have re-created their institutions of local self-governance and communal economic organization: "The Zapotecs outmaneuver the slumlords by buying apartment buildings—which the church dutifully blesses—listing multiple names on the titles and paying for them jointly."[9] The Zapotecs are simultaneously **reinhabiting** places in Los Angeles and Oaxaca. The transplanting of community self-governance, cooperative economic development, and **mutual aid** is accompanied by the replanting of maize, chiles, and calabacitas in urban milpas. México desconocido is a transborder community of Zapotecs called Oaxacalifornia, sustaining itself in two places—Los Angeles and the mountains of Oaxaca. This example of transnationalism from below marks a new phase in the self-organization of Mexican immigrant communities. How are transnational Mexican-origin communities remaking urban and rural places in the United States and Mexico? What are the implications of this grassroots urbanism (and new ruralism) in the struggle for autonomy and just sustainability?

Environmental Security

The field of environmental security studies is relatively unknown within environmental justice activist circles and grassroots organizations. Instead, the study of environmental security has been dominated by conservative social scientists from the fields of international and national security studies. These individuals tend to approach both environmental protection and ecological degradation as factors in national security risk models. The point is not to eliminate environmental risks or dismantle regulatory regimes, but to understand and manage them within the context of national and international security policy. The national security framework is already blocking public access to information about environmental risks as a consequence of the Patriot Act of 2001.

Some critical approaches to environmental security studies have emerged over the past five years. Some of this newer research focuses on how environmental security discourses take a colonialist or imperialist slant and reinforce the inequalities between the First and Third Worlds.[10] Critics of the dominant environmental security framework debunk the idea that Third World countries are a security threat to the First World due to overpopulation, poverty, and fundamentalism. This conventional view fails to acknowledge First World overconsumption and overdevelopment as principal sources of environmental insecurity for Third World communities subject to the stress, poverty, and conflict associated with modernist development programs and neoliberal restructuring. Given the context and aftermath of the 9-11 attacks, environmental security needs to be addressed from environmental justice vantage points.

■ Final Words

Aquí nos juntamos todos pa' rezarle al sol,
a nuestra madre tierra,
y al agua que nos dan vida
pa' recibir el amor que nos da Dios,
y para amarnos los unos a los otros.

We join together here to pray to the sun,
to our mother earth,
and to the water that provide us with life
so that we can receive God's love,
and love one another.
—Annual prayer to San Isidro Labrador[11]

In 2001, more than 120 million Mexicans and Mexican Americans lived in the binational territory composed of Mexico and the United States. By 2040, one in every six persons in the United States is predicted to have a degree of Mexican-origin cultural heritage. The implications of this demographic change for future forms of protest, direct action, mobilization, and discourses of community and sustainability merit consideration.

If Mexican-origin communities demand autonomy—the right to control their own local places—does that mean rejecting other rights? Men in the Zapotec village of Santa Ana del Valle, Oaxaca, are reportedly refusing to let women vote, claiming women's suffrage is not in accordance with local customary law. The mainstream media reporting on this and similar conflicts frame the issue as a "clash of villagers' law with modern rights."[12] This conflict is construed as a case of "rule by force and exclusion, machetes and machismo." But the rule of force by machetes and machismo is an ideological and even racist construct. It can be read as an expression of the neoliberal backlash against local indigenous communities seeking autonomy. The exclusion of women is *not* an inherent quality of indigenous customary law in Mexico (or El Norte), even if some of the men in Santa Ana del Valle make that claim. In contrast, women are fully integrated at all levels of the military, political, and economic organization of Zapatista indigenous communities in Chiapas. Many of the most fervent defenders of customary law are indigenous women who vote, organize, and participate in social movements for indigenous autonomy.

Despite the attacks on the legitimacy of customary law, the ecological worldviews of Mexican-origin cultures may in the end provide alternative vantage points for the critical evaluation of the culture-nature interrelation as a historical, political, and scientific problem. The final epigram is from a prayer (*oración*) delivered every year during the May 15 Feast Day of San Isidro Labrador in San Luis, Colorado. San Isidro, the patron saint of the farmer, is a symbol of the unity among humans, land, and water. The oración calls on the people of the Culebra villages "to pray to the sun, to our mother earth, and to the water that provide us with life so that we can receive God's love and love one another." Somehow this prayer reassures me that the Mexican-origin people can continue to play a positive and active role in shaping a sustainable and just future guided in part by *querencia*—their love and respect for each other and *la tierra y vida*.

■ **Notes**

1. D. G. Peña, "Identity, Place, and Communities of Resistance," in *Just Sustainabilities: Development in an Unequal World,* ed. J. Agyeman, R. D. Bullard, and B. Evans (London: Earthscan; Cambridge: MIT Press, 2003), 146–67.

2. C. Rechtschaffen and E. Gauna, *Environmental Justice: Law, Policy and Regulation* (Durham, NC: Carolina Academic Press, 2002), 351, 369–73.

3. D. G. Peña, "The 'Brown' and the 'Green': Chicanos and Environmental Politics in the Upper Rio Grande," *Capitalism, Nature, Socialism* 3 (1992): 79–103; L. Pulido, "Sustainable Development at Ganados del Valle," in *Confronting Environmental Racism: Voices from the Grassroots,* ed. R. D. Bullard (Boston: South End Press, 1993), 123–40.

4. J. Agyeman, R. D. Bullard, and B. Evans, eds., *Just Sustainabilities: Development in an Unequal World* (London: Earthscan, 2003).

5. D. G. Peña, *The Terror of the Machine: Technology, Work, Gender, and Ecology on the U.S.–Mexico Border* (Austin: CMAS Books, 1997), 319–24; A. Sampaio,

"Transforming Chicana/o and Latina/o Politics: Globalization and the Formation of Transnational Resistance in the United States and Chiapas," in *Transnational Latina/o Communities: Politics, Processes, and Cultures,* ed. C. G. Vélez-Ibáñez and A. Sampaio (London: Rowman and Littlefield, 2002), 47–72.

6. J. Nash, *Mayan Visions: The Quest for Autonomy in an Age of Globalization* (London: Routledge, 2001).

7. G. Esteva and M. Prakash, *Grassroots Postmodernism: Remaking the Soil of Cultures* (London: Zed, 1999), 41–42.

8. G. Hunn, "The Value of Subsistence for the Future of the World," in: *Ethnoecology: Situated Knowledge/Located Lives,* ed. V. D. Nazarea (Tucson: University of Arizona Press, 1999), 23–36.

9. *Los Angeles Times,* 25 March 1998, as cited in M. Davis, *Magical Urbanism: Latinos Reinvent the U.S. Big City* (London: Verso, 2000), 85.

10. See S. Dalby, *Environmental Security* (Minneapolis–St. Paul: University of Minnesota, 2002).

11. Recorded by Rowena Rivera in San Luis, Colorado, May 13, 1995, for the Rio Grande Bioregions Project, "Upper Rio Grande Hispano Farms: A Cultural and Environmental History of Land Ethics in Transition, 1598–1998." Collection of the Project Archive, Department of Anthropology, University of Washington.

12. M. Stevenson, "Villagers' Laws Clash with Modern Rights," *Seattle Post-Intelligencer* (4 February 2004), A7.

GLOSSARY

acequia: A communal irrigation ditch used by Mexican-origin farmers in el Norte. Acequias are collectively maintained by the association of irrigators under the customary law of self-governance based on the principle of one person/one vote. The word *acequia* derives from the Arabic root word *as-Saquiya* or the water bearer.

agency: The capacity for individuals or groups to act purposefully to bring about change in the social world.

allelopathic: A characteristic of certain plants that prevents other plants from growing too close to them. This is usually done using chemicals that the plant produces and releases into its surroundings.

anthropocentrism: A moral philosophy based on the supremacy and primacy of humans and on their dominion over nature.

anthropogenesis: Changes in the environment that result from human activities.

barrio: A predominantly Mexican, Mexican American, or Latina/o neighborhood.

biocentrism (or **ecocentrism**): A moral philosophy based on the equality of all living organisms and the intrinsic value of nature independent of human use and need.

biological corridors: In conservation biology, a pattern of vegetation linking habitat islands to facilitate the movement of plants and animals among them.

biome: A division of the world's vegetation that corresponds to a particular climate and is characterized by certain types of plants and animals (e.g., tropical rain forest).

bioregion: An area of the biosphere defined by watershed boundaries, a unique mix of biota, cultural distinctiveness, and a sense of place.

biosphere: The space on earth inhabited by living organisms.

biota: Living organisms within an ecosystem, including animals, plants, fungi, bacteria, and other microorganisms.

brownfield: Any vacant land area designated as too polluted and damaged for viable human use.

built environment: The physical stocks of buildings, streets, bridges, power plants and grids; the spatial and temporal patterns in urban and rural localities, neighborhood designs, and street layouts; and the flows of people, goods, and services with demands for energy, transport, materials, waste handling, and so on.[1]

carrying capacity: The capacity of the land to sustain human life without loss of biodiversity or ecosystem integrity.

chaos theory: A theory stating that the complexity of the biophysical world is such that humans cannot easily predict, manipulate, or control natural processes without provoking unintended and unanticipated consequences.

chaotic ecology: The study of complexity, uncertainty, and catastrophe in ecosystems affected by patterns of natural and human disturbance.

Chicana/o: A person of Mexican-origin heritage born and raised in the United States. The label is often used to designate a self-identity based on oppositional or militant ethics and an activist orientation toward social change and justice.

colonia: Any subdivision constructed in the absence of regulations related to housing standards and usually lacking in public drinking water and sewage systems.

commodity (commodification): An underlying principle of capitalism that everything (land, water, labor, etc.) is a thing with a price and that it can be bought and sold on the market for money. The process of converting an object into a commodity by market forces is called *commodification* or *commoditization*.

commons: The idea that the natural environment inhabited by a culture is considered a home place and all members of the group have rights to make use of it.

community: In organismic ecology, the associated flora and fauna in a locality as an interconnected whole.

cultural adaptation: The process through which a culture adapts to its environment.

cultural ecology: The anthropological study of the interaction (mutual influence) of culture and ecology.

cultural landscape: The spaces to which a group belongs and from which its members derive some part of their shared identity and meaning or sense of place.[2] The interaction of people and place produces patterns of land use, spatial organization, and settlement unique to each inhabited space.

culture: Culture has numerous definitions. This textbook emphasizes two ideas: The concept of *symbolic culture* refers to the ideas, values, norms, beliefs, and discourses a people share. Eugene Hunn states that "culture is what one must know to act effectively in one's environment."[3] The concept of *material culture* refers to the artifacts and practices involved in the production of subsistence goods and services in a community. Together these constitute culture as a "whole way of life."

customary law: The institutional authority structures that indigenous and other local cultures use to resolve disputes, manage resources, and allocate rights to common-use areas. Traditional aboriginal societies continue to have a definable body of rules, norms, and traditions that the community accepts as law.

deep ecology: An environmental philosophy first proposed by Arne Naess; it is based on the idea that humans are not at the center of life and embraces the ideal of equality among all species.

discourse: According to Foucault, the "games of truth" created by the interaction of knowledge and power whenever social groups and institutions use language and other means of communication to create meaning and impose particular interpretations and political projects on others.[4]

ecofeminism: A radical environmental philosophy based on the idea that the domination and exploitation of nature and of women are interconnected.

ecological democracy: The principle of local grassroots participation in environmental policy and decision making.

ecological life zone: A concept developed by C. Hart Merriam to delineate zones dominated by vegetative communities of characteristic physiognomy and composition.

ecological niche: The role or function of an organism in its habitat and surrounding ecosystem.

ecological revolutions: The historical processes through which societies change their relationship to nature.[5]

ecological services: Fundamental life-support services that natural ecosystems, and some human keystone communities, perform and without which civilizations would cease to thrive. These include the purification of air and water, detoxification and decomposition of wastes, regulation of climate, regeneration of soil fertility, and production and maintenance of biodiversity.

ecology: The scientific study of the relationship between organisms and their surrounding environment.

ecology of disturbance: The study of processes of dynamic change that emphasizes the "inherent unpredictability of ecosystems" and how natural uncertainties play havoc with conventional resource management.[6]

ecosocialism: A radical philosophy and social movement based on the Marxist critique of capitalism. It emphasizes Marx's second contradiction, which states that the need for the capitalist system to expand production and accumulation inevitably destroys the natural conditions of production.

ecosystem: A dynamic and complex structure consisting of the biota (plants, animals, fungi, and microorganisms) and the abiota (nonliving factors) interacting as an ecological unit.[7]

ecosystem integrity: The ability of an ecosystem to maintain natural processes of interaction and change that allow for the continued functioning of the different components as a whole.

ecosystem management: Any land (or aquatic) management system that seeks to protect viable populations of all native species, perpetuate natural-disturbance regimes on a regional scale, adopt a planning time line of centuries, and allow human use at levels that do not result in long-term ecological degradation.[8]

enclosure: The expropriation of a common pool resource by the state or the market for public or private use.

encomienda: The authority to exploit aboriginal labor in designated native communities that was conveyed to conquistadors by the Spanish crown; essentially rights to forced labor.

endemic: Inhabiting or pertaining to only one, limited biogeographical area; found nowhere else.

environmental equity: The elimination of discrimination in the development and enforcement of environmental regulations, laws, and policy-making; implies the equitable distribution of risks and amenities as an endpoint goal.

environmental ethics: A field of moral philosophy that focuses on the effects and quality of the relationship between humanity and nature.

environmental impact study (EIS): A scientific assessment of the predicted environmental, social, and economic effects of any given action or policy of the federal government or of federally funded activities by other governmental and private agencies, required under NEPA.

environmental justice: The abolition of racial discrimination in environmental laws and regulations. This includes elimination of patterns of disproportionate environmental risk and harm based on race.

environmental justice movement (EJM): A recent social movement that seeks to end environmental racism and establish a sustainable and equitable society based on grassroots ecological democracy.

environmental managerialism: A top-down model of ecosystem management and conservation based on the expert knowledge of development planners and environmental scientists.

environmental racism: Racial discrimination in enforcement of environmental regulations and laws; deliberate targeting of communities of color for toxic waste disposal and the siting of polluting industries; official sanctioning of pollutants in communities of color; and historical exclusion of people of color from environmental groups, decision-making bodies, commissions, and regulatory bodies.[9]

environmental risk: Any activity, substance, or facility that poses a threat to human and nonhuman health and safety.

equilibrium: The idea that ecosystems exist in a natural state of balance and harmony.

Executive Order 12898: Regulation signed by President Clinton on February 11, 1994, to establish guidelines for implementation of a federal environmental justice policy.

food web: A network of interrelations of living organisms—including producers, consumers, decomposers, and transformers—in energy exchange.

fragmentation: *See* habitat fragmentation.

globalization: The process through which the economic system of capitalism becomes established on a worldwide scale.

habitat: The living space of an organism.

habitat fragmentation: The process, usually caused by human activity, that results in the subdivision of habitat into smaller, disconnected areas.

homeostasis: A state of ecological balance (or dynamic equilibrium) maintained through the biochemical feedback loops of a given ecosystem.

invasive species: Plants and animals introduced to a new area through human activities tied to invasion, conquest, and colonization.

keystone communities: Local cultures that provide a variety of ecological goods and services to other species, including habitat and movement corridors, as a result of their material livelihood activities.

land ethic: The philosophy that the land is a member of the community of life and is worthy of respect and protection.

land organism: The philosophical idea that the land is organized as a living thing.

land race: A native cultivar adapted to the environmental conditions of the locality where it grows.

landscape mosaic: The shifting patterns of random plant associations that produce a mosaic-like structure in ecosystems.

legitimation: In discourse, the political process that qualifies a norm, value, or belief system as truthful and authoritative.

maquiladora: An assembly-line factory on the U.S.–Mexico border usually owned by a transnational corporation or under contract to such an entity.

Mega-Mexico (also **Greater Mexico**): A biogeographical province defined by the presence of endemic species of Mexican flora and fauna.

Mestiza/o: A Mexican-origin person of mixed Spanish-Indian descent.

Mexican-origin people: The population of people belonging to a number of ethnic groups native to Mexico, including Spanish-origin, mestiza/o, and indigenous groups.

mode of production: The combination of the social relations of production, the forces of production, and the technology used to transform natural products into goods and services.

monocultures: Agricultural systems that produce only one type of crop.

mutual aid: A customary practice in which members of a community or association share pooled resources; it may include some forms of cooperative labor.

National Environmental Policy Act (NEPA): A law passed in 1969 and amended as Public Law 91-190 42 U.S.C.4321-4347, January 1, 1970. NEPA establishes a federal policy to encourage "productive and enjoyable harmony" between humans and the environment and "promote efforts which will prevent or eliminate damage to the environment." It establishes the Council on Environmental Quality to advise the president on public law and policy and defines the procedures, standards, and criteria to be used in official environmental impact studies.

natural conditions of production: The land, water, animals, plants, and other living organisms that are the material sources of human production.

natural resource conservation: An anthropocentric philosophy of conservation in which nature (the land, water, and living organisms) is defined in terms of its utility to humans and as a commodity, a thing to be bought and sold in the marketplace and to be consumed.

new social movements (NSMs): Collective actions arising from civil society rather than formal organizations with vested interests in the status quo. NSMs involve new forms of identity politics in which individuals from cultures and other social groups that have been excluded, exploited, or subordinated by the dominant institutions of society articulate their collective identities. NSMs seek alternatives to the dominant institutions and may work to reclaim the autonomy of the civil society by liberating local places from encroachment from market and state forces.

North American Free Trade Agreement (NAFTA): A trilateral agreement among Canada, Mexico, and the United States designed to eliminate tariff and nontariff barriers to free trade.

Norteña/o: A Mexican-origin person residing in the area north of the present-day U.S.–Mexico border.

paradigm: A general research model composed of the methods and theories for the scientific study of any given phenomenon.

polyculture: A farm that grows a diversity of native cultivars adapted to local environmental conditions.

rancho: A ranch; sometimes used to refer to any form of agriculture including a farm.

re-inhabitation: The philosophical idea that sustainability is possible only if people inhabit a place without exceeding its ecological limits.

set-point control: A mechanism like a thermostat or chemostat that allows for the regulation of environmental conditions in a given cybernetic system. In Odum's ecosystems ecology, feedback is internal and has no fixed goal. Set-point controls exist at the level of ecosystems, but there are none at the level of the biosphere to regulate change and prevent collapse. Ecosystem control, where manifested, is the result of a network of internal feedback processes as yet little understood.

shifting cultivation (also **swidden**): A traditional agroecological practice in which farmers clear forested areas to plant crops, then move on to another area to repeat the process, allowing previously cleared areas to become reforested.

social ecology: A political philosophy and social movement that proposes radical changes in the organization of political and economic institutions based on elimination of all forms of hierarchical social domination.

social movement: Any formal or informal effort at collective action to promote or resist social change by a group with a shared ideology.

sustainable: a complex and highly contested concept, usually referring to the idea that human activities are organized in a manner that does not damage the environment, reduce biodiversity, or undermine ecosystem integrity.

sustainable development: As defined by the United Nations, development that does not deprive future generations of the resources needed to survive.

traditional environmental knowledge (TEK): A particular form of place-based knowledge of the diversity and interactions among plant and animal species, landforms, watercourses, and other qualities of the biophysical environment in a given place.

traditional use area: An area of common property that local inhabitants use as a source of materials for their rightful livelihood.

uncertainty: The idea in chaos theory that tiny differences in initial conditions can result in an infinite and thus ultimately unknowable set of possible outcomes.

wilderness preservation: A philosophy within American environmentalism, associated with John Muir, that argues nature has intrinsic value and should be preserved in as pristine and undisturbed a state as possible.

workplace democracy (or **worker self-management**): A form of organization in which workers have control over the full range of managerial decisions related to the process of production.

World Trade Organization (WTO): An international organization created in 1995 to oversee a large number of agreements covering the rules of trade between its member states.

■ Notes

1. M. Smith, J. Whitelegg, and N. Williams, *Greening the Built Environment* (London: Earthscan, 1998), p. 3.

2. P. Groth, "Frameworks for Cultural Landscape Study," in *Understanding Ordinary Landscapes,* ed. P. Groth and T. W. Bressi (New Haven: Yale University Press, 1997), 1.

3. E. Hunn, "Ethnoecology: The Relevance of Cognitive Anthropology for Human Ecology," in *The Relevance of Culture,* ed. M. Freilich (New York: Bergin and Garvey, 1989), 145.

4. M. Foucault, *Discipline and Punish* (London: Penguin, 1977) and *Power/Knowledge: Selected Interviews and Other Writings* (New York: Pantheon, 1980).

5. Carolyn Merchant, *Ecological Revolutions: Nature, Gender, and Science in New England* (Chapel Hill: University of North Carolina Press, 1989), 23.

6. C. S. Holling, F. Berkes, and C. Folke, "Science, Sustainability and Resource Management," in *Linking Social and Ecological Systems: Management Practices and Social Mechanisms for Building Resilience,* ed. F. Berkes and C. Folke (Cambridge: Cambridge University Press, 1998), 342–62.

7. R. F. Noss and A. Y. Cooperrider, *Saving Nature's Legacy: Protecting and Restoring Biodiversity* (Washington, DC: Island Press, 1994), 391.

8. Grumbine, *Ghost Bears,* 276–77.

9. B. F. Chavis Jr., foreword to *Confronting Environmental Racism: Voices from the Grassroots,* ed. Robert D. Bullard (Boston: South End Press, 1993), 3.

■ SOURCE CREDITS

Chapter 1

Topic Highlight 1 from Harvard University, Missouri Botanical Garden, and National Museum of Natural History as cited in "World Faces Mass Extinction Unseen since Dinosaur Age," *International Wildlife* 17, no. 5 (September–October 1987), p. 29. J. Edward Grumbine, *Ghost Bears: Exploring the Biodiversity Crisis* (Washington, DC: Island Press, 1994).

Figure 1 used with permission from the *American Midland Naturalist*.

Figure 2 used with permission of Sinauer Associates.

Chapter 2

Figure 3 used with permission of the Ecological Society of America.

Figures 4, 5, and 6 are based on R. F. Noss and A. Y. Cooperrider, *Saving Nature's Legacy* (Washington, DC: Island Press, 1994).

Chapter 3

Figure 7 is used with permission of Columbia University Press.

Chapter 4

Figure 9 was prepared by Robert K. Green based on the author's original drawing.

Figures 10 and 11 were taken by the author.

Chapter 6

Topic Highlight 3 is from C. Lee, ed., *Proceedings: The First National People of Color Environmental Leadership Summit* (New York: United Church of Christ, Commission for Racial Justice, 1992).

Chapter 7

Map 2 is from the 1992 Census of Agriculture.

Figure 12 photo is by the author.

■ INDEX

The letter f *following a page number denotes a figure, the letter* t *denotes a table.*

171, 172; biodiversity in, 74, 75; exotic species in, 99–100; farmworkers in, 103, 157; gold rush in, 98–99; land loss in, 92, 115
Camino Real, 78, 86, 88
Cananea mine strike, 101
capitalism, xxxiii, 10, 26, 27, 71, 90, 107n22, 131, 133, 134–35
carrying capacity, 35, 53, 135, 171, 192
Carson, Rachel, xxxii, 111, 123; *Silent Spring,* 120–22
Castillo, Aurora, xxi, xxiii, 170
cattle, 81, 89, 93
Central Plateau, 57
Central Valley, 78, 98, 105n1
Chaco Canyon, 76
Chalco, 51, 54, 55
chaos theory, xxix, 18, 192
Chávez, César, xxi, xxiii, 102–3
Chávez Ravine, 101
chemical industry, 121
Chiapas, xxxiii, 67n36, 189
Chicago, 167
Chicano Park, 101–2
Chihuahua, 58, 63
Citizen's Clearinghouse for Hazardous Wastes, 137–38
Ciudad Juárez, xx, 160, 173
Civil Rights Act: Title VI, 183
Clean Air and Water Acts, 113
Clements, Frederic, xxviii, 6–7
Clinton, Bill, 144
Coahuila, 58, 63
collective bargaining, xxiii, 103
colonialism, 26–27, 35, 36, 78–79, 133–34; Spanish, 57–64
colonias, 172–73, 192
Colorado, xix, xxi, xxii, 74, 77, 78, 81, 103, 105n1, 115, 136, 159; acequias in, 166–67

Colorado Acequia Association (CAA), 137, 165–66
Colorado River, 70
Colorado Supreme Court, 163
commodities, 133, 167, 192; nature as, xxxi, 27, 117
common property resources (CPRs), 35
commons, 35, 36, 71, 81, 82, 161, 163–64, 192
communities, 82, 132, 192; economies of, 86–88; endemic, 75, 194; in social ecology, 131–32; sustainable, 184–85
community grants, 79, 81
Community Justice Organizing, xxi
Compañía Ocho, La, 162
complexity theory. *See* chaos theory
Comprehensive Environmental Response, Compensation, and Liability Act (CERCLA), 138–39
computer chip industry, 170–71
congregaciónes, congregas, 63
Congreso de Acequias, 166
conquest, 44–45, 69; impacts of, 57–64
conservation, xxxi, 10, 111; Mexica, 55–56; natural resource, 113–16, 197
conservation biology, 19, 21–23, 30–31
cooperation, 71, 88
cooperatives, 86, 132, 162–63
Coronado Bay Bridge, 101–2
corporations, 118–19, 125n17, 170–71, 184
Cortés, Hernán, 44, 57
Costa Rica, 161
Court of Private Land Claims, 91
crops, 69; diversity of, xxxi, 33, 45–46, 48–49; monoculture, 61–62, 94–95; Norteño, 86, 87t; Old World, 59t, 60, 77; pre-contact, 53, 55
Crosby, Alfred, 26
Culebra coalition, 165, 174, 189
cultivation: shifting, 50, 198

cultural exchange, 77
culture(s), xxv–xxvi, 36, 132, 146, 167, 193; conservation and, 115–16; diversity of, 28–29, 45, 49–50, 51; and ecology, xix, xx, 23, 31–33; and keystone communities, 30–31
cybernetics, 13–14, 18, 20f

dams, 94, 95, 103
DDT, 120, 122
Defenders of Wildlife, 111
deforestation, 3, 4, 49t, 50–51, 76, 89
democracy, xxxiii, 131; acequias and, 82–83, 132; ecological, 141, 186, 193; workplace, 159, 199
Denver, xxii, 105n1
desertification, 3, 4
development, xxxi; sustainable, 34–36, 184–85, 198
Díaz del Castillo, Bernal, 44–45
direct-action campaigns, 128
discrimination, 134; racial, 139–41, 168
displacement: enclosure and, 91–92
Dodger Stadium, 101
domination, 131, 133–34
Dow Chemical, 119
DuPont, 119
Durango, 58, 63

Earth Day, 118
Earth First!, 128, 164
Earth Island Institute, 169
East Los Angeles, xxi, xxii, 102, 170
Ebright, Malcolm, 91–92
Echlin Corporation, 160–61
Echo Amphitheater, 102
ecofeminism, xxxii, 132–34, 149n15, 193
ecological niches, 5, 7, 53, 193
ecological revolutions, xxx–xxxi, 27,

61, 104, 193; in El Norte, 68, 70–72; industrial, 90–103; Norteño, 77–90
ecology, xxx, xxxii, xxxiii, 3, 4, 15–16n1, 186, 192; chaotic, 18–19; cultural, xix, xx, 29; cybernetic, 13–14; deep, 127–29, 193; disturbance, xxix, 20–24, 194; Lake Texcoco, 44–45; political, xxxi, 34–38, 167–72; principles of, 5–6; scientific and political, xxviii–xxix; social, 129–32, 198; traditional knowledge, xxv–xxvi
economics: and land ethic, 10–11
economy, xxxiii; Norteña/o, 86–88
ecosocialism, xxxii, 134–35, 194
ecosystems, xxviii, xxix, 3, 7–8, 18, 53, 119–20; after conquest, 57–64; homeostasis, 11–12; integrity of, 22–23, 194; management of, 21, 194; Mexica, 54–57
ejidos, 71, 81
El Paso, 93, 100
El Paso Interreligious Sponsoring Organization, 173
Elton, Charles, 8
enclosure, xx, 35, 36, 71, 90, 91–92, 95, 115, 163, 194
encomienda, 61, 194
Endangered Species Act, 21, 113
environment, 4, 75–76; built, 6, 123, 138, 168, 191; Mexica and, 54–57; Norteñas/os and, 88–90
Environmental Agenda for the Future, An, 118
Environmental Defense Fund, 111
environmental equity, 144–45, 194
environmental impact studies, 119–20, 141, 169, 194–95
environmentalism, xxiv, 111, 148n5; antitoxics movement, 137–39; bioregionalism, 135–37; conservation, xxxi–xxxii; deep ecology, 127–29;

ecofeminism, 132–34, 149n15; ecosocialism, 134–35; professional, 118–20, 122–23; social ecology and, 129–32

environmental justice movement, xix, xxii, xxvi, xxxii, 120, 123, 127, 134, 153, 154–55t, 164, 170, 171, 174, 183, 184, 186, 195; and acequia systems, 165–66; equity in, 144–45; identity and, 145–46; precursors of, 100–103; principles of, 142–44; racism and, 139–41; security and, 187, 188

Environmental Leadership Summit, xxii, 141

Environmental Policy Institute, 111

Environmental Protection Agency, xxiv, 113, 122, 123, 145, 169

environmental risks, xx, xxxiii, 159–60, 184, 195

environmental security, 187–88

ethic(s): environmental, 136, 194; land, xix, xxviii, 10–11, 23, 136, 196

ethnobiology, 29

ethnobotany, 53, 55

ethnoecology, xxix, 19, 28–30; and agroecology, 31–33

ethnolinguistic families, 45

Eubonne, Françoise d', 132

Executive Order 12898, 144, 169, 195

extinction: rates of, 22

Exxon Chemical, 119

FAB 11 plant, 171

factories, 62, 159–60

Farm Labor Organizing Committee, 156, 159

Farm Worker Network for Economic and Environmental Justice, 141, 159, 176n12

farmworkers, xxiii, 102–3, 120, 156–57, 159, 176n13

fire, 21, 89

First National People of Color Environmental Leadership Summit, 141

food web, xxviii, 8–10, 195

Foreman, Dave, 128, 148n5

Forest Guardians, 162

forests, xx, 22, 90, 162. *See also* logging

Friends of the Earth, 111

Fuerza Unida, 161

Fundamentals of Ecology (Odum), 11

fur trade, 88

Gallegos, Joseph C., xxi, xxiv–xxv, 174, 182

Ganados del Valle, 162–63

gardens, 45, 46, 51, 52f, 54–55, 62

General Accounting Office, 161, 172

genetic engineering, 157, 159

genomics, 184

gentrification, 101, 186

Gibbs, Lois, 137

Gleason, Herbert, xxviii, 7

globalization, xxxiii, 3, 5, 153, 185–86

gold rush, 98–99

Gorras Blancas, Las, 100–101, 161

Granado, Lorraine, xxi–xxii, xxvi

grasslands, 58, 60, 89–90

grazing, 89–90, 162–63

Green Party–USA, 131, 135

Greenpeace, 128, 164

Green Revolution, 31, 33

Group of Ten, xxxii, 111, 113, 118–20, 122–23, 125n17, 146

GTE Lenkurt, 160

Gutiérrez, Juana, xxii, xxiii, 170

habitat(s), xxx, 3, 5, 58, 136; acequia, 84–85; fragmentation of, 22, 99, 195

haciendas, 60, 61–62

Haenke, David, 136

hazardous waste disposal, 167

Head, Lois, xxii, xxiv

healers: Mexica, 55, 56, 67n23
health, xxiii, 4, 55, 56, 57, 128, 138, 157, 159, 160, 169–70, 173
highways, 101–2
history: environmental, 19, 25–28
homeostasis, xxviii, 11–12, 18–21, 195–96
hortaliza (herb patch), 51, 62
Huerta, Dolores, 102
huertas familiares, 62
huertos familiares, 46, 62
Hughes Aircraft Corporation, 169–70
Humboldt, Alejandro von, 63
hunting, 86, 88, 90
hydrology: Mexica, 55–56

identity, xxvii, 38, 145–46
immigration, 96, 98, 128–29, 156, 172
imperialism, 26–27, 35
Imperial Valley, 157
Indian Camp Dam, 103
indigenous cultures, 28, 35, 70, 75, 76–77, 90, 105n1; colonialism and, 57–64; conservation and, 30–31; knowledge in, 45, 48t
Indigenous Environmental Network, 141
industrialization, xx, xxxi, 71, 90; impacts of, 93–96
industry, 170–71
Intel, 170–71
Interstate 10, 102
invasive species, 22, 27, 58, 60, 89, 99–100, 196
irrigation systems, 77, 85. *See also* acequias
Izaak Walton League, 111

Jalisco, 48–49
Jaramillo, Teresa, xxii, xxv–xxvi, 69–70, 117

Kaber, Adelmo, xxii-xxiii, xxvi
Kettleman City, 169
keystone communities, 31, 196
keystone species, 30–31
Kit Carson National Forest, 92, 115, 162
knowledge, 48t, 60; Mexica, 56, 67n25; place-based, 29–30, 186. *See also* traditional environmental knowledge

labor, 62, 88; forced, 57–58, 61; migratory, 71, 90, 92, 96, 98
Labor and Community Strategy Center, 171
labor market, 71, 96, 98
labor movement, 72, 98, 102–3
La Manga timber sale, 162
land, xix, xx, 117; communal, xxvi, 100–101; restoration of, 161–62; Spanish colonial control of, 60, 62–63; use rights to, 70–71
landfills: hazardous waste, 167
land grants, xxiv–xxv, 102; El Norte, 79, 81; enclosed, 90, 95, 115, 163; Las Gorras Blancas and, 100–101; restoration of, 161–62; U.S. treatment of, 91–92
land races, xxxi, 33, 49, 60, 196
land rights, 70–71, 91–92, 115, 165–66; commons, 163–64; traditional use and, 162–63, 178n29
landscape mosaic, 21, 56, 196
landscapes, 22, 53; cultural, 63–64, 136, 192; Mexica cultural, 60–61; precontact, 75–76; Spanish colonial, 61–62
land trusts, 165
land use, 37, 170
law, 69, 88; customary, 30, 58, 81, 82, 83, 166–67, 185, 188, 189, 193; environmental protection, 112t, 113; land, 91–92

legal system: U.S., 91–92

legitimation, 37, 163, 196

Leonard, George M., 70

Leopold, Aldo, xxviii, 6, 10, 11, 98

Levidow, Les, 119

Levi Strauss, 161

libertarian municipalism, 131

life forms, 128

life zones, 45, 72–74, 193

Lindeman, Raymond, 8–10

livestock, 58, 59t, 60, 62, 77, 86, 92, 165; cooperatives, 162–63; impacts of, 89–90

localism, 132

logging, xxvi, 95, 96t, 98–99, 163, 174, 182; protests against, xxii, xxvii, 164, 174

Los Angeles, xxxiii, 78, 101, 102, 105n1, 132, 170, 171, 187

Los Angeles Metropolitan Transit Authority, 171

Love Canal, 137

madre de maíz, 48–49

Madres del Este de Los Angeles, xxi, xxii, xxiii–xxiv, 170

Maestas, Aubin, xxii, xxvii

maize (maíz), 46, 48, 50

management, 117; ecosystem, 146, 186, 194; environmental, 36–37; sustainable, 13

managerialism, 36, 185, 195

Manes, Christopher, 128

Man in the Biosphere, 23

maquiladoras, xx, 159–60, 196

Martínez, Enrico, 60, 61

Maya, xxxiii, 66n15, 67n25; agriculture, 45, 50–53

Mega-Mexico, xxviii, xxix–xxx, 45–46, 74, 196; pre-contact civilizations in, 50–57

Mexica, 67n25; environmental manipulation by, 54–57

Mexico, xxix–xxx, 46t, 48t, 63, 76, 173; conquest of, 44–45; pre-contact civilizations in, 50–57

Mexico, Valley of, 54–57

Mexico City, 45, 60–61

Mexico City–Veracruz corridor, 60

microelectronics, 160, 170–71

migration: bird, 74; labor, 71, 90, 92, 96, 98

milpas, 51–52, 66n15, 180n51

mining, 58, 62, 92, 98–99, 101

Mixteca, 58, 172

modes of production, xxx–xxxi, 133, 163, 196; environmental history and, 26–27; Mayan, 51–53; in El Norte, 78–79, 86, 88

Molycorp molybdenum mine, 165

monocultures, 22, 94–95, 100, 196

Monsanto, 119

Moore, Richard, xxii, xxiv, 141

mosaic: Maya agricultural, 51–53

Muir, John, xxxi, 111, 116–17, 121, 122

mutual aid, 71, 76, 131–32, 196

Naess, Arne, 127–28

National Conservation Association, 114

National Environmental Justice Advisory Committee, 144, 169

National Environmental Policy Act, 113, 119, 169, 197

National Parks and Conservation Association, 111

National Park System, 115, 122

National People of Color Environmental Leadership Summits, xxii, 141, 184–85

National Toxics Campaign, 138

native peoples. *See* indigenous cultures

natural resources, 86; conservation of, 111, 113–16, 197

Natural Resources Defense Council, 111

nature, 133, 146; Mexica view of, 56–57; social construction of, 25–28, 69–70, 117–18, 129, 131

Navajo Dam, 103

neoliberalism, 185, 189

New Ecology, 13–14

New Mexico, xix, xxii, 68, 69, 74, 76–77, 78, 88, 89, 103, 105n1, 115, 116, 136, 159, 172; acequias, 166–67; Intel in, 170–71; land grants in, 81, 91–92, 102, 161–62; logging in, 95, 96t; resistance in, 100–101

New Mexico Acequia Association, 166

new social movements, 38, 197

Norteños/as, xxxi, 68; ecological revolution of, 70–71, 77–90, 104; and native peoples, 76–77; worldview, 69–70

North American Bioregional Congress, 136

North American Free Trade Agreement, xxxiii, 153, 161, 185, 197

Northeast Environmental Justice Network, 141

Oaxaca, xxxiii, 67n36, 187

Oaxacalifornia, xxxiii, 187

obrajes, 62

Odum, Eugene, xxviii, 6, 11–13, 19

Office of Environmental Justice, 169

Office of the Surveyor General, 91

orchards, 62, 77

overgrazing, 58, 89

Ozark Area Community Congress, 136

ozone depletion, 3, 4

Pai, Lou, 163

parciantes, 82, 83

pastures, 89–90

patriarchy, 131, 132

Patriot Act, 187

pesticides, xx, xxiii; farmworkers and, 156–57; opposition to, 103, 111, 120–22

Pinchot, Gifford, xxxi, 111, 113–14, 121, 122

piperos, 173

place-names, 29, 69

plantations, 61, 66n15

plant communities, 6–7, 60, 72, 74–75, 80f, 89–90

plants, xxxi, 49t, 87t; domesticated, 45–46; exotic, 22, 27, 58, 59t, 60, 89, 99–100, 196; as guides, 69, 70

plant succession, 6–7

politics, 71; ecological, xxxi–xxxii, 34–38

pollution, xx, xxiii, 45, 165, 184; air and water, 3, 4, 169–70; antitoxics movement and, 138–39

polycultures, 33, 53, 54–55, 197

population: Hispanic, 95–96, 97t, 168t

poverty, xx, 34, 35–36, 134, 163

predator control, 98, 100

Principles of Environmental Justice, 142–44, 145

privatization, xx, 35, 36

production. *See* modes of production

Progressive Reform Movement, 114

property rights, 70–71, 167

Pueblo cultures, 75, 76, 77, 79

Pueblo de San Joaquín de Chama, 102

Pueblo para el Aire y Agua Limpio, El, 169

Pulido, Laura, 145, 163

Questa (N.M.), 165

Quintana Roo, 23, 67n36

Tansley, Arthur, xxviii, 7–8
Taos, 103, 162, 166
Taylor, Dorceta, 134
Taylor, Zachary, Jr., 174, 182
Taylor Ranch, 163–64, 165–66, 182
TCE (trichloroethylene), 169–70
Tenochtitlan, 55–56, 57, 60–61
Tewa: worldview, 68–69
Texas, xxii, 68, 77, 78, 81, 88, 92, 98, 100, 105n1, 136, 159; biodiversity in, 74, 75; colonias in, 172, 173
Texas Rangers, 92
Texas Water Development Board, 172
Texcoco, Lake, 44–45; manipulation of, 54–56, 66–67n22; Spanish conquest and, 57, 60, 61
Third World, 34–35, 128; First World relations, 159, 187–88
Tierra Amarilla, 102, 124n6, 163, 177–78n23
Tijerina, Reies López, 102, 124n6, 177–78n23
timberlands, 95, 162, 163–64
Title VI, 183
Tohono O'odham, 169–70
tourism, 167
toxic wastes, xx, 141, 145, 170, 184
Toxic Wastes and Race, 141
trade, 86, 107n22
traditional environmental knowledge, xxv–xxvi, 19, 28–30, 31, 33, 36, 38, 45, 50, 51, 172, 186, 198
traditional use areas, 71, 198
transnationalism, 187
Treaty of Guadalupe Hidalgo, 78, 91, 102, 115
Tucson, 78, 169–70
Turtle Island Bioregional Congress, 136

uncertainty, xxix, 22, 198
Union Carbide, 119

unions, 98, 102–3, 160–61
United Church of Christ Commission for Racial Justice, 141
United Electrical Workers, 160–61
United Farmworkers Organization, xxi
United Farmworkers Organizing Committee, xxi, 102–3
United States v. Sandoval, 91–92
UN World Commission on Environment and Development, 34–35
urban centers, 62, 71, 101; agriculture in, 171–72, 180n51; pollution in, 169–70; reclamation in, 168–69
urbanization, 71, 90, 92, 95–96
U.S. Air Force, 169, 170
U.S. Forest Service, 113, 115, 116, 124n6, 161–62
U.S. Supreme Court, 91–92, 183

Vallecitos Federal Sustained Yield Unit, 162
Vavilov Center, 46
Velasquez, Baldemar, 156

water, 70, 76, 88, 93–94, 173; pollution of, 3, 4, 169–70
water rights, xxiv–xxv, 115, 171; for acequias, 81, 82, 83, 164–67
watersheds, 69–70, 76, 90; damage to, xx; Lake Texcoco, 55–56, 61, 66–67n22; and land grants, 79, 81; Taylor Ranch, 165–66
water trusts, 165
web of life, 8–10
weeds: Spanish introduced, 58, 60
wheat, 61–62, 77
wilderness, 146; deep ecologists and, 128–29; native peoples and, 28, 75; preservation of, xxxi–xxxii, 31, 116–18, 199

■ ABOUT THE AUTHOR

DEVON G. PEÑA is a professor of anthropology and American ethnic studies at the University of Washington, where he is associated with the Inter-disciplinary Graduate Program in Environmental Anthropology. An internationally recognized research scholar and environmental justice activist, Peña is the author of award-winning books, including *The Terror of the Machine: Technology, Work, Gender, and Ecology on the U.S.–Mexico Border* (Texas University Press, 1997) and *Chicano Culture, Ecology, Politics: Subversive Kin* (University of Arizona Press, 1998).

Mexican Americans and the Environment is a volume in the series The Mexican American Experience, a cluster of modular texts designed to provide greater flexibility in undergraduate education. Each book deals with a single topic concerning the Mexican American population. Instructors can create a semester-length course from any combination of volumes, or may choose to use one or two volumes to complement other texts.

Additional volumes deal with the following subjects:

Mexican Americans and Health
Adela de la Torre and Antonio L. Estrada

Chicano Popular Culture
Charles M. Tatum

Mexican Americans and the U.S. Economy
Arturo González

Mexican Americans and the Law
Reynaldo Anaya Valencia, Sonia R. García, Henry Flores, and José Roberto Juárez Jr.

Chicana/o Identity in a Changing U.S. Society
Aída Hurtado and Patricia Gurin

For more information, please visit
www.uapress.arizona.edu/textbooks/latino.htm